"Language Is a Place of
STRUGGLE"

"Language Is a Place of
STRUGGLE"

Great Quotes by People of Color

~

Edited by Tram Nguyen

Beacon Press, Boston

A complete list of quote sources for *"Language Is a Place of Struggle"* can be located at www.beacon.org/nguyen

Beacon Press
25 Beacon Street
Boston, Massachusetts 02108-2892
www.beacon.org

Beacon Press books
are published under the auspices of
the Unitarian Universalist Association of Congregations.

This book is printed on acid-free paper that meets the uncoated paper ANSI/NISO specifications for permanence as revised in 1992.

Text design by Susan E. Kelly at Wilsted & Taylor Publishing Services

Library of Congress Cataloging-in-Publication Data
    Language is a place of struggle : great quotes by people of color / edited by Tram Nguyen.
    p. cm.
    Includes bibliographical references and index.
    ISBN-13: 978-0-8070-4800-9 (hardcover : alk. paper)
    1. Minorities—United States—Quotations. 2. Immigrants—United States—Quotations. 3. United States—Race relations—Quotations, maxims, etc. 4. United States—Ethnic relations—Quotations, maxims, etc. 5. United States—Social conditions—Quotations, maxims, etc. 6. Social change—United States—Quotations, maxims, etc. 7. Community life—United States—Quotations, maxims, etc. 8. Social justice—United States—Quotations, maxims, etc. 9. Spirituality—Quotations, maxims, etc. I. Nguyen, Tram.
    E184.A1L259 2008
    305.8—dc22   2008015487

Contents

FOREWORD vii

CHAPTER 1 ROOTS 1
History 1
Race, Ethnicity, and Racism 7
Surviving 30
Migrations 42

CHAPTER 2 SELVES 53
Identities 53
Education 67
Gender and Sexuality 77
Wisdom 88

CHAPTER 3 RELATIONSHIP 112
Love 112
Family and Friendship 120
Community 130

CHAPTER 4   WORK AND PLAY 138

                              Labor 138

                              Economic Justice 142

                              Arts and Culture 151

CHAPTER 5   MAKING CHANGE 169

                              Organizing and Activism 169

                              Leadership 192

                              Peace and Justice 200

                              Environmental Justice 230

CHAPTER 6   INNER VISIONS 239

                              Spirit 239

                              Faith 244

                              Inspirations 250

                              ACKNOWLEDGMENTS 263

                              NAME INDEX 265

Foreword

Why a book of quotes by people of color? Well, first of all, we've said a lot and have a lot worth saying. And secondly, at the time of this printing, there still has yet to be such a multiracial, multicultural collection dedicated specifically to quotes from across communities of color in the U.S.

Like many people, I suspect, I keep my own little collection of memorable words by others. My notebooks and diaries are full of these jottings of words—words that I came across while reading something, seeing something on TV or listening to someone talk—along with cuttings that I've pasted onto my computer and onto my desk. Something about a good quote manages to capture a feeling, a situation, or an observation just so. They can be short quips, funny, or profound, or sometimes long and thoughtful ... There isn't any one formula for what makes a quote something you want to remember and want to share. I suppose what good quotes have in common seems to be their ability to speak to a larger truth that resonates with almost everyone, truths about the condition of human life filtered through all the wonderfully distinct perspectives and voices of the speakers.

Of course, gathering such a collection was an entirely subjective process, and in many ways a matter of personal taste. I let myself be guided by what struck me as true, insightful or valuable, and what delighted my ear. Being an ardent book lover, this collection became an extension of the feeling I have toward my books—companions for the journey of life. I like to think of a quote book as a condensed library in that sense, and sort of like having friends at your fingertips—smart, wise, funny and diverse friends from the historically significant to up-and-coming contemporary voices.

Having said that, there is more of a guiding principle to this book than just my own whimsies. The quotes have been organized into six chapters: Roots, Selves, Relationship, Work and Play, Making Change, and Inner Visions. As you can see, the chapters are meant to tell a larger story about people of color in the context of history, culture, and community, becoming oneself and relating to others, realizing social injustice and doing something about it, and finally, as with all good quotes, imparting some wisdom and inspiration at the end of it all.

To quote from a quote itself, by longtime educator Glenn Omatsu, this book is shaped by "three main themes in the history of people of color in America: first, the significance of mass movements and the role of individuals in relation to these movements; second, the enduring vision of a new society that propels these movements forward; and third, the fundamental link between changing society and transforming oneself."

The quotes are drawn primarily from Black, Latino, Asian American, American Indian, and immigrant sources. To keep things simple, I've listed authors' racial identities according to these broad categories, realizing the vast diversity encompassed within each one. And as for why these particular terminologies, I must refer to scholar (and quote source) Beverly Daniel Tatum's book *Why Are All the Black Kids Sitting Together in the Cafeteria?* for an excellent and succinct explanation of racial categories. To paraphrase, *Black* is used in order to be inclusive of all people of African descent, such as those from the Caribbean and African immigrants as well as Black Americans. *Latino* is used as a term that is broad and widely accepted enough to encompass people of Latin American descent, including the Mexican American movement identity of *Chicano*. *Asian American* and *American Indian* are also widely used and accepted umbrella terms for Asian and Pacific Islander communities and indigenous peoples. But aside from practical considerations, these terms are also closer to the liberation movements that defined racial justice struggles for people of color, and produced many of the writers, scholars, poets, activists, and artists whose words grace these pages.

CHAPTER 1

Roots

History

1 I have noticed that whenever you have soldiers in the story it is called history. Before their arrival it is called myth, folktale, legend, fairy tale, oral poetry, ethnography. After the soldiers arrive, it is called history.

—PAULA GUNN ALLEN, AMERICAN INDIAN WRITER

2 Yesterday is gone, but we must hold on to it anyway. Its meaning is the sense of our lives. We must be careful not to fictionalize and romanticize our stories. We must look at the beauty and the failures of our history with equal love and understanding.

—WALTER MOSLEY, BLACK NOVELIST

3 The Gringo, locked into the fiction of white superiority, seized complete political power, stripping Indians and Mexicans of their land while their feet were still rooted in it. *Con el destierro y el exilo fuimos desuñados, destroncados, destripados*—we were jerked out by the roots, truncated, disemboweled, dispossessed, and separated from our identity and our history.

—GLORIA ANZALDÚA, LATINA WRITER

4   America is filled with people whose histories have deep and complicated roots. Their stories give us alternative views to the grand narrative of Western European progress, modernization, and enlightenment. Often, they directly contradict the fictions the United States tells about itself as a nation as benevolent abroad and inclusive at home.

—ELAINE KIM, ASIAN AMERICAN SCHOLAR

5   Who could possibly have more stories to tell than we—a resilient and indestructible people with a catastrophic, prophetic and almost unbelievable history?

—KALISHA BUCKHANAN, BLACK NOVELIST

6   History has determined our lives, and we must work hard for what we believe to be the right thing … life is something we borrow and must give back richer when the time comes.

—CARLOS BULOSAN, ASIAN AMERICAN WRITER

7   Americans, in addition to their staggering ignorance, also seem to think that everything happened yesterday.

—RANDALL ROBINSON, BLACK ACTIVIST

8   Anecdotes, / The poor man's history.

—RITA DOVE, BLACK POET

9   Our tribe unraveled like a coarse rope, frayed at either end as the old and new among us were taken.

—LOUISE ERDRICH, AMERICAN INDIAN NOVELIST

10　A misunderstanding of the Black freedom movement—and therefore of the history of this country—had dire consequences for everyone, especially for all of us who believe that there is still the possibility of creating a "more perfect Union" in this land.

　　　　　　　　　　—VINCENT HARDING, BLACK SCHOLAR

11　I suppose in the final analysis, that is what history is about—what we remember, what perspective our memory reflects, and what we lie about to make the point we want to make.

　　　　—CHRIS IIJIMA, ASIAN AMERICAN LAW PROFESSOR AND SINGER

12　I guess I would have been a completely different person had I not gone to [the internment] camp. Maybe I would have been something worthwhile.

　　　　—HENRY MIYATAKE, ASIAN AMERICAN REDRESS ACTIVIST

13　I learned a history not then written in books but one passed from generation to generation on the steps of moonlit porches and beside dying fires in one-room houses, a history of great-grandparents and of slavery and of the days following slavery; of those who lived still not free, yet who would not let their spirits be enslaved.

　　　　　　　　　　—MILDRED TAYLOR, BLACK WRITER

14　It's so important to maintain a historical perspective and understand our own struggles in relation to others, and to understand what realities shape our uneasy proximities.

　　　　　　　　—VIJAY IYER, SOUTH ASIAN MUSICIAN

15　There is no life that does not contribute to history.

　　　　　　　　　—DOROTHY WEST, BLACK WRITER

16 All History is current; all injustice continues on some level, somewhere in the world.

—ALICE WALKER, BLACK WRITER

17 White folks always want to forget the past, but you can't forget the past because the present is always the result of the past.

—REV. FREDERICK K.C. PRICE, BLACK MINISTER

18 We are not makers of history. We are made by history.

—MARTIN LUTHER KING, JR., BLACK CIVIL RIGHTS ACTIVIST

19 We were stolen from our mother country and brought here. We have tilled the ground and made fortunes for thousands. This land which we have watered with our tears and our blood, so it is now our mother country.

—RICHARD ALLEN, BLACK ABOLITIONIST

20 Diaspora does not describe the black experience. We came here as slaves, not as a diaspora people.

—YOSEF BEN-JOCHANNON, BLACK SCHOLAR

21 Civil Rights opened the windows. When you open the windows, it does not mean that everybody will get through. There are people of my generation who didn't get through. We must create our own opportunities.

—MARY FRANCES BERRY, BLACK SCHOLAR

22 The story of Asian American history, in these ways, is a story of not-belonging, of alienation, from America and Asia. Yet, despite all this ambivalence and contradiction about our place in U.S. society, Asian Americans have played upon the broader American stage, and have made lives and history change as a result.

—SONIA SHAH, SOUTH ASIAN WRITER

2 3   Dissonance is our way of life in America. We are something apart, yet an integral part.

— DUKE ELLINGTON, BLACK MUSICIAN

2 4   The Creator didn't mention reservations. Where does it say we have to live on a reservation to live the way we want?

— WINONA LADUKE, AMERICAN INDIAN ACTIVIST

2 5   The history of the capitalist era is characterized by the degradation of my people: despoiled by their lands ... denied equal protection of the law, and deprived of their rightful place in the respect of their fellows.

— PAUL ROBESON, BLACK ACTOR

2 6   America's real contribution to the world is a vision of individual importance and liberty that is as revolutionary today as it was 200 years ago. It is up to us to make this generation the one that transforms that vision into a universal reality. And when we work together to do that, we give life to the noblest tradition that makes us all Americans.

— CAROL MOSELEY BRAUN, BLACK POLITICIAN

2 7   Within our society there are hierarchies of need because there have been hierarchies of oppression.

— MARTHA P. COTERA, LATINA WRITER

2 8   We are on Indian land. Throughout this entire hemisphere, wherever anyone lives, these are the original homelands of peoples indigenous to what is now known as the Americas. The spirits of the original peoples have been forgotten. One of the teachings from traditional people is to pay your respects to the spirits of the lands you are visiting or traveling over. Some do this with an offering of tobacco or with song. There is an understanding with the offering that you are asking permission to be on the land.

— INÉS HERNÁNDEZ-ÁVILA,
NATIVE-CHICANA WRITER AND SCHOLAR

29   This country was founded by white men of means. But sometimes my tongue slips and I say it was founded by mean white men!

—MEL KING, BLACK ACTIVIST

30   The history of racial terrorism continues to shape the relationship between and among blacks and whites in communities all over this country. If we are honest, we know that it is this history—not that of affirmative action or busing—that lurks in the dim, gray area of distrust, fear, and resentment between and among blacks and whites. It is there—where overwhelming anger, insistent denial, shame, and guilt lie—there, where our reconciliation efforts must be targeted.

—SHERRILYN A. IFILL, BLACK LAW PROFESSOR

31   Contemporary America is a multicultural and multireligious political community that has yet to come to grips with its settler origins.

—MAHMOOD MAMDANI, SOUTH ASIAN SCHOLAR

32   First of all, athletes black/red/brown/yellow and white need to do some research on their history; their own personal family. They need to find out how many people in their family were maimed in a war. They need to find out how hard their ancestors had to work. They need to uncloud their minds with the materialism and the money and study their history. And then they need to speak up.

—JOHN CARLOS, BLACK ATHLETE

33   We have yet to completely overcome our colonial past, our master-slave past, our xenophobic past, but our hubris knows no bounds—with it we construct our militaristic foreign policy and our draconian immigration laws. If America is ever to truly become the exception it claims to be, it must confront the tragic contradiction of being a "race-less" and racist, a "class-less" and classed society. Once again, America must, as it did during the Civil Rights Movement, recognize its failures—the distance between its ideals and its reality.

—RUBÉN MARTÍNEZ, LATINO JOURNALIST

34 The United States does not need to be defended; it needs to be cured. The collective denial of guilt in this country weighs so heavily upon its national psyche that soon the day will come when not one scapegoat (neither Muslim fundamentalist, Mexican immigrant, nor lesbian of color) will be able to carry it.

—CHERRÍE MORAGA, LATINA WRITER

35 Humanity is now left with a challenge: how to subdue and hold accountable the awesome power that the United States built up during the Cold War.

—MAHMOOD MAMDANI, SOUTH ASIAN SCHOLAR

36 Indians think it is important to remember, while Americans believe it is important to forget.

—PAULA GUNN ALLEN, AMERICAN INDIAN WRITER

37 No movement can thrive if it doesn't recall its birth.

—NAS, BLACK HIP-HOP ARTIST

Race, Ethnicity, and Racism

38 America must respect its own diversity. Our nation's inclusion and future in the world community may count on it.

—ABU QADIR AL AMIN, BLACK IMAM

39 Everybody remembers the first time they were taught that part of the human race was Other. That's a trauma. It's as though I told you that your left hand is not part of your body.

—TONI MORRISON, BLACK NOVELIST

40   A lot of the athletes thought that winning medals would supercede or protect them from racism. But even if you won the medal it ain't going to save your momma. It ain't going to save your sister or children. It might give you 15 minutes of fame, but what about the rest of your life?

—JOHN CARLOS, BLACK ATHLETE

41   An odd thing happens in the minds of Americans when Indian civilization is mentioned: little or nothing.

—PAULA GUNN ALLEN, AMERICAN INDIAN WRITER

42   I laugh when people tell me, "I just want you to know, I'm colorblind." Why shouldn't they notice my color? I'm proud of being what I am. It is essential. I just don't want to be held back because of it.

—GWEN IFILL, BLACK JOURNALIST

43   Broken are the barriers of geography and technology that caused races and cultures to develop in millenniums of isolation, and this world will not pass that way again. And so those who wish to separate from others who are not their kind will find that there is no place to go.

—J. DOUGLAS ALLEN TAYLOR, BLACK JOURNALIST

44   I do not feel remorseful about the act on the victory stand as it was an act of "faith." Because I believe in "hope" for our changing society, the evidence of non-equality had to be challenged. At the time, my "visual" on the victory stand was not thought of as a portrait to be classified as a picture of history, but as a cry for freedom.

—TOMMIE SMITH, BLACK ATHLETE

45   I am visible—see this Indian face—yet I am invisible. I both blind them with my beak nose and am their blind spot. But I exist, we exist. They'd like to think I have melted in the pot. But I haven't, we haven't.

—GLORIA ANZALDÚA, LATINA WRITER

46   The first thing we have to understand is that racism is not a "mental quirk" or a "psychological flaw" on an individual's part. Racism is the systematized oppression by one race of another.

—JAMES AND GRACE LEE BOGGS,
BLACK AND ASIAN AMERICAN ACTIVISTS

47   As a black man, you often think that things can go either way. You could be that guy in the penitentiary, or you could be that guy on everybody's television screen.

—TODD BOYD, BLACK SCHOLAR

48   There is Indian time and white man's time. Indian time means never looking at the clock ... .There is not even a word for time in our language.

—MARY CROW DOG, AMERICAN INDIAN ACTIVIST

49   The Black emphasis must not be *against white* but *FOR Black*.

—GWENDOLYN BROOKS, BLACK POET

50   The resort to stereotype is the first refuge and chief strategy of the bigot.

—BAYARD RUSTIN, BLACK CIVIL RIGHTS ACTIVIST

51   If a society is a just society, if it is one which places a premium on social justice and human rights, then racism and intolerance cannot survive.

—BAYARD RUSTIN, BLACK CIVIL RIGHTS ACTIVIST

52   It seems likely that the problem of the twenty-first century will be that of the multiple color lines embedded in the American social order.

—CLAIRE JEAN KIM, ASIAN AMERICAN SCHOLAR

53   Racism is so universal in this country, so widespread, and deep-seated, that it is invisible because it is so normal.

—Shirley Chisholm, Black politician

54   In the end, antiblack, antifemale, and all forms of discrimination are equivalent to the same thing—antihumanism.

—Shirley Chisholm, Black politician

55   It always seemed to me that white people were judged as individuals. But if a negro did something stupid or wrong, it was held against *all* of us.

—Annie Elizabeth "Bessie" Delany, Black dentist

56   When I heard there was a shooter, I thought, "Please don't let him be Korean. Please don't let him be Korean." Not only was he Korean, but his name was Cho.

—Margaret Cho, Asian American comedian

57   I don't think we did well. I think we totally underestimated how entrenched racism was in this country. I know I did.

—Kenneth B. Clark, Black psychologist

58   The joke used to be that in every Indian home, there is the mother, father, children, grandparents, and the anthropologist.

—Elizabeth Cook-Lynn, American Indian writer

59   When Negroes are average, *they fail*, unless they are very, very lucky. Now, if you're average and *white*, honey you can go far. Just look at Dan Quayle. If that boy was colored, he'd be washing dishes somewhere.

—Annie Elizabeth "Bessie" Delany, Black dentist

60   Despite the fact that the U.S. is no longer a relatively homogenous population of white, two parent, English speaking, Christian heterosexuals, our venues for cultural reflection still produce only ill conceived caricatures of a new America.

—GARY DELGADO, BLACK ORGANIZER

61   A not-insignificant part of the reality of Black males is our relationship to the police. We do not have to run. We do not have to engage in high-speed chases. We just have to look Black. And, if we try to assert our "rights," we just get "a little extra on the baton." In a very basic way, we are all Rodney King.

—GARY DELGADO, BLACK ORGANIZER

62   There's a great deal of mental stress for black men who want to fulfill the demands of a dominant culture that tells us to walk and then cuts our legs off.

—MICHAEL ERIC DYSON, BLACK SCHOLAR

63   A stereotype is the lazy person's way of engaging the other.

—MICHAEL ERIC DYSON, BLACK SCHOLAR

64   We are, quite simply, disqualifying, jailing, and burying an increasing number of our potential black football players, basketball players, baseball players, and other prospective athletes—right along with our potential black lawyers, doctors, and teachers.

—HARRY EDWARDS, BLACK EDUCATOR

65   The master's tools will never dismantle the master's house.

—AUDRE LORDE, BLACK WRITER

66   On the one hand, they're disillusioned by the racial realities of America, which hates blacks and the poor; on the other hand, they're still in love with the idea and the hope of achieving white folks' American dream.

—NATHAN McCALL, BLACK JOURNALIST

67   The whites stole the whole country. Sure as hell they did. They stole the air, the grass, whatever they could get their hands on. Why should we go on licking their damn butts? I'm getting old and cranky, so I say anything that runs through my mind.

—MARTHA GRASS, AMERICAN INDIAN ACTIVIST

68   The practice of self-love is difficult for everyone in a society that is more concerned with profit than well-being, but it is even more difficult for black folks, as we must constantly resist the negative perceptions of blackness we are encouraged to embrace by the dominant culture.

—BELL HOOKS, BLACK WRITER

69   In many ways Arabs replaced Mexicans overnight in the old stereotype of the seditious brown man with a mustache.

—GUILLERMO GÓMEZ-PEÑA, LATINO PERFORMANCE ARTIST

70   Jim Crow is still around, but Jim Crow is old. That's not who I'm mindful of today. The problem is that Jim Crow has sons. The one we've got to battle is James Crow, Jr., Esquire. He's a little more educated. He's a little slicker. He's a little more polished. But the results are the same. He doesn't put you in the back of the bus. He just puts referendums on the ballot to end affirmative action where you can't go to school. He doesn't call you a racial name, he just marginalizes your existence. He doesn't tell you that he's set against you, he sets up institutional racism, when you have a nation respond looking for weapons in Iraq that are not there, but can't see a hurricane in Louisiana that is there.

—REV. AL SHARPTON, BLACK MINISTER

71 Within commodity culture, ethnicity becomes spice, seasoning that can liven up the dull dish that is mainstream white culture.

— BELL HOOKS, BLACK SCHOLAR

72 Mutual recognition of racism, its impact both on those who are dominated and those who dominate, is the only standpoint that makes possible an encounter between races that is not based on denial and fantasy.

— BELL HOOKS, BLACK SCHOLAR

73 We need to continually break the silence about racism whenever we can. We need to talk about it at home, at school, in our houses of worship, in our workplaces, in our community groups. But talk does not mean idle chatter. It means meaningful, productive dialogue to raise consciousness and lead to effective action and social change.

— BEVERLY DANIEL TATUM, BLACK EDUCATOR

74 The language we use to categorize one another racially is imperfect... Yet it is difficult to talk about what is essentially a flawed and problematic social construct without using language that is itself problematic. We have to be able to talk about it in order to change it.

— BEVERLY DANIEL TATUM, BLACK EDUCATOR

75 Because racism is so ingrained in the fabric of American institutions, it is easily self-perpetuating. All that is required to maintain it is business as usual.

— BEVERLY DANIEL TATUM, BLACK EDUCATOR

76 The idea of systematic advantage and disadvantage is critical to an understanding of how racism operates in American society.

— BEVERLY DANIEL TATUM, BLACK EDUCATOR

77   The United States is obsessed with race for oppressive reasons.

—Christine C. Iijima Hall, Black-Asian scholar

78   Like many who have gone before you, you must struggle against injustice with all your might. You must refuse to be racialized or to racialize others. But at the same time you must also live as if the world were otherwise. You must reach out and claim it as your own. I know that is a lot to ask. It will certainly require a difficult heroism and a subtle resistance, as well as exposure to the risk of being misunderstood by your peers and elders. But perhaps ... just perhaps ... when enough people do as you do, racism will indeed have no future.

—Thomas C. Holt, Black scholar

79   Sometimes, I feel discriminated against, but it does not make me angry. It merely astonishes me. How *can* any deny themselves the pleasure of my company. It's beyond me.

—Zora Neale Hurston, Black writer

80   Light came to me when I realized that I did not have to consider any racial group as a whole. God made them duck by duck and that was the only way I could see them.

—Zora Neale Hurston, Black writer

81   Racial categories are inherently unstable and shifting. We can never have categories that will be conceptually valid, measurable, and reliable over time. Yet we cannot simply abandon the use of racial and ethnic categories. Without them, we cannot monitor and track racial inequality and discrimination—for example, racial profiling. However "unscientific" and imprecise these categories may be, some form of racial classification is needed to discern trends and discriminatory patterns.

—Michael Omi, Asian American scholar

82   Lots of brown folks getting publicity, but behind the scenes it's still white folks setting the rules.

— WALIDAH IMARISHA, BLACK WRITER

83   I hear that melting-pot stuff a lot, and all I can say is that we haven't melted.

— JESSE JACKSON, BLACK POLITICIAN

84   We have all been physically, mentally, and emotionally spent, so hurt by the remarks that were uttered by Mr. Imus ... It's not about the Rutgers women's basketball team, it's about women. Are women hos? Think about that. Would you have wanted your daughter to have been called that? It's not about they as black people or as nappy headed, it's about us as a people, black, white, purple or green ... when there's been denied equality for one, there's been denied equality for all.

— C. VIVIAN STRINGER, BLACK COACH

85   I realize that many people see no problem with the use of American Indians as sports mascots. However, I think the danger of this use is more than just its potential to offend. It is representative of an endemic problem of racism against America's First Peoples.

— KIMBERLY ROPPOLO, AMERICAN INDIAN EDUCATOR

86   The average American doesn't even realize the Washington Redskins emerges from a history of the literal bloody skins of American Indian men, women, and children being worth British Crown bounty money—no one's skin is red. American Indian skin is brown, at least when it is on our bodies and not stripped from us in the name of profit and expansionism.

— KIMBERLY ROPPOLO, AMERICAN INDIAN EDUCATOR

87   We, the Blacks or Coloured People, are treated more cruel by the white Christians of America, than devils themselves ever treated a set of men, women and children on this earth.

—David Walker, Black abolitionist

88   That system founded on racism might now and again rouse up to correct itself, but it does so only after crippling the victim.

—Edward P. Jones, Black novelist

89   If we are always seen as "ethnic" and "particular," then no one else ever has to imagine that they have any points of contact with us, outside of what they see as our quaint little sphere. We are rarely permitted to have any larger impact in the world. We should work to confound all of that, by claiming our place in a larger conversation.

—Vijay Iyer, South Asian musician

90   Most Negroes have a little black militancy swimming around in them and most white people have a little Ku Klux Klan swimming around in them. If we'd be honest with each other, we would discover we are all victims of the racism that is historically part of this country.

—Barbara Jordan, Black politician

91   To be a minority in America, even in the 21st century, is to be always on trial. An evil act by one indicts the entire community. Whoever doubts this need only look at the spike in hate crimes against Muslims and South Asian communities after 9/11.

—Andrew Lam, Asian American writer

92   It's hard to be an Indian these days. Whether you choose a middle-class American lifestyle, or remain devoted to your traditional beliefs, a Native

American today lives a life embroiled on one side by a violent history and on the other by romanticized notions of Native culture. Our lives are made difficult for one simple reason: America is Indian land, a fact that still confounds.

— JULIAN LANG, AMERICAN INDIAN ARTIST

93   No meaningful dialogue can take place when some whites still think about race as a "zero-sum game," where any economic or political advances by racial minorities must come at their expense.

— MANNING MARABLE, BLACK SCHOLAR

94   The greatest struggle of any oppressed group in a racist society is the struggle to reclaim collective memory and identity. At the level of culture, racism seeks to deny people of African, American Indian, Asian, and Latino descent their own voices, histories, and traditions.

— MANNING MARABLE, BLACK SCHOLAR

95   Arabs are generally to be avoided, despised, incarcerated. In moments of generosity, however, the Arab is transformed in the liberal imagination from alien presence into tolerable object of curiosity. Because Arabs have been subject to the competing (but not necessarily antagonistic) strategies of castigation and toleration, they have been marked as different.

— STEVEN SALAITA, ARAB AMERICAN SCHOLAR

96   Obviously, I too believe in a colorblind society; but it has been and remains an aspiration. It is a goal toward which our society has progressed uncertainly, bearing as it does the enormous burden of incalculable injuries inflicted by race prejudice and other bigotries which the law once sanctioned, and even encouraged. Not having attained our goal, we must face the simple fact that there are groups in every community which are daily paying the cost of American injustice.

— THURGOOD MARSHALL, BLACK SUPREME COURT JUSTICE

97 You know they don't like Muslims much these days. We're the new black people. But I'm not worried because soon they're gonna be wearing our clothes and playing our music.

—Shazia Mirza, South Asian comedian

98 I wear a hijab. Since September 11, people look at me differently. They prejudge me and I am always looking over my shoulder . . . We feel rejected, we experience hatred and violence. This community is desperately seeking peace and safety like all of us. Today we are here to say, as a community, enough is enough, enough with the targeting, enough with the harassment. We are not terrorists but we are your neighbor, co-worker, schoolmate. We are here for the same reason your ancestors came here, fear of persecution, freedom of religion.

—Asha Mohamed, Black immigrant

99 Anything I have ever learned of any consequence, I have learned from Black people. I have never been bored by *any* Black person, ever.

—Toni Morrison, Black novelist

100 There is an incredible amount of magic and feistiness in black men that nobody has been able to wipe out. But everybody has tried.

—Toni Morrison, Black novelist

101 Maybe I'm wrong about the impact of the white gaze on African American literature, but I know that eliminating it from my imagination was an important thing.

—Toni Morrison, Black novelist

102 Anti-Arab racism has existed in the United States since the arrival of the first Arab in North America, but since 9/11 anti-Arab racism is, to use a cliché, America's elephant in the living room—an enormous elephant, at that.

—Steven Salaita, Arab American scholar

103   It's as if the Black man's got an illness, and we need to cure him, fit him into some category and make him functional in society. It makes it seem like there's something wrong with us, and not something wrong with society.

—OMOWALE MOSES, BLACK EDUCATOR

104   Although black men are conspicuously successful in many arenas of American life, they are facing a social emergency. Throughout America, but especially in the inner cities, African-American men are disproportionately surrounded by poverty, violence, mass incarceration and disease. A confluence of ills has long conspired to marginalize black men and track them into a trajectory of failure.

—SALIM MUWAKKIL, BLACK JOURNALIST

105   Now I like telling people that I am Muslim, I want to shatter their stereotypes and preconceived notions and show them that there are people fighting for change.

—ASRA Q. NOMANI, SOUTH ASIAN JOURNALIST

106   I am to be the perpetual solution to what is seen as the crisis of black America. I am to be a weapon in the war against black America. Meanwhile, white America can take its seat, comfortable in its liberal principles, surrounded by state-selected Asians, certain that the culpability for black poverty and oppression must be laid at the door of black America. How does it feel to be a solution?

—VIJAY PRASHAD, SOUTH ASIAN SCHOLAR

107   I am here and you will know that I am the best and will hear me. The color of my skin or the kink of my hair or the spread of my mouth has nothing to do with what you are listening to.

—LEONTYNE PRICE, BLACK OPERA SINGER

108   Black folklore is so much a part of the entire heritage of this country. It is the spiritual heartbeat of America. From it trials have been withstood, problems have been solved, roots have been strengthened, progress has been made.

—LEONTYNE PRICE, BLACK OPERA SINGER

109   Racism is used *both* to create false differences among us *and* to mask very significant ones.

—MIRTHA QUINTANALES, LATINA WRITER

110   "Black man in America" is a role beyond even Shakespeare's imagination, open to more interpretations than Hamlet. Those of us born to play this multifaceted, often self-contradictory role have to do what all actors do: We make choices.

—EUGENE ROBINSON, BLACK JOURNALIST

111   You try to steer a course in American society that's not self-destructive. But America is a country that inflicts injury. It does not like to see anything that comes in response, and accuses one of anger as if it were an unnatural response. For anyone who is not white in America, the affronts are virtually across the board.

—RANDALL ROBINSON, BLACK ACTIVIST

112   This country was built on two things: competitiveness and racism—how can you *not* be prejudiced?

—BRENT ROLLINS, BLACK-ASIAN GRAPHIC DESIGNER

113   The average American's limited ability to think about race results in a limited ability to converse about race.

—MARIA P. ROOT, ASIAN AMERICAN SCHOLAR

114   You get racism crossing the street, it's the very fabric of American society.

—NINA SIMONE, BLACK SINGER-SONGWRITER

115   When I came back from the South, I decided that I needed to understand not the how and what of racism but the why. Why did it continue to exist? How had it managed to transform itself from its very beginnings to what it is now, which is so endemic and such a part of our society that it is now impossible to imagine American society without racism.

—PAT SUMI, ASIAN AMERICAN ACTIVIST

116   Multiculturalism is just a fact of life. It's not a case or an argument.

—ZADIE SMITH, BLACK NOVELIST

117   We are always presented with other people's images of the future. Whether it's Star Wars or Star Trek or whatever, they always speak in this language, somehow they have British accents, somehow they all look a certain way. Too often, the whole [Black] community never makes it to the future or it doesn't exist. We're rarely together. We're either one Black man or one Black woman, alone. I envision a future where we are together and where our communities remain intact. Our culture is legitimate, is valid, is important, should be cherished and continued and I think our language, Blackspeak is what I call it, is a part of that.

—SHEREE THOMAS, BLACK WRITER

118   Racism is so extreme and so pervasive in our American society that no black individual lives in an atmosphere of freedom.

—MARGARET WALKER, BLACK EDUCATOR

119   Only ways you can keep folks hating is to keep them apart and separate them from each other.

—MARGARET WALKER, BLACK EDUCATOR

1 2 0   One can spy multilingual store signs in New York or Los Angeles, eat food from all over the world, listen to the rhythms of every culture and time on the airwaves, but the fires of nationalism still rage, and in the cities of the United States, blacks and Koreans and Latinos and Anglos live in anything but a multicultural paradise.

—RUBÉN MARTÍNEZ, LATINO JOURNALIST

1 2 1   Some say that multiculturalism will not die. The numbers tell us and the demographics warn us of a more multicultural society in the twenty-first century. Of course, numbers do not mean sharing power. Numbers do not mean cultural equity. Numbers do not mean a varied identity. Numbers do not mean that all identities will be recognized. Numbers do not mean that all will have the right to speak. Numbers do not tell us who can speak for whom and about what. Numbers do not ensure an open conversation.

—ANNA DEAVERE SMITH, BLACK PLAYWRIGHT, PERFORMER

1 2 2   The increased racial profiling of Arabs and Muslims and the further erosion of our civil liberties since September 11 have merely exacerbated long-standing racist domestic policies targeted against our communities. Yet within U.S. racial categories, we are rendered racially invisible by our current classification as "white, non-European." Arab and Middle Eastern groups have lobbied unsuccessfully for an alternative category. Still, our racial ambiguity within U.S. society has left us politically disempowered and marginalized.

—THERESE SALIBA, ARAB AMERICAN SCHOLAR

1 2 3   Look at most of the major cities that have Black mayors and you'll find the same thing. What can we do about racism? We can talk about it, not in an acrimonious way, but in a clinical way. And maybe by talking about it, we can reach a few of those borderline white people who have never consciously thought about racism or prejudice to think about it and maybe want to do something about it.

—HAROLD WASHINGTON, BLACK POLITICIAN

124 Islam is about faith, indeed, but in our contemporary world it is also about race.

— VIJAY PRASHAD, SOUTH ASIAN SCHOLAR

125 The specificity of black culture—namely, those features that distinguish black culture from other cultures—lies in both the *African* and *American* character of black people's attempts to sustain their mental sanity and spiritual health, social life and political struggle in the midst of a slaveholding, white-supremacist civilization that viewed itself as the most enlightened, free, tolerant and democratic experiment in human history.

— CORNEL WEST, BLACK SCHOLAR

126 Most of the time when "universal" is used, it is just a euphemism for "white": white themes, white significance, white culture.

— MERLE WOO, ASIAN AMERICAN WRITER

127 If the majority culture knows so little about us, it must be *our* problem, they seem to be telling us; the burden of teaching is on us.

— MITSUYE YAMADA, ASIAN AMERICAN POET

128 Asian Americans have been played both as the bystander and the weapon. Indeed, one of the miracles of modern media was the overnight conversion of Asian Americans from the Fifth Column and the Enemy Within, to the Modern American Success Story.

— HELEN ZIA, ASIAN AMERICAN JOURNALIST

129 As a member of a minority group everywhere in my country except among family or through the self-conscious effort to find other Asian Americans, I alternate between being conspicuous and vanishing, being stared at or looked through. Although the conditions may seem contradictory, they have in common the loss of control. In most instances, I am how others perceive me to be rather than how I perceive myself to be.

—Frank H. Wu, Asian American scholar

130   Before Emmett Till's murder, I had known the fear of hunger, hell, and the Devil. But now there is a new fear known to me—the fear of being killed just because I was Black. This was the worst of my fears.

—Anne Moody, Black writer

131   Color is an act of God that neither confers privileges nor imposes a handicap. A man's skin is like the day: day is neither clear or dark. There is nothing more to it until external agencies come in and invest it with special meaning and importance.

—Peter Abrahams, Black novelist

132   I hate racial discrimination most intensely and in all its manifestations. I have fought it all along my life. I fight it now, and I will do so until the end of my days.

—Nelson Mandela, Black president of South Africa

133   What's so frightening about the diminished life chances of young Black Americans at home is not that so many of our citizens are not aware, but that so many are aware and do not care.

—Julian Bond, Black civil rights activist

134   In the animal world it indicates danger: the most colorful creatures are often the most poisonous. Color is also a way to attract and seduce a mate. In the human world color triggers many more complex and often deadly reactions.

—Judith Ortiz Cofer, Latina writer

135   I put myself out there so far that when I fail it's very painful. Overcoming racism has certainly made me smarter and wiser.

—RAE DAWN CHONG, BLACK-ASIAN ACTRESS

136   America is a rainbow. America is European and African and *much more*. It is the "much more"—Indians, Asians, Latinos, and others—which makes this country a rainbow.

—JAMES H. CONE, BLACK MINISTER

137   Genocide is the logical conclusion of racism.

—JAMES H. CONE, BLACK MINISTER

138   Being black in America has nothing to do with skin color. To be black means that your heart, your soul, your mind and your body are where the dispossessed are.

—JAMES H. CONE, BLACK MINISTER

139   Just pushing "multiculturalism" without political content is not helpful.

—MARIA JIMÉNEZ, LATINA ACTIVIST

140   Our enemies don't show their colors as they once did. Today's Bull Connors smile a lot, don't have hoses, and may even invite you to lunch.

—CAMILLE COSBY, BLACK PHILANTHROPIST

141   I find that I am actuated by a strong sense of race consciousness. This grows upon me as I grow older, and though I struggle against it, it colors my writing in spite of everything I can do. There may have been many things in my life that have hurt me and I find the surest relief from these hurts is in writing.

—COUNTEE CULLEN, BLACK WRITER

142   You cannot talk about race without class and look at class without race. If you do that, you fall into the trap of racializing, or the other side of the coin, become ethnocentric or nationalistic.

—Roy Hong, Asian American organizer

143   Hate is not inborn; it has to be constantly cultivated, to be brought into being, in conflict with more or less recognized guilt complexes. Hate demands existence, and he who hates has to show his hate in appropriate actions and behaviors...That is why the Americans have substituted discrimination for lynching.

—Frantz Fanon, Black revolutionary

144   The real problem is not the Negro but the Nation. It is whether the republic shall be a republic in fact or in stupendous shame.

—T. Thomas Fortune, Black journalist

145   Racism is a scholarly pursuit, it's taught, it's institutionalized.

—Toni Morrison, Black novelist

146   Much as Jim Crow racism served as the glue for defending a brutal and overt system of racial oppression in the pre-Civil Rights era, color-blind racism serves today as the ideological armor for a covert and institutionalized system in the post-Civil Rights era. And the beauty of this new ideology is that it aids in the maintenance of white privilege without fanfare, without naming those who it subjects and those who it rewards.

—Eduardo Bonilla-Silva, Latino scholar

147   Whatever obstacles I found made me fight all the harder. But it would have been impossible for me to fight at all, except that I was sustained by the personal and deep-rooted belief that my fight had a chance.

—Jackie Robinson, Black athlete

148   Unless minority communities have alternative leadership that critically challenges this fostering of racial tension by the dominant force of society, we cannot counter it in an effective manner.

—ROY HONG, ASIAN AMERICAN ORGANIZER

149   Little do the Amadou Diallos of the world know that the black man in America bears the curse of Cain, and that in America, they, too, are considered black men, not Fulanis, Mandingos, or Wolofs. In America, no taxi will stop to pick them up; putting a price on their heads elects politicians; and the police will hunt them down.

—MANTHIA DIAWARA, BLACK SCHOLAR

150   Racism has been described as the American metaphor. In fact, racism in America is not only alive and well; it is a growth industry.

—HAKI MADHUBUTI, BLACK POET

151   Beware of those who compliment us on how clean, hard-working, and self-reliant we are. Beware of those who tempt us with compliments about our old and venerable culture. Beware of those who speak sympathetically about how Korean and other Asian Americans are losing ground because of affirmative action for African Americans and Latinos.

—ELAINE KIM, ASIAN AMERICAN SCHOLAR

152   If we don't watch out, we may find ourselves one day schooled, credentialed, and trapped in the old "buffer zone" or "middleman" position, attempting an ultimately impossible mediation between those mostly white people who have the power to make the rules and those mostly black and brown people who are oppressed by them.

—ELAINE KIM, ASIAN AMERICAN SCHOLAR

153   There are no readily available "good" Muslims split off from "bad" Muslims, which would allow for the embrace of the former and the casting off of the latter, just as there are no "good" Christians or Jews split off from "bad" ones. The presumption that there are such categories masks a refusal to address our own failure to make a political analysis of our times.

— MAHMOOD MAMDANI, SOUTH ASIAN SCHOLAR

154   The boundaries of one's skin become the crude starting point for negotiating access to power and resources within a society constructed around racial hierarchies.

— MANNING MARABLE, BLACK SCHOLAR

155   One of the luxuries of being white in a racist society is that you never have to talk about *being white*. When something is viewed as normal, then there's nothing unusual about it, so there's nothing to talk about.

— MANNING MARABLE, BLACK SCHOLAR

156   More than anything else that unites us, everyone with an Asian face who lives in America is afflicted by the perpetual foreigner syndrome. We are figuratively and even literally returned to Asia and ejected from America.

— FRANK H. WU, ASIAN AMERICAN SCHOLAR

157   Anytime you stand up for human or civil rights and happen to have a bit of color pigmentation, they will call you by a racist name when attacking your ideas.

— MAGDALENO ROSE-AVILA, LATINO ACTIVIST

158   Although conservatives see separate lunch tables of blacks, whites, and Asians as symbolic of resentment between different racial groups, I think it more likely that such scenes represent the loss of language and hope necessary to talk and act on racial differences. The retreat from race, though well intentioned, only exacerbates that loss and does nothing to bridge the differences that separate society by race.

—DANA TAKAGI, ASIAN AMERICAN SCHOLAR

159   In our hearts, most Americans will acknowledge that racism is still at work in the body politic and in our individual lives, regardless of our race or cultural identity. But most would also acknowledge that we haven't yet found a way to move forward to redress the impact of racism, or even a way to productively talk about race in our society or in our lives. We have been stuck for far too long.

—REV. WILLIAM G. SINKFORD, BLACK MINISTER

160   Neither Asian Asians (the cousins overseas) nor "real" Americans (the neighbors next door) seem ready to accept the authenticity of Asian American lives. They are prepared to accept a white American or a black American, and perhaps they can adjust to a Puerto Rican or Mexican American. Each of these ethnicities can claim to belong to the body politic, however awkwardly, and all of them can lay claim to a birthplace within shared borders.

—FRANK H. WU, ASIAN AMERICAN SCHOLAR

161   The main pillars of structural racism throughout American history have been prejudice, power, and privilege.

—MANNING MARABLE, BLACK SCHOLAR

162   People are too busy running around proclaiming, "I am not a racist." Either they get over their blindness and see the pink elephant, or they'll get run over in a stampede they don't see coming.

—JANET ROBIDEAU, AMERICAN INDIAN ACTIVIST

163   The real deal, I think, is "white supremacy," because it's an institutionalized thing with long historical roots that goes beyond individual bad attitudes and shapes the development of the policies and cultures of institutions. The term "white supremacy" indicates more of a structural phenomenon than "racism."

—JEROME SCOTT, BLACK ACTIVIST

164   Viva the children of all colors! *Punto*!

—PIRI THOMAS, LATINO WRITER

165   For racism to die, a totally different America must be born.

—KWAME TOURE, BLACK ACTIVIST

Surviving

166   It's an instinct to try to hide if you're feeling like you're under attack, to be quiet. And you learn that, unfortunately, what looks like the easy way is often a really bad choice. If you silence yourself, if you try to be good, if you try to be polite, or toe a party line, you end up paying for that in the long run. You pay for it ... with your homeland, or with your soul, or with your artistic vision.

—DIANA ABU-JABER, ARAB AMERICAN NOVELIST

167   When I look back on reservation life it seems that I spent a great deal of time attending the funerals of my relatives or friends of my family ... Death was so common on the reservation that I did not understand the implications of the high death rate until after I moved away and was surprised to learn that I've seen more dead bodies than my friends will probably ever see in their lifetime.

—BARBARA CAMERON, AMERICAN INDIAN WRITER

168   Black ice is the smoothest naturally occuring ice there is, as if nature were condescending to art...Black ice is an act of nature as elusive as grace, and far more rare...I have never skated on black ice, but perhaps my children will. They'll know it, at least, when it appears: that the earth can stretch smooth and unbroken like grace, and they'll know as they know my voice that they were meant to have their share.

— LORENE CARY, BLACK WRITER

169   Adaptation, not accommodation, has become a reality.

— VINE DELORIA, JR., AMERICAN INDIAN WRITER

170   I'm now just beginning to understand that taking care of myself is not selfish (as in, going to the dentist, asking for help, deducting $15 from my rent because I haven't had running water in 2 years) which is, I think, the worst legacy which women have to cope with we are so busy defending ourselves from on-going traumas violence to ourselves, our families & our friends that we remain traumatized & frozen

— CHRYSTOS, AMERICAN INDIAN POET

171   Those of us who are Indian understand that it is the telling of stories, our very breath, that brings forth tribal identity and defines purpose.

— KATHRYN LUCCI-COOPER, AMERICAN INDIAN WRITER

172   Diseases have no eyes. They pick with a dizzy finger anyone, just anyone.

— SANDRA CISNEROS, LATINA WRITER

173   One pain like this should be enough to save / the world forever.

— TOI DERRICOTTE, BLACK POET

174   They were so strong in their beliefs that there came a time when it hardly mattered what exactly those beliefs were; they all fused into a single stubbornness.

—Louise Erdrich, American Indian novelist

175   You know, some people fall right through the hole in their lives. It's invisible, but they come to it after time, never knowing where.

—Louise Erdrich, American Indian novelist

176   Homicide, often involving guns, is a disease that is the leading cause of death for young black men, and the second-leading cause of death for all people aged fifteen to twenty-four. That *makes* it the leading health issue, particularly when guns are used in combination with drugs and alcohol.

—Joycelyn Elders, Black Surgeon General

177   Those who are racially marginalized are like the miner's canary: their distress is the first sign of a danger that threatens us all.

—Gerald Torres, Latino scholar

178   To live is to suffer; to survive is to find some meaning in the suffering.

—Roberta Flack, Black singer

179   The government was supposed to wipe us out, commit a war of genocide and kill every last one of us. But we survived, and we survived because the creator has a plan for us. We're bringing the old ways back, ways that teach about the spirit, about community, about justice, about love for the Earth. And we're bringing them to the world in a time when it needs them.

—William Underbaggage, American Indian activist

180 At least if I can stay mad I can stay alive.

—Magdalena Gómez, Latina poet

181 The ability to laugh, not in ridicule but in amusement, at oneself, at situations, at anything and everything, even what is considered sacred, in a way that acknowledges the potential for the absurd, the ridiculous everywhere … Humor is one of the major ways Native people have been able to survive.

—Inés Hernández-Ávila,
Native-Chicana writer and scholar

182 Life is short, and it's up to you to make it sweet.

—Sarah Louise "Sadie" Delany, Black educator

183 You've got to have something to eat and a little love in your life before you can hold still for any damn body's sermon on how to behave.

—Billie Holiday, Black singer

184 There was a time, after a particularly tough rash of getting roughed up, that I was afraid to walk alone. After a couple of weeks of refocusing, I talked myself through this fear and exercised my confidence to understand that I needed to be who I am and still be able to survive. So I overcame that fear and took a long stroll down the street, and I fell in love with this city again.

—YK Hong, Asian American activist

185 It is not the big, dramatic things so much that get us down, but just being Indian, trying to hang on to our way of life, language, and values while being surrounded by an alien, more powerful culture.

—Mary Crow Dog, American Indian activist

186   The written word is the only record we will have of this our present, or our past, to leave behind for future generations. It would be a shame if that written word in its creative form were to consist largely of defeat and death.

—LANGSTON HUGHES, BLACK POET

187   It is from our communities that much of this consumption comes. It is almost impossible for us to retain our cultural practices, our cultural diversity, our sacred sites, as long as this level of consumption continues. We must wake up every day and fight a mine.

—WINONA LaDUKE, AMERICAN INDIAN ACTIVIST

188   I have been in Sorrow's kitchen and licked out all the pots. Then I have stood on the peaky mountain wrapped in rainbows, with a harp and a sword in my hands.

—ZORA NEALE HURSTON, BLACK WRITER

189   I been through living for years. I just ain't dead yet.

—ZORA NEALE HURSTON, BLACK WRITER

190   Blues are the songs of despair, but gospel songs are songs of hope.

—MAHALIA JACKSON, BLACK SINGER

191   That there should be a purpose to suffering, that a person should be chosen for it, special—these are houses of the mind, in which whole peoples have found shelter.

—GISH JEN, ASIAN AMERICAN NOVELIST

192   Americans in general and African Americans in particular desperately need to start giving a damn about each other.

—BRANDON ASTOR JONES, BLACK PRISONER

193 None of us necessarily count in this "new world order" where corporations and the rich have stacked the deck in their own favor and see most of us as marginal and expendable. To survive, to get the kinds of wages and programs that we'll need to survive this transition to a global economy, all of us on the bottom need to stick together.

—VAN JONES, BLACK ACTIVIST

194 We should take care so that we will lose none of the jewels of our soul. We must begin, now, to reject the white, either/or system of dividing the world into unnecessary conflict.

—JUNE JORDAN, BLACK POET

195 The Civil Rights generation feels like this younger generation has no drive, is suicidal, especially Black males. But think about this generation coming up with almost no jobs, access to firearms, thanks to the N.R.A., and no hope. Imagine people saying you'll never get the kind of jobs our parents had, and by the way, here's some malt liquor and crack cocaine.

—ROBIN D.G. KELLEY, BLACK SCHOLAR

196 This culture was born in the ghetto. We were born here to die. We're surviving now, but we're not yet rising up. If we've got a problem, we've got to correct it. We can't be hypocrites. That's what I hope the hip-hop generation can do, to take us all to the next level by always reminding us: It ain't about keeping it real, it's about keeping it right.

—DJ KOOL HERC, BLACK HIP-HOP ARTIST

197 I learned to combat the rancor in my heart by embracing my losses, accepting the tragedies of my life—my lost homeland, my dead friends and relatives, my traumatized family, my broken heart—as a kind of inheritance. Over time, I learned to give it aesthetic expression, and this gives me solace, a center, and ultimately a sense of direction.

—ANDREW LAM, ASIAN AMERICAN WRITER

198   Growing up Fat Black Female and almost blind in america requires so much surviving that you have to learn from it or die.

—AUDRE LORDE, BLACK WRITER

199   "Soul" helps us to navigate the hostile currents of an unequal and unfair world, a world stratified by color and class, where all too frequently there seems to be no justice. "Soul" reminds us that we are a people who possess history and memory, and that we have the capacity to discover and know our own truths.

—MANNING MARABLE, BLACK SCHOLAR

200   Your ammunition is your imagination and your technique.

—WYNTON MARSALIS, BLACK MUSICIAN

201   I know we're living in difficult times. People who don't understand that, they're not gonna survive. You have to have faith, and that's basically what I'm living on day by day, faith.

—JOCQUELYN MARSHALL,
BLACK SURVIVOR OF HURRICANE KATRINA

202   Anger stirs and wakes in her; it opens its mouth. And like a hot-mouthed puppy, laps up the dredges of her shame. Anger is better. There is a sense of being in anger. A reality and presence. An awareness of worth.

—TONI MORRISON, BLACK NOVELIST

203   Being a minority in both caste and class, we moved about anyway on the hem of life, struggling to consolidate our weakness and hang on, or to creep singly up into the major folds of the garment.

—TONI MORRISON, BLACK NOVELIST

204 Just as our ancestors sang their songs in a strange land when they were kidnapped and sold from Africa, we must, now and in the future, continue to sing our songs under strange stars.

—CHARLES R. SAUNDERS, BLACK WRITER

205 our dreams draw blood from old sores.

—NTOZAKE SHANGE, BLACK WRITER

206 We is terrific.

—THE SUPREMES, BLACK SINGERS

207 When asked, most folks will gladly tell us about ourselves, who we are, what we're feeling, and where we should be heading. And if we don't honor ourselves by listening to our lives, we'll believe them.

—SUSAN L. TAYLOR, BLACK WRITER

208 In order to be able to live at all in America I must be unafraid to live anywhere in it, and I must be able to live in the fashion and with whom I choose.

—ALICE WALKER, BLACK WRITER

209 This tragicomic sense—tragicomic rather than simply "tragic," because even ultimate purpose and objective order are called into question—propels us toward suicide or madness unless we are buffered by ritual, cushioned by community or sustained by art.

—CORNEL WEST, BLACK SCHOLAR

2 I 0   The blues records of each decade explain something about the philo-sophical basis of our lives as black people...Blues is a basis of historical conti-nuity for black people. It is a ritualized way of talking about ourselves and passing it on.

—SHERLEY ANNE WILLIAMS, BLACK WRITER

2 I I   This is what I hold against slavery. May come a time when I for*give*—cause I don't think I'm set up to for*get*—the beatings, the selling, the killings, but I don't think I ever forgive the ignorance they kept us in.

—SHERLEY ANNE WILLIAMS, BLACK WRITER

2 I 2   It amazes me that black people have managed over the course of their long history on these shores to keep their humanity intact. For surely all the signs and signals around us told us otherwise; told us that we were less than human, a people cursed by God to live degraded lives; told us that we were lazy, stupid, and unfit for society.

—JAN WILLIS, BLACK WRITER

2 I 3   There is a great existential difficulty in attempting to count oneself a human being equal with all others after having suffered through the experi-ence of centuries of slavery. Our very humanity was challenged and degraded at every turn and yet, through it all, we have maintained the desire to stand tall, with dignity and love of self.

—JAN WILLIS, BLACK WRITER

2 I 4   You see, even with the new drugs, we are still dying in droves—and most of us don't seem to care. What makes me so sad and so terrified is that I just don't know what else to do to get Black folks to make ending the AIDS epidemic a top priority.

—PHILL WILSON, BLACK ACTIVIST

2 1 5   The ceremony will continue. This is a testament to the faith of the Indian people. No matter how badly the salmon have been treated, no matter how serious the decline. It has only made Native people deeper in their resolve. It has doubled their commitment. It has rekindled the hope that today is beginning to grow in many young people.

—TED STRONG, AMERICAN INDIAN ACTIVIST

2 1 6   Hunger steals the memory.

—LOUISE ERDRICH, AMERICAN INDIAN NOVELIST

2 1 7   I got well by talking. Death could not get a word in edgewise, grew discouraged, and traveled on.

—LOUISE ERDRICH, AMERICAN INDIAN NOVELIST

2 1 8   Vile habits acquired in a state of servitude are not easily thrown off.

—RICHARD ALLEN, BLACK ABOLITIONIST

2 1 9   Despite the murders, rapes, and suicides, we had survived the middle passage, and the auction block had not erased us. Not humiliations, nor lynchings, individual cruelties, nor collective oppression had been able to eradicate us from earth.

—MAYA ANGELOU, BLACK POET

2 2 0   My life, my *real* life, was in danger, and not from anything other people might do but from the hatred I carried in my own heart.

—JAMES BALDWIN, BLACK WRITER

2 2 1   In a time of chaos, in a time of trouble, we're asking for unity, as defense against these mad white people who continue to run the world.

—AMIRI BARAKA, BLACK POET

222 Given the three-hundred-year war against Black manhood and womanhood, and given the circumstances under which most Black fathers and mothers are forced to live, the mystery is that so many still stand and love.

— Lerone Bennett, Jr., Black writer and historian

223 Life in the Apple doesn't allow much time for reminiscing and pining for the good old days. The snap, pop, and hassle of tomorrow hits faster than a rimshot from Tubbal's tom-tom and is upon you as persistently as a landlord with the rent receipt.

— Herb Boyd, Black journalist

224 "You're mine." And Blackness—the red of it, the milk and cream of it, the tan and yellow-tan of it, the deep-brown middle-brown high-brown of it, the "olive" and the ochre of it!—Blackness marches on.

— Gwendolyn Brooks, Black poet

225 I've been in slavery all my life. Ain't nothing changed for me but the address.

— James Brown, Black singer

226 Our grandfathers and fathers had to run, run, run. My generation is out of breath. We ain't running no more.

— Stokely Carmichael, Black activist

227 A crust of bread and a corner to sleep in, / A minute to smile and an hour to weep in, / A pint of joy to a peck of troubles / And never a laugh but the moans come double; / And that is life.

— Paul Lawrence Dunbar, Black poet

228 I have been offered Black quasi-heroes who get hanged at the end. I won't do a part like that. If I do a hero, he's going to live to the end of the movie.

— MORGAN FREEMAN, BLACK ACTOR

229 Indian nations are forced to cope with difficult decisions regarding economic development, cultural preservation, and national sovereignty within a society that never meant for them to survive. For many nations, gaming is a partial answer to the problems they face. For others, it is part of the problem. However, the decision to pursue gaming or not is a choice that only Indian tribes have the right to make.

— ANDREA SMITH, AMERICAN INDIAN ACTIVIST

230 None who leave here are normal. If I leave here alive, I'll leave nothing behind. They'll never count me among the broken men, but I can't say that I am normal either. I've been hungry too long. I've gotten angry too often. I've been lied to and insulted too many times. They've pushed me over the line from which there can be no retreat. I *know* that they will not be satisfied until they've pushed me out of this existence altogether.

— GEORGE JACKSON, BLACK PRISONER

231 Like many Cheyenne, I feel as if I have already lived a lifetime of fighting strip mining. We live in fear, anger, and urgency. And we long for a better life for our tribe. I've been told that if we mined our coal, we'd be millionaires. We want to keep our homeland, to keep it intact.

— GAIL SMALL, AMERICAN INDIAN ACTIVIST

232 Maybe survival isn't our only goal anymore. Maybe we can aim at success.

— WALTER MOSLEY, BLACK WRITER

Migrations

233   As long as everything remains this way, we'll keep crossing. If they throw out two by Nogales, ten will enter by Mexicali. And if they deport five by Juarez, seven will come through Laredo. If today they throw me out, tomorrow I'll come back.

—ANONYMOUS, MIGRANT

234   The border has never been a gentle place. On that history and myth agree.

—EARL SHORRIS, LATINO WRITER

235   I tell my students that these "illegal" immigrants are foreign aid from Mexico.

—SERGIO ELIZONDO, LATINO EDUCATOR

236   Migration is the story of my body.

—VICTOR HERNÁNDEZ CRUZ, LATINO POET

237   I think that America is such an incredibly dynamic place because of immigration. We fundamentally have been a culture that's been put together from the explosions of other cultures. But it's hard for us to see. We have blinded ourselves to the reality of what our country is.

—JUNOT DIAZ, LATINO WRITER

238   The real problem is the inability of America to acknowledge that our borders are already permeable, they're already flexible. Let's stop the xenophobia.

—MICHAEL ERIC DYSON, BLACK SCHOLAR

239   You see there are hundreds and hundreds and hundreds of ethnic groups that represent where our people came from. Our people who were dragged out of Africa as slaves. And in the New World, imagine, it is like a gumbo. That's a wonderful metaphor for it.

—HENRY LOUIS GATES, JR., BLACK SCHOLAR

240   The world is made up of those who move and those who do not, and increasingly it's populated by the former.

—ANDREW LAM, ASIAN AMERICAN WRITER

241   When you move a lot, you travel through space at the same rate you travel through time. Everything becomes relative. You pick things up along the way. You leave things behind and you miss them later. Some things you carry with you, even if they were never yours. You cling to things that weren't important in the first place. You hedge your bets. You are not one thing and you are not another. You are everything to all people. You are, as the American kids at school used to say when asked about their religion, "nothing." You find you can't listen to a national anthem sung with sloppy sentimentality without blushing or cringing or both. You are literally neither here nor there.

—CARINA CHOCANO, LATINA WRITER

242   Home, did I say. I forgot I have no home.

—IDA B. WELLS, BLACK JOURNALIST

243   The interesting thing I had come to learn quickly about America was that life got more complicated and therefore more difficult by the day. When you first landed, everything seemed so much easier than where you had come from—no matter where in the world that was. There seemed to be more freedom, and people acted nicer than you were used to. Everything appeared brighter and merrier in America, as long as you remained innocent and the laws were invisible to you. But once you had become aware of the different laws, how easy it was to break them, and the consequences of breaking them, then you would begin to wish sometimes that you were back home. It was like being caught in a spider web of legal maneuvers. The laws also invariably seemed to work against those with less education and less money. In other words, laws could be bought in America.

—MANTHIA DIAWARA, BLACK SCHOLAR

244   The truth is that state and local policies that reach out to try to incorporate newcomers—documented and undocumented—are in the best interest of society.

—BILL ONG HING, ASIAN AMERICAN SCHOLAR

245   Why treat a person like they are a criminal? For me it has been difficult to think why they treat us in this way, all of us who are immigrants.

—ELVIRA ARELLANO,
LATINA UNDOCUMENTED WORKER AND ACTIVIST

246   It makes absolutely no sense to go after these working people in the name of homeland security when they all know they had absolutely nothing whatsoever to do with 9/11 or any type of terrorist activity in this country.

—EMMA LOZANO, LATINA ACTIVIST

247   The great human migration within the Americas cannot be stopped; human beings are natural forces of the earth, just as rivers and winds are natural forces.

—LESLIE MARMON SILKO, AMERICAN INDIAN WRITER

248   It is no use; borders haven't worked, and they won't work, not now, as the indigenous people of the Americas reassert their kinship and solidarity with one another.

—LESLIE MARMON SILKO, AMERICAN INDIAN WRITER

249 With the policies of the past century Indians have seen a constant migration of people beyond the traditional homelands to the cities of America. Whether seeking employment or education, the Indians have become a constant source of immigrants and, like other groups, have had to begin at the bottom of the economic pyramid and work their way toward economic stability.

— Vine Deloria, Jr., American Indian writer

250 Amnesty from what? We die in the desert, we die in the workplace, and we sacrifice our lives for our families' survival—why should they "forgive" us? I prefer to describe our struggles as a fight for the rights of residency and mobility, and for demilitarization of borders.

— Maria Jiménez, Latina activist

251 I think the notion of identifying yourself as a non-immigrant, which I think we're losing, frankly, is very important. Saying that you were here before they were is a very radical perspective. Chicanismo aligned us as indigenous people, which is something I feel we're losing.

— Cherríe Moraga, Latina writer

252 It has been argued that our immigration system is broken and open for exploitation by any potential immigrant. In fact, our immigration system is cruel and contravenes basic ethical principles of an open society.

— Deepa Fernandes, South Asian journalist

253 Just as there are no "good" guest worker programs, there are no "good" free-trade agreements.

— Gilbert G. Gonzalez, Latino scholar

254   A battle line is being drawn within nations and across continents. The people versus free trade and its varying identities—such as free markets, globalization, the Washington Consensus, and neoliberalism—has emerged as a key political battle of the twenty-first century.

—GILBERT G. GONZALEZ, LATINO SCHOLAR

255   The world today is divided not just between haves and have-nots, but also between those who must move to survive and those who move because they want to and because they can, between global exiles and globe-trotters. The global exiles are socially positioned on the margins no matter what shore they arrive on. The globe-trotting vacationers are lavishly received by those global subjects who haven't yet made their pilgrimage into exile. The globe-trotters have a great time abroad, while the global exiles sing songs, write poems and novels and essays, produce plays and films, and fill canvases with the metaphors of their never-ending journeys.

—RUBÉN MARTÍNEZ, LATINO JOURNALIST

256   My quest for a true center, for a cultural, political and romantic home, is stripped of direction.

—RUBÉN MARTÍNEZ, LATINO JOURNALIST

257   America is defined by movement—literally, every step of the way. The cliché is belabored before it is uttered: to be an American is to come from elsewhere and to be afflicted by restlessness forever after. It is to be part of the lines embarking at Ellis Island in the East or Angel Island in the West, the wagon train across the plains, the trail of tears, white flight, suburban sprawl, the exodus from the dust bowl portrayed by John Steinbeck in *The Grapes of Wrath*, the Middle Passage of slavery, the Underground Railroad to freedom in the North, the Great Migration of African Americans toward economic opportunity, the marches for civil rights, the smuggler's human cargo packed into vans or container-ships, and the Beat Generation on the road.

—FRANK H. WU, ASIAN AMERICAN SCHOLAR

258   We had already acquired the habit of doubting ourselves as well as the place we came from. To this day, after three decades of living in America, I feel like a stranger in what I now consider my own country.

—JULIA ALVAREZ, LATINA WRITER

259   In this decade of large-scale diasporic movements, it is imperative that we come to some agreement about who "we" are now that the community includes old-timers, newcomers, many races, languages, and religions; about what our expectations of happiness and strategies for its pursuit are; and what our goals are for the nation.

—BHARATI MUKHERJEE, SOUTH ASIAN NOVELIST

260   Others often talk of diaspora, of arrival as the end of the process. They talk of arrival in the context of loss, the loss of communal memory and the erosion of an intact ethnic culture. They use words like "erosion" and "loss" in alarmist ways. I want to talk of arrival as gain.

—BHARATI MUKHERJEE, SOUTH ASIAN NOVELIST

261   In migrating, and in imagining the difference between the places we have come to and the places we have left behind, new knowledges are created.

—HENRY YU, ASIAN AMERICAN SCHOLAR

262   California, and especially Los Angeles, a gateway to both Asia and Latin America, poses the universal question of the coming century: how do we deal with the Other?

—CARLOS FUENTES, LATINO WRITER

263   Those who seek remittances from abroad continue to stake their belonging to a country they left, not merely for some forlorn sense of community at a time when immigrants feel unwelcomed in America, but because many have family who depend on their labor.

—FRANCIS CALPOTURA, ASIAN AMERICAN ORGANIZER

264   The single mothers who are coming to this country, and the children who follow them, are changing the face of immigration to the United States. Each year, the number of women and children who immigrate to the United States grows. They become our neighbors, children in our schools, workers in our homes. As they become a greater part of the fabric of the United States, their troubles and triumphs will be a part of this country's future.

—Sonia Nazario, Latina journalist

265   Immigrants who come to the United States are by nature optimists. They have to be in order to leave everything they love and are familiar with for the unknown.

—Sonia Nazario, Latina journalist

266   Latina migrants ultimately pay a steep price for coming to the United States. They lose their children's love. Reunited, they end up in conflicted homes. Too often, the boys seek out gangs to try to find the love they thought they would find with their mothers. Too often, the girls get pregnant and form their own families. In many ways, these separations are devastating Latino families. People are losing what they value most.

—Sonia Nazario, Latina journalist

267   I would say that we've had a guest worker program for the last 500 years. I don't think there's going to be much change unless you break down the borders altogether.

—Ana Castillo, Latina writer

268   Before a person can become an emigrant, he must first become expert in the study of his own condition, for emigration is made of despair and dreams, despair over life at home and dreams of life in another place.

—Earl Shorris, Latino writer

269 For the moment, the method of communication beyond the immediate stimuli of economics and politics is unknown, although something is surely going on, something draws the people down out of the mountains and sends them into a world they could not have dreamed. The pattern is clear; it has been observed; the people are coming north.

—EARL SHORRIS, LATINO WRITER

270 The experience of displacement is a profound one and is one that so many people have gone through. Displacement in relation to refugeeism that comes out of a war experience is present now. It's a huge human landscape. So many people are being moved through that landscape right now.

—LÊ THI DIEM THÚY, ASIAN AMERICAN WRITER

271 Immigrant communities blend domestic and homeland issues, and make the experience of globalization painfully real. To meet these challenges, one of the key areas of concentration is developing an infrastructure for a new, emerging leadership in immigrant communities.

—MARIA JIMÉNEZ, LATINA ACTIVIST

272 I feel that especially in the political gestalt we're in right now, exile has become a particularly pointed question, more so than immigration. Immigration, at least from the Arab-American point of view, was just more innocent and—I don't want to say naïve—but it had a kind of hopefulness and optimism that wasn't as charged by issues of race and politics as it is now.

—DIANA ABU-JABER, ARAB AMERICAN NOVELIST

273 Water will run to a dry spot, like labor will run to where there is work, this is true for everybody, no matter what your trade is or what your profession is. But we migrants want the same thing as everybody else; the ability to feed, educate and clothe our families, no matter what it takes. Some of us come poor, illegal or contracted, all sharing one dream to better the lives of that next generation.

—BALDEMAR VELASQUEZ, LATINO ORGANIZER

274   Migrant farmworkers suffer probably the worst living and working conditions of any workers in the United States. Not only are you talking substandard wages, but you are talking about essentially a plantation arrangement. Workers live in housing provided by the growers. They have the status of indentured servants; they are obligated to do anything the farmer tells them to, or else lose their homes.

—BALDEMAR VELASQUEZ, LATINO ORGANIZER

275   We were born on this continent. We built those cities in the West and Southwest. We didn't cross anybody's borders—everybody's borders crossed us.

—BALDEMAR VELASQUEZ, LATINO ORGANIZER

276   The government has violently raided homes and workplaces, sanctioned slave-like working conditions and denied historic and fundamental human rights. Migrants see and feel the slow, gradual dawn of a mutating American dream.

—ROBERTO LOVATO, LATINO WRITER

277   If our displacement was brought about by decades of maltreatment under the dictates of U.S.-crafted policies, and that we've paid for it with our broken families and with the ravaged natural resources of our countries, and that we're relegated to work in treacherous jobs and to live in squalor in urban America, then we have more than "earned" the right to be here.

—FRANCIS CALPOTURA, ASIAN AMERICAN ORGANIZER

278   We have to replace the moniker "immigrant" with the term "displaced"—casting our lot with the millions in motion around the world.

—FRANCIS CALPOTURA, ASIAN AMERICAN ORGANIZER

279   You can pass a million legalization programs, but as long as we have restrictive laws that don't move with our economies, we'll still have migration. Our goal is a community that doesn't discriminate against people based on status.

—MARCELA DÍAZ, LATINA ORGANIZER

280   When people have sacrificed so much and left their country, they want their children to conform and lead what they think of as a good, stable life. If you're not doing that, there's fear that not only will you fail, but the whole family, the whole enterprise will fail.

—EDWIDGE DANTICAT, BLACK NOVELIST

281   We live in a world where people float between borders. When you come from such different circumstances and you end up in the United States, it's like space travel. Within hours, you're on a different planet.

—EDWIDGE DANTICAT, BLACK NOVELIST

282   Railroad tracks divided us from communities where white people lived, such as South Gate and Lynwood across from Watts. We were invisible people in a city which thrived on glitter, big screens and big names, but this glamour contained none of our names, none of our faces. The refrain "this is not your country" echoed for a lifetime.

—LUIS J. RODRIGUEZ, LATINO WRITER

283   It's not an easy thing—moving your whole life, leaving your friends and family for something completely unknown on pure hope and faith that life might be better somewhere else.

—ISHLE YI PARK, ASIAN AMERICAN POET

284   "Ana del Aire," my mother calls me. Woman of the air, not earthbound, rooted to one place—not to Mexico, where Mami's mother died, not to Chicago, where I was born, not to New Mexico, where I've made a home for my son, but to everywhere at once.

—ANA CASTILLO, LATINA WRITER

285   I came to the U.S. alone. I started empty handed, and now I am empty handed again.

—ANH HOANG, ASIAN AMERICAN FISHERMAN AND HURRICANE
KATRINA SURVIVOR

286   For decades the message has been: We have a job for you. Today it is: We have a job for you but you'll have more trouble getting across the line.

—RUBÉN MARTÍNEZ, LATINO JOURNALIST

287   The migrant trail is a loop not only in space but in time. The future lies in America, the past in Mexico. The past is tolerable only for so long, especially in the impoverished lands of the south. But the future can also be painful for a migrant in America; the distance from loved ones in the homeland can become unbearable. It all works out perfectly for the migrant who shuttles between the two. It is best to stay on the road, to keep moving.

—RUBÉN MARTÍNEZ, LATINO JOURNALIST

288   When my homeland faces difficulties, I do not allow myself to leave it.

—SHIRIN EBADI, IRANIAN LAWYER AND ACTIVIST

289   Who is a settler and who a native? Who is the enemy and who are we?

—MAHMOOD MAMDANI, SOUTH ASIAN SCHOLAR

CHAPTER 2

Selves

Identities

1　I had to leave home so I could find myself, find my own intrinsic nature buried under the personality that had been imposed on me.

—Gloria Anzaldúa, Latina writer

2　All I knew for sure was that I was drowning, a constant pressure on my chest to choose between things I could not choose between—black or white America, material or spiritual gain, gender or racial allegiance, beauty or safety, myself or others—choose, choose! With each dichotomy I sputtered, taking on water. For the first time in my life, I was lost. Even if I could swim, where was the shore?

—Faith Adiele, Black writer

3　Living on borders and in margins, keeping intact one's shifting and multiple identity and integrity, is like trying to swim in a new element, an "alien" element.

—Gloria Anzaldúa, Latina writer

4   We are the only true Pan-African people in the whole world, the African-American people. And by African-American I mean Black people anywhere in the New World, whether it's Latin America, the Caribbean, or in North America.

—HENRY LOUIS GATES, JR., BLACK SCHOLAR

5   To separate from my culture (as from my family) I had to feel competent enough on the outside and secure enough inside to live life on my own. Yet in leaving home I did not lose touch with my origins because lo mexicano is in my system. I am a turtle, wherever I go I carry "home" on my back.

—GLORIA ANZALDÚA, LATINA WRITER

6   I think it's important for everyone, including so-called white people, to be more precise about who you are, to just be truthful and sane.

—JUNE JORDAN, BLACK POET

7   Everyone claims to be part Cherokee.

—SHERMAN ALEXIE, AMERICAN INDIAN WRITER

8   The primary thing that people need to know about Indians is that our identity is much less cultural now and much more political—that we really do exist as political entities and sovereign political nations. We are separate politically and economically. And should be.

—SHERMAN ALEXIE, AMERICAN INDIAN WRITER

9   I grew up with occasional bhajans and Michael Jackson, brief doses of Karnatak music and Hindu ritual, a lot of Beethoven, Saturday Night Fever, math club, rice & sambar, Pizza Hut, the Police, Star Wars, Prince, and (more than anything else) the experience of being dark-skinned with a "foreign" name in suburban America, trying to figure out how to *be*.

—VIJAY IYER, SOUTH ASIAN MUSICIAN

10 They [Iranian women] are trying to show the world that it is possible to be Muslim and modern. That it is possible to be Muslim and to believe in the equality of rights between men and women.

— SHIRIN EBADI, IRANIAN LAWYER AND ACTIVIST

11 Listen how they say your name. If they can't say that right, there's no way they're going to know how to treat you proper, neither.

— RITA DOVE, BLACK POET

12 When we lose destiny, we forfeit obvious markers of what is supposed to constitute a successful life. We might even begin to question the true value of our professional or scholastic achievements, or our faith in the strategies that were supposed to have earned us respect. When that happens, what remains is only the essence of who we are, stripped of camouflage. Is the person that remains someone we know? What does she stand for? What is she worth to herself?

— PHOEBE ENG, ASIAN AMERICAN LECTURER

13 I speak with no authority; no assumption of age nor rank; I hold no position. I have no wealth. One thing alone I own and that is my own soul.

— W.E.B. DU BOIS, BLACK SCHOLAR AND ACTIVIST

14 Mexicans! Spicy, wabby, drunk, dreamy. The downfall of the United States. Its salvation. Mexicans mow our lawns, graduate from college, fleece us dry. They're people with family values—machismo, many kids, big trucks. Our neighbors south of the border. Our future. Tequila!

— GUSTAVO ARELLANO, LATINO WRITER

15 To be a colored man in America ... and enjoy it, you must be greatly daring, greatly stolid, greatly humorous and greatly sensitive. And at all times a philosopher.

— JESSIE REDMOND FAUSET, BLACK WRITER

16   I think I'll keep my mixed up, multicultural (this is not a bad word), bastardized, poly-religious, integrated and even miscegenated American identity, thank you anyway.

—Suheir Hammad, Arab American poet

17   I don't know what Palestine looks like, what Palestine tastes like, but it is something that is in your blood and we all carry ancestry around with us. As a child I was told that I was different from everyone else around me, I was Palestinian. I think that becoming a woman and understanding myself, being Palestinian becomes what I make it. I may not be like every other Palestinian and that is good. It is also something that I realize I have to claim for we are not living in a perfect society where we do not have to claim nationalities or religions.

—Suheir Hammad, Arab American poet

18   No matter what I did, or where I was, or how I lived, I had considered myself a writer … Foremost a writer. Above all else a writer. It was my salvation, and is. The world can deny me all other employment, and stone me as an ex-convict, as a nigger, as a disagreeable and unpleasant person. But as long as I write, whether it is published or not, I'm a writer, and no one can take that away.

—Chester Himes, Black novelist

19   Many children create a false self early in life. In the case of black children the idea of a false self has become a norm in many families wherein folk believe that survival depends on wearing a mask, never letting anyone know how you feel or who you really are.

—bell hooks, Black writer

20   Ethnic writers, those of us from communities that are being newly discovered by a white industry, have to remember that we are so much more than our buzz. We are voices of translation and resistance, vast reservoirs of untold stories. Our generation, whatever that is, should never be reduced to one voice—even our own.

—MINAL HAJRATWATA, SOUTH ASIAN WRITER

21 I see myself as a Black man and as an artist, and when I think about art, I think about it in a broader scope. I explore it as a way of living, of transcending the hype that surrounds us, and I'm able to become a better human being.

—DANNY GLOVER, BLACK ACTOR

22 Awareness of our situation must come before inner changes, which in turn come before changes in society.

—GLORIA ANZALDÚA, LATINA WRITER

23 America's dilemma has been our resistance to ourselves—our denial of our immensely varied selves.

—RONALD TAKAKI, ASIAN AMERICAN SCHOLAR

24 To become visible is to see ourselves and each other in a different mirror of history.

—RONALD TAKAKI, ASIAN AMERICAN SCHOLAR

25 We have the capability to pick and choose and pastiche and sample from our multiple selves to construct a better human being.

—GUILLERMO GÓMEZ-PEÑA, LATINO PERFORMANCE ARTIST

26 I wish I could buy you for what you are really worth and sell you for what you think you're worth. I'm sure I would make money on the deal.

—ZORA NEAL HURSTON, BLACK WRITER

27   People are prone to build a statue of the kind of person that it pleases them to be. And few people want to be forced to ask themselves "What if there is no me like my statue?"

—Zora Neal Hurston, Black writer

28   If I pass for other than what I am, do you feel safer?

—Lani Ka'ahumanu, Native Hawaiian poet

29   I never said I was an angel. Nor am I innocent or holy like the Virgin Mary. What I am is natural and serious and as sensitive as an open nerve on an ice cube. I'm a young black sister with an unselfish heart who overdosed on love long ago. My closest friends consider me soft-spoken. Others say I have a deadly tongue. And while it's true that I have a spicy attitude like most of the ghetto girls I know, I back it up with a quick, precise, and knowledgeable mind. My memory runs way back and I'm inclined to remind people of the things they'd most like to forget.

—Sister Souljah, Black hip-hop artist

30   Themes of power, or lack of it, provide the drumbeat for every aspect of our lives.

—Phoebe Eng, Asian American lecturer

31   Power is about knowing what we stand for, breathing it into every activity of the day, and being clear.

—Phoebe Eng, Asian American lecturer

32   Acting black. Looking black. Being a real black. This debate among us is almost a parody. The fact is that I am black, so why do I need to prove it?

—Roberto Santiago, Latino writer

33 Indigenismo, the embracing of an indigenous identity, has less to do with any innate merit in being an Indian, than with the concept of accepting yourself for who you are.

—JESÚS SALVADOR TREVIÑO, LATINO FILMMAKER

34 Identity must not become an end. It must be an empowering experience that motivates struggle.

—JESÚS SALVADOR TREVIÑO, LATINO FILMMAKER

35 The first step in claiming yourself is anger.

—JAMAICA KINCAID, BLACK WRITER

36 When people say you're charming you are in deep trouble.

—JAMAICA KINCAID, BLACK WRITER

37 In the transformation of silence into language and action, it is vitally necessary for each one of us to establish or examine her function in that transformation, and to recognize her role as vital within that transformation.

—AUDRE LORDE, BLACK WRITER

38 I am not *just* a lesbian. I am not *just* a poet. I am not *just* a mother. Honor the complexity of your vision and yourselves.

—AUDRE LORDE, BLACK WRITER

39 Writing helped me reconcile a lot of the contradictions in my life, because it meant I would actually take note of them. And traversing that world made me recognize that you can really be anything you want to be.

—ASRA Q. NOMANI, SOUTH ASIAN JOURNALIST

40   I know that truth needs no evidence, because what comes of the dust of sacred tablets is only what has ever been in the air. I have walked for twenty-eight days to enter this cave of my own skin, which is really but a cloth lent to me by ancestors. It is, my skin, steeped in their herbs and the voices of their lives. Inside myself, I reenter them who gave me life in the first.

—Bahiyyih Maroon, Black writer

41   There is no way to enter Blackness, for it is that which is never absent— ever present, no? But through channels, the mind can rejoin the texture of its skin's history. A texture of braids, plaited around and about the skull as a nest ready for a basket to be perched. The texture of a womon's head/hair.

—Bahiyyih Maroon, Black writer

42   I return to the place I live with cloth under my arm. Before it fades, I will have memorized its pattern and tattooed the pictures onto bone. The patterns speak of past and visions. They speak a code within code. As with a line like touchstone, poised in the air for thousands to see. For some it will be the symbol of the bed they share. For me it will be like a moment back inside the oldest cave, witness to a fine black mark etched forever into the rock which holds eternity, a black mark shaped as a pubic bone, a triangle, a womon's center, a man's beginning.

—Bahiyyih Maroon, Black writer

43   Without road maps and compasses, we have grown accustomed to defining our experiences and our validity individually, through blind trial and error, often without mentors, often without hearing the stories of others that might help us understand our own lives. In my life, I have often found myself swinging back and forth, alone and searching for a stabilizing center.

—Phoebe Eng, Asian American lecturer

44 My work requires me to think about how free I can be as an African-American woman writer in my genderized, sexualized, wholly racialized world.

— TONI MORRISON, BLACK NOVELIST

45 Do more than: Stop self-destructing. Save each other. Not have a nervous breakdown or six by twenty-five. Decolonize our minds, our hair, our hearts. Transform into the phoenixes we were all meant to be.

— LEAH LAKSHMI PIEPZNA-SAMARASINHA, SOUTH ASIAN WRITER

46 At the time, I found it hilarious that the one time I found myself totally holy and totally Muslim was when I was at a conference for Lesbian, Gay, Bi-Sexual, Transgendered, and Queer people.

— KHALIDA SAED, IRANIAN AMERICAN ACTIVIST

47 There are no anglicized accents in this name, no long vowel sounds, and definitely no generic naming associations. There is only Spanish seasoning and a mouth full of mambo when you utter my name. Make no mistake about it— I carry the island of Borinquen not only in my heart, but also in my name. What's in a name? Well, everything.

— CELIA SAN MIGUEL, LATINA WRITER

48 Is Black masculinity defined by hypersexuality, anti-social behavior and a propensity towards sports, or is it something that is more authentic and elusive?

— KEHINDE WILEY, BLACK PAINTER

49 I think now that whatever people call me doesn't really affect me. I know in my heart that my spirit is broader than any category, so it's okay. Sticks & stones.

— ISHLE YI PARK, ASIAN AMERICAN POET

50   To speak as black, female *and* commercial lawyer has rendered me simultaneously universal, trendy, and marginal.

—Patricia Williams, Black law professor

51   You don't know what you're giving if you don't know what you have and you don't know what you're taking if you don't know what's yours and what's somebody else's.

—Ntozake Shange, Black poet

52   If people who look like me and talk like me can be inspired by me, then I've done my job.

—Tom Shimura (aka Lyrics Born),
Asian American hip-hop artist

53   I slip among classifications like water in cupped palms, leaving bits of myself behind. I am quick and deft, for there is no greater fear than the fear of being caught wanting to belong. I am a chameleon. And the best chameleon has no center, no truer sense of self than what he is in the instant.

—Andrew X. Pham, Asian American writer

54   No other group in America has so had their identity socialized out of existence as have black women ... When black people are talked about the focus tends to be on black *men*; and when women are talked about the focus tends to be on *white* women.

—bell hooks, Black writer

55   The Black artist. The Black man. The holy man. The man you seek. The climber, the striver. The maker of peace. The lover. The warrior. We are they whom you seek. Look in. Find yourself. Find the being, the speaker.

—Amiri Baraka, Black poet

56 When you believe in the righteousness of your path, you take firmer steps. At the same time, being a Muslim and believing in God, I gain more strength as well.

—SHIRIN EBADI, IRANIAN LAWYER AND ACTIVIST

57 Asian American individuals give "Asian American" meaning as they define it to suit themselves.

—FRANK H. WU, ASIAN AMERICAN SCHOLAR

58 We realized that ultimately, it is up to us to decide that we are Latina, to individually determine what the term means. We grappled with the implications of this on our greater culture, and argued about the word's ability to entirely define us. At the end of this process, we realized that no matter how loaded, conflicted, and difficult the term may be, we are Latinas. Through heritage and by choice.

—MICHELLE HERRERA MULLIGAN, LATINA WRITER

59 Being a man is the continuing battle of one's life. One loses a bit of manhood with every stale compromise to the authority of any power in which one does not believe.

—H. RAP BROWN, BLACK ACTIVIST

60 Growing up as a refugee child and a child of color, it's inescapable that I'm always carrying a political identity wherever I go. For me, I've always been a political billboard.

—MEE MOUA, ASIAN AMERICAN POLITICIAN

61 If you look at Africa, the whole continent of Africa, I have one little dot, one little exact DNA match, and it's in Egypt, in the delta of the Nile River, but if you lift your eyes and look at northern Europe, I have ten thousand matches ... my mitochondrial DNA goes back to northern Europe, which means that I am descended from a white woman who slept with a black man between 1619 and 1750 ... I set off on this series trying to prove that I was a Yoruba from western Nigeria and it turns out that I'm a Jew from northern Germany.

—HENRY LOUIS GATES, JR., BLACK SCHOLAR

6 2   It's important for women to have a healthy definition of themselves. You should not look to the men you meet, or to your girlfriends, for your sense of yourself, your self-esteem, your role as a woman. You should cultivate your mind, spirit, body, heart, and soul.

—SISTER SOULJAH, BLACK HIP-HOP ARTIST

6 3   When we play to the demands of others, we are putting through our heads what we think they want and we are using our energies to do that. When we are freed from that, we are free to move on to the job of defining ourselves.

—CAMILLE COSBY, BLACK PHILANTHROPIST

6 4   In our first and second waves of feminism as well as in our first and second generations as immigrants and as newly minted Latinos, we sometimes trap ourselves in too-rigid definitions of what it means to be who we are.

—JULIA ALVAREZ, LATINA WRITER

6 5   You don't have to accept those media labels. You need not settle for any defining category. You don't have to be merely a taxpayer or a red state or a blue state or a consumer or a minority or a majority. Of course, you're general, but you're also specific. A citizen and a person, and the person you are is like nobody else on the planet ... You are your own stories and therefore free to imagine and experience what it means to be human without wealth ... And although you don't have complete control over the narrative (no author does, I can tell you), you could nevertheless create it.

—TONI MORRISON, BLACK NOVELIST

66 When you know your name, you should hang on to it, for unless it is noted down and remembered, it will die when you do.

—Toni Morrison, Black novelist

67 Books after books, that is how I have come to best describe myself— a place where words have no boundaries and titles change. A place with many places, different names, endless endings, and beginnings ...

—Nathalie Handal, Arab American poet

68 We've been battered, in very different ways, by racism, sexism, classism, homophobia, and other forms of physical/psychic oppression and abuse. Identity politics has been extremely useful: we've invented and found specific names and labels that affirm us, give us self-confidence, agency, a sense of belonging, a place to call "home." But at some point—no matter how effective these labels seem to be—they will fail us. They will be walls rather than doorways.

—AnaLouise Keating, Latina scholar

69 Some days I wonder if anyone sees that I am all of these at once, and other days it doesn't matter what anyone sees because I am comfortable being a contrary, existing at the margins of categories.

—Shefali Milczarek-Desai, South Asian scholar

70 My identity, the most intimate of feelings about my own body, were directly tied to what had happened nearly fifty years ago—the signing of Executive Order No. 9066 and the internment of the Japanese American community.

—David Mura, Asian American writer

71   There are moments in my life when I feel as though a part of me is missing. There are days when I feel so invisible that I can't remember what day of the week it is, when I feel so manipulated that I can't remember my own name, when I feel so lost and angry that I can't speak a civil word to the people who love me best. Those are the times when I catch sight of my reflection in store windows and am surprised to see a whole person looking back. Those are the times when my skin becomes gummy as clay and my nose slides around my face and my eyes drip down to my chin. I have to close my eyes at such times and remember myself, draw an internal picture that is smooth and whole; when all else fails, I reach for a mirror and stare myself down until the features reassemble themselves, like lost sheep.

—Patricia Williams, Black law professor

72   Very little in our language or culture encourages looking at others as parts of ourselves.

—Patricia Williams, Black law professor

73   All of us, and I mean ALL of us, are the inheritors of European, African, Native American, and even Asian pasts, even if we can't exactly trace our blood lines to all of these continents.

—Robin D. G. Kelley, Black scholar

74   We are all Americans who have toiled and suffered and known oppression and defeat, from the first Indian that offered peace in Manhattan to the last Filipino pea pickers.

—Carlos Bulosan, Asian American writer

75   For us, the ability to use identity in a purely expressive way is, finally, the surest mark of freedom.

—Geoffrey Jacques, Black poet

76 I am an American Muslim from India. My adolescence was a series of rejections, one after another, of the various dimensions of my heritage, in the belief that America, India, and Islam could not coexist within the same being. If I wanted to be one, I could not be the others. My struggle to understand the traditions I belong to as mutually enriching rather than mutually exclusive is the story of a generation of young people standing at the crossroads of inheritance and discovery, trying to look both ways at once. There is a strong connection between finding a sense of inner coherence and developing a commitment to pluralism. And that has everything to do with who meets you at the crossroads.

—EBOO PATEL, SOUTH ASIAN ACTIVIST

Education

77 I try to learn as much as I can because I know nothing compared to what I need to know.

—MUHAMMAD ALI, BLACK BOXER

78 Learning made me painfully aware of life and me. I began to dig what was inside of me. What had I been? How had I become that way? What could I be? How could I make it?

—PIRI THOMAS, LATINO WRITER

79 "Sticks and stones will break my bones, but words will never harm me." The first part about "stones breaking my bones" is right, but the part about "words will never harm me" is bullsheet!!

—PIRI THOMAS, LATINO WRITER

80   A cynical young person is almost the saddest sight to see, because it means that he or she has gone from knowing nothing to believing in nothing.

—MAYA ANGELOU, BLACK POET

81   Education takes place in the combination of the home, the community, the school and the receptive mind.

—HARRY EDWARDS, BLACK EDUCATOR

82   I can forgive bad parents! Because maybe it was an accident! Maybe they didn't even want to be parents! But teachers are no accident! You study to become a teacher! You work at it for years. So I cannot, and will not forgive teachers who are abusive, mean, and torture kids with commas and periods and misspelling, making them feel like they are less than human because they don't or can't seem to get it right.

—VICTOR VILLASEÑOR, LATINO WRITER

83   The truth was that they really didn't even want to educate us. They wanted to train us.

—VICTOR VILLASEÑOR, LATINO WRITER

84   The chief task now, it seems to me, is for teachers and educationists to ensure quality education, to foster the ideal of communication and compassion among all the young people of our society, and to view the teaching process as an integral part of the effort to bring about social change and social justice in our society.

—BAYARD RUSTIN, BLACK CIVIL RIGHTS ACTIVIST

85   What we require is not a formal return to tradition and religion, but a rereading, a reinterpretation, of our history that can illuminate the present and pave the way to a better future. For example, if we delve more deeply into ancient Egyptian and African civilisations we will discover the humanistic elements that were prevalent in many areas of life. Women enjoyed a high status and rights, which they later lost when class patriarchal society became the prevalent social system.

—NAWAL EL SAADAWI, ARAB WRITER

86 Grown people know that they do not always know the why of things, and even if they think they know, they do not know where and how they got the proof. Hence the irritation they show when children keep on demanding to know if a thing is so and how the grown folks got the proof of it. It is so troublesome because it is disturbing to the pigeonhole way of life.

—ZORA NEALE HURSTON, BLACK WRITER

87 The loss of the dominant language of the hemisphere is an intellectual and economic waste. If there is any injustice in bilingual education in the United States, it is that children who speak the majority or dominant language are not often exposed to education in two languages.

—EARL SHORRIS, LATINO WRITER

88 I learned to make my mind large, as the universe is large, so that there is room for paradoxes.

—MAXINE HONG KINGSTON, ASIAN AMERICAN NOVELIST

89 We must recognize that, to the extent that change is possible, it is more likely to occur in education than in any other sector. This is because, despite its faults, public education remains the most democratic and accessible institution in this country. In fact, in the post-welfare reform period, it is all that remains of the social safety net for poor children.

—PEDRO AND ANTWI AKOM NOGUERA, LATINO SCHOLARS

90   It's good to learn from people that have been doing it, but also you have things to offer. You have new ideas. It's a lot about training. Some people say everything is theory. That's not everything. It's about doing the work. This is a two-way thing. You learn—but you also have to teach.

—WANDA SALAMAN, BLACK ORGANIZER

91   When we say that American education must be as multinational and multicultural as the reality of American society, we are just saying that what is taught in the schools should be the whole culture of the American people.

—AMIRI BARAKA, BLACK POET

92   Education is the most powerful weapon which you can use to change the world.

—NELSON MANDELA, BLACK PRESIDENT OF SOUTH AFRICA

93   The wording of the 1954 Supreme Court decision says, in essence, that segregated schools are damaging to Black children and what they really need is to be in a school with white children. This is the message our parents heard. Nowhere does it say that segregated schools are also damaging to white children.

—NA'IM AKBAR, BLACK PSYCHOLOGIST

94   The purpose of education is to create in a person the ability to look at the world for himself, to make his own decisions.

—JAMES BALDWIN, BLACK WRITER

95   It is becoming increasingly clear that urban high schools are graduating hundreds of thousands of undereducated Black students who need the motivation that only Black colleges can provide.

—LERONE BENNETT, JR., BLACK WRITER AND HISTORIAN

96 An individual who can't relate to the Black community, understand and be understood by her own people, isn't well educated.

—JOHNETTA COLE, BLACK EDUCATOR

97 If the purpose of education is to make one person better off, it's going to take us forever to do what we need to do.

—JOHNETTA COLE, BLACK EDUCATOR

98 An error means a child needs help, not a reprimand or ridicule for doing something wrong.

—MARVA COLLINS, BLACK EDUCATOR

99 A little learning, indeed, may be a dangerous thing, but the want of learning is a calamity to any people.

—FREDERICK DOUGLASS, BLACK ABOLITIONIST

100 Education is a precondition to survival in America today.

—MARIAN WRIGHT EDELMAN, BLACK ACTIVIST

101 Our children's allegiance to high goals and standards will be principally established and enforced, not on the campus, but in the home.

—HARRY EDWARDS, BLACK EDUCATOR

102 Although anyone may speak two languages, no man or woman, no child can dream in more than one. Therefore, the logic of the proponents of bilingual education is indisputable: A child sitting at a schoolroom desk in Spanish Harlem or a kindergarten table in Texas is in danger of losing hope, unless that child is permitted, in the moonlit gardens of the soul, a serenade.

—EARL SHORRIS, LATINO WRITER

103   Clearly, English is a better language for conquerors than Spanish, for it is so difficult that no man can speak it fluently without changing his soul.

—EARL SHORRIS, LATINO WRITER

104   There is no standard by which the education of Latino children in the United States can be considered adequate, fair, or morally acceptable.

—EARL SHORRIS, LATINO WRITER

105   In the real world there is nothing romantic about the place known as *el labor*. The work is so hard, the pay so poor, and the conditions so abominable that the fathers of Mexican-American children in the valley towns of California and Texas often urge their sons or daughters to work for a day, a week, even a summer in the fields so that they will know the alternative to education.

—EARL SHORRIS, LATINO WRITER

106   Children who do not think well of themselves will fail; it is as simple as that.

—EARL SHORRIS, LATINO WRITER

107   I hear adults saying that the "youth of today don't want anything, and don't care about anything. They're a lost generation." But adults have to remember that they led us here. These situations were set into motion a long time ago. We are actually cleaning up the mess that our ancestors have left for us. But we have to look past that and get to the point where we can lay the groundwork for the generations that are going to follow us.

—SHERMAN SPEARS, BLACK ACTIVIST

108   Students had no choice but to take their education in their own hands. We have been miseducated and lied to from the very first time we stepped into a classroom.

—ANTONIO GARCIA, LATINO STUDENT ACTIVIST

109   We must get beyond textbooks, go out into the bypaths and untrodden depths of the wilderness of truth and explore and tell the world the glories of our journey.

—JOHN HOPE FRANKLIN, BLACK SCHOLAR

110   Real education consists in drawing the best out of yourself. What better book can there be than the book of humanity?

—MOHANDAS GANDHI, INDIAN ACTIVIST

111   You can be educated in some vision and feeling, as well as in mind. To see your enemy and know him is part of the complete education of man; to spiritually regulate oneself is another form of the higher education that fits man for a nobler place in life, and still to approach your brother by the feeling of your own humanity, is an education that softens the ills of the world and makes us kind indeed.

—MARCUS GARVEY, BLACK ACTIVIST

112   Education means to bring out wisdom. Indoctrination means to push in knowledge.

—DICK GREGORY, BLACK COMEDIAN

113   A man without knowledge of himself and his heritage is like a tree without roots.

—DICK GREGORY, BLACK COMEDIAN

114   It is possible to create a curriculum that encompasses the complexity of contemporary American reality in all its diversity.

—LIZA FIOL-MATTA

115   Asian Americans have functioned as a wild card in the racial politics of higher education—their educational experiences could be and have been incorporated into arguments both for and against discrimination, diversity, and affirmative action.

—DANA TAKAGI, ASIAN AMERICAN SCHOLAR

116   We must treat all with love, care, and respect. We must make them feel welcomed and invited by allowing their interests, culture and history into the classroom. We must reconnect them to their own brilliance and gain their trust so that they will learn from us. We must respect them, so that they feel connected to us.

—LISA DELPIT, BLACK SCHOLAR

117   We don't humbly ask for fairness. We demand educational equity and justice for all children and their families.

—PAM MARTINEZ, LATINO ACTIVIST

118   The "successful" colonized person understands, with the help of her family's and her community's experience of colonization, that the survival technique for the subjugated group involves double realities. She must be in two places at the same time, ovuh dyuh and here too, and not give any indication that her attention is divided. She must operate from behind the mask of the "white" language. Her lot is to act as a channeler of languages, a mere imitator of the sounds and belief systems, not one who makes sense of the ideas.

—JOANNE KILGOUR DOWDY, BLACK EDUCATOR

119   One of the great tragedies of modern education is that most people are not taught to think critically. The majority of the world's people, those of the West included, are taught to believe rather than to think. It is much easier to believe than to think.

—HAKI MADHUBUTI, BLACK POET

1 2 0 Affirmative action is neither the real problem or the whole solution. The challenge for public education is to rethink how they admit everyone.

— LANI GUINIER, BLACK LAW PROFESSOR

1 2 1 Could it be we stifle our children's genius by languaging them too quickly away from their hearts and into the straight and narrow confines of linear thinking?

— VICTOR VILLASEÑOR, LATINO WRITER

1 2 2 So could it be that we live in a very small and limited world by only speaking one language? Could it be that "only one" of anything imprisons the mind—religiously, socially, and politically—and only one in language is the first sign of the end of any nation?

— VICTOR VILLASEÑOR, LATINO WRITER

1 2 3 American Indian scholarship is, by necessity, an act of self-preservation —whether it is fighting for tribal water rights or putting a pow-wow into a poem.

— JACQUELINE KEELER, AMERICAN INDIAN WRITER

1 2 4 By supporting affirmative action even if we are not directly included in the specific program, Asian Americans strengthen the argument for affirmative action as a matter of principle ... Asian Americans can set an example—not one that defeats affirmative action, one that rescues it.

— FRANK H. WU, ASIAN AMERICAN SCHOLAR

1 2 5 At a loss for words really describes the feeling of the soul in the "white" language world. Thoughts come into her head in her family's intimate vocabulary, and she strains to translate those ideas into the acceptable form expected in public conversation. She expects that her usual facility with language will be available to her when she begins to speak in public. Instead, there are cold, metal sounds bouncing off her teeth, the act of translation cooling the passion of the thought. Where she expected to create an easy access to her listeners' acceptance, she finds that her efforts create a glistening wall, icy with dangerous foreign sounds and echoes of the unfamiliar tones of strangers.

—JOANNE KILGOUR DOWDY, BLACK EDUCATOR

126 Public education alone has the potential capacity for building pluralistic communities and creating a lively civic culture that promotes the fullest possible engagement and participation of all members of society. In this sense, the public school is a true laboratory for democracy.

—MANNING MARABLE, BLACK SCHOLAR

127 People know what is good in education and what a good education is. The lengths to which working-class parents and youth go to secure education and to preserve schools are extraordinary. Families undergo long commutes and harsh struggles to ensure that children get the means to understand and transform their reality.

—VIJAY PRASHAD, SOUTH ASIAN SCHOLAR

128 I think the biggest challenge for us is to ensure that our children have a better future than what we've had. That our children, our future, have an opportunity to be respected, to be treated as equal human beings, to get a decent education, to have opportunities that we did not have in our lifetime, and we need to fight for that.

—ARTURO RODRIGUEZ, LATINO LABOR ACTIVIST

129 As a nation and individually, we must recognize that Latino and Black students are not expendable for our future. They are critical to the growth and success of our country. Educating these students must be a central focus on our national, state, and local agendas. It is not a choice; it's a necessity.

—JOHN JACKSON, BLACK FUNDER

1 3 0   I'd organize my boot camp curriculum around three main themes in the history of people of color in America: first, the significance of mass movements and the role of individuals in relation to these movements; second, the enduring vision of a new society that propels these movements forward; and third, the fundamental link between changing society and transforming oneself.

—GLENN OMATSU, ASIAN AMERICAN EDUCATOR

Gender and Sexuality

1 3 1   Deviance is whatever is condemned by the community. Most societies try to get rid of their deviants. Most cultures have burned and beaten their homosexuals and others who deviate from the sexual common. The queer are the mirror reflecting the heterosexual tribe's fear: being different, being other and therefore lesser, therefore sub-human, in-human, non-human.

—GLORIA ANZALDÚA, LATINA WRITER

1 3 2   In the best friendships I have had with women, there is a closeness that is unique, a sympathy that comes from somewhere deep and primal in our bodies and does not need explanation, perhaps because of the life-changing experiences we share—menstruation, childbirth, menopause. The same tragedies, physical or emotional, threaten us: the infidelity of a spouse or boyfriend, rape, breast cancer, the death of a child who had grown inside our body. Whether any of these strike us personally or not, if we hear of it happening to a woman we love, we feel its reality like an electric shock along our own spine.

—CHITRA BANJEREE DIVAKARUNI, SOUTH ASIAN WRITER

1 3 3   We cannot go to the police for protection against domestic violence and then rally against them for brutality as if they are two different institutions.

—ANANNYA BHATTACHARJEE, SOUTH ASIAN ACTIVIST

134   Are there women who both cook and write? Kitchen poets, they call them. They slip phrases into their stew and wrap meaning around their pork before frying it. They make narrative dumplings and stuff their daughters' mouths so they say nothing more.

—EDWIDGE DANTICAT, BLACK NOVELIST

135   Women are not valued in this society, are attacked, objectified, traumatized, and exploited. So of course it's difficult to value ourselves. These experiences install little land mines of self-hate, self-doubt, self-sabotage, and self-destruction.

—AYA DE LEON, LATINA ARTIST

136   To be honest, being an outspoken, sensual Asian American woman is interesting and difficult territory to negotiate. On one hand, I want to be free to be my whole self onstage, and that means sometimes being reckless, bawdy, and carefree. On the other hand, I don't want to feed into the stereotype of the oversexualized Asian girl because I myself can't stand it when we're only seen in a sexualized context.

—ISHLE YI PARK, ASIAN AMERICAN POET

137   The black female body is the site where white supremacist thinking about beauty is reinscribed again and again.

—BELL HOOKS, BLACK WRITER

138   I have lived long enough now to see big changes. The older generation's fears and prejudices have given way, and today's young people realize that if someone loves someone they have a right to marry.

—MILDRED LOVING, BLACK PLAINTIFF

139   Usually, when people talk about the "strength" of black women they are referring to the way in which they perceive black women coping with oppression. They ignore the reality that to be strong in the face of oppression is not the same as overcoming oppression, that endurance is not to be confused with transformation ... The tendency to romanticize the black female experience that began in the feminist movement was reflected in the culture as a whole.

— BELL HOOKS, BLACK WRITER

140 The new self-help books for women suggest that individual relationships between men and women can be changed solely by women making the right choices.

— BELL HOOKS, BLACK WRITER

141 For ambitious women in the United States, being beautiful will only jeopardize their reputation in any professional field aside from Hollywood. I don't come from a long line of Protestant cool, suffragette movements and the 1960's feminist revolution. My heritage is hot Catholicism, where men and women are so intricately tangled that feminism becomes a dirty word.

— ADRIANA LOPEZ, LATINA WRITER

142 I, as a modern feminist, straddle the contradictions of U.S. and Latin American identities—I'm not curvaceous and polished enough for Latin American standards and I'm too sexy and well dressed for white-American standards. As a U.S. Latina, I can dance and think my way out of any situation, but for my sisters in the South, the economic chaos in Latin America is still inhibiting their movement towards sexual equality.

— ADRIANA LOPEZ, LATINA WRITER

143 I say *muchisimas gracias* to [these] difficult *chicas*, my Tia, grandmother and mother, for never being silent, for being happily unmarried, for enjoying sex and for never suffering in pain like so many have. I thank them for showing me a new kind of feminism, one that includes plenty of pleasure.

— ADRIANA LOPEZ, LATINA WRITER

144 But there are no new ideas waiting in the wings to save us women, as human. There are only old and forgotten ones, new combinations, extrapolations and recognitions from within ourselves, along with the renewed courage to try them out.

— ADRIANA LOPEZ, LATINA WRITER

145 In each story, the beauty that Yellow Woman possesses is the beauty of her passion, her daring, and her sheer strength to act when catastrophe is imminent.

— LESLIE MARMON SILKO, AMERICAN INDIAN WRITER

146 Black feminism was about flying in the face of a black male political establishment that was still very much in place on the heels of the black civil rights and black liberation struggle.

— BARBARA SMITH, BLACK ACTIVIST

147 I think it's really hard to organize around sexual politics whatever one's race. It is especially difficult to organize around issues of sexual politics as women of color because what you're doing is drawing attention to negative interactions, power relationships, and violence within communities of color.

— BARBARA SMITH, BLACK ACTIVIST

148 No matter how headstrong I had been, I, like most women of my generation, had had the desire to be alluring to men ingrained into me. And that longing had always worked like a brake on my behavior. When what men think of me ceased to be compelling, I gained greater freedom to be myself.

— SUCHENG CHANG, ASIAN AMERICAN SCHOLAR

149   And what Woman of Color in america over the age of 15 does not live with the knowledge that our daily lives are stitched with violence and with hatred, and to naively ignore that reality can mean destruction?

—AUDRE LORDE, BLACK WRITER

150   Domestic violence occurs because of social power structures where the roles of men and women are predefined, and domestic violence is how that power is played out.

—INHE CHOI, ASIAN AMERICAN ACTIVIST

151   Where is the political outcry for those women who are raped, beaten, and harassed by police? Where is the political prisoner movement for those women who are imprisoned for retaliating against abusive fathers, uncles, lovers, and others? I think the absence of these types of campaigns speaks volumes about our movement's gender politics. As long as we continue to frame criminal justice issues as an attack on our brothers, we will be unable to critique violence against women as an institutional problem.

—KAI LUMUMBA BARROW, BLACK ACTIVIST

152   All too often, the anti-prison movement has forgotten that women are specific targets of state violence.

—KAI LUMUMBA BARROW, BLACK ACTIVIST

153   For women of color all over the world, the most common and destructive experiences of violence have come from war.

—ELIZABETH (BETITA) MARTINEZ, LATINA ACTIVIST

154   Gay *rights* are not enough for me, and I doubt that they're enough for most of us. Frankly, I want the same thing now that I did thirty years ago when I joined the civil rights movement and twenty years ago when I joined the women's movement, came out, and felt more alive than I ever dreamed possible: Freedom.

— BARBARA SMITH, BLACK ACTIVIST

155   I take offense at the notion that feminism and issues of concern to gays and lesbians are only of concern to white communities because I believe that gives white people one more piece of our power and history that they are going to walk away with.

— BETH RICHIE, BLACK ACTIVIST

156   If we continue to downplay the importance of these powerful histories and social forces, we will keep them alive; we will mask and sustain their impact on our lives. Intimate justice comes from our working through, not around, these histories.

— TRICIA ROSE, BLACK SCHOLAR

157   Race, class, gender and nation are all relational categories. They're all about relationships. They are not things that are embedded in you. So race is not something that is embedded in brown people. Gender is not something that is embedded in women. Gender is about relationships among and between men and women, women and women, women of different classes, men and men. It's about all those things.

— CHANDRA TALPADE MOHANTY, SOUTH ASIAN SCHOLAR

158   And she had nothing to fall back on; not maleness, not whiteness, not ladyhood, not anything. And out of the profound desolation of her reality she may very well have invented herself.

— TONI MORRISON, BLACK WRITER

159   The apparent hypocrisy and condescension that white Western feminists held for Arab women confused me. I felt betrayed by a movement that claimed to create a global sisterhood of women; it seemed that the Arab woman was the poor and downtrodden stepsister in this family. Where was my feminism?

—Susan Muaddi Darraj, Arab American writer

160   This experience—feeling emotionally torn between my culture and what white Western feminism told me I had to be—relates almost inversely to another conflict that obstructed the recognition of my feminist identity: America's exoticism of Arab women. Although we were considered veiled and meek, we were simultaneously and ironically considered sultry, sexual and "different." People, especially white feminists, were often intrigued by my "exoticness" and asked me silly questions, like whether Arab women knew how to belly-dance or whether I knew of any women who lived in harems.

—Susan Muaddi Darraj, Arab American writer

161   The belief that Black procreation is the problem remains a major barrier to radical change in America.

—Dorothy Roberts, Black scholar

162   Basically, the men in my religion have certainly made a mess of things, and we want to go from the back rows to the front rows—we want to go from the back of the mosque to the front of the mosque. We believe that we are fulfilling Islam's teachings that men and women are spiritual equals—and we don't have to just sit deaf, dumb and blind in the mosque and the community while Osama bin Laden defines our religion for the world.

—Asra Q. Nomani, South Asian journalist

163   Where there is woman there is magic.

—Nitzoka Shange, Black poet

164 She pronounced her words in unashamed Black English and she danced her unchoreographed unladylike steps with class.

— SISTER SOULJAH, BLACK HIP-HOP ARTIST

165 If racism ended right this second, African and African American women, Arab women, Asian women, Pacific Islander women, Latinas, South Asian women, indigenous women would not be safe.

— AISHAH SHAHIDAH SIMMONS, BLACK FILMMAKER

166 To say, like our men, black women experience racism as blacks, and like white women, we experience sexism as female, erases our total life experiences.

— MONNETTE SUDLER, BLACK MUSICIAN

167 Being a woman and a mother really colors how I spend my time. I am most concerned with passing information to generations and very interested in how women are either cut off or reconnected with themselves.

— SHEREE THOMAS, BLACK WRITER

168 Abortion, for many women, is more than an experience of suffering beyond anything most men will ever know, it is an act of mercy, and an act of self-defense.

— ALICE WALKER, BLACK WRITER

169 I believe all Americans, no matter their race, no matter their sex, no matter their sexual orientation, should have that same freedom to marry.

— MILDRED LOVING, BLACK PLAINTIFF

170 Womanist is to feminist as purple is to lavender.

—ALICE WALKER, BLACK WRITER

171 The trouble with most women is they get old in their heads. They think about it too much.

—JOSEPHINE BAKER, BLACK ENTERTAINER

172 [T]here is a great space where sex ought to be; and what usually fills this space is violence.

—JAMES BALDWIN, BLACK WRITER

173 I've been living outside my body for so long I'm not sure how to make it back. I want to be back inside my body. I miss it.

—CARIDAD SOUZA, LATINA RESEARCHER

174 If men could get pregnant, abortion would be a sacrament.

—FLORYNCE RAE KENNEDY, BLACK LAWYER

175 We fight our own forms of patriarchal traditions, religious fundamentalism, and western intolerance. We may not be allowed into the streets without a veil in some Arab countries, and we are vilified for wearing the veil in the U.S. Yet I sincerely doubt that many Arab or Arab-American women would name the veil as their greatest inhibitor, even though it may be the most outwardly obvious one.

—NADIA ELIA, ARAB AMERICAN WRITER

176 When women get together and talk about men, the news is almost always bad news.

—BELL HOOKS, BLACK SCHOLAR

177 Today it should be obvious to any thinker and writer speaking about black males that the primary genocidal threat, the force that endangers black male life, is patriarchal masculinity.

— BELL HOOKS, BLACK SCHOLAR

178 I believe that men have to somehow find out what our role is in the modern world. The woman still carries forth the children, still understands that creative principle, still has that connection to the Earth and the powers of the moon. Their role is more easily defined. But I find a lot of brothers, no matter what race, are out of balance, searching to find out who they are as a man.

— TOM GOLDTOOTH, AMERICAN INDIAN ACTIVIST

179 We need to turn the question around to look at the harasser, not the target. We need to be sure that we can go out and look anyone who is a victim of harassment in the eye and say, "You do not have to remain silent anymore."

— ANITA HILL, BLACK LAWYER

180 While western feminism creates the illusion that I must either choose to be a strong, independent woman or play a role in my family and community, Third World feminism allows us to embrace and express several identities.

— SHEFALI MILCZAREK-DESAI, SOUTH ASIAN SCHOLAR

181 Like racism, sexism and misogyny are not mere aberrations in an otherwise healthy U.S. body politic; they are thoroughly necessary to the functioning of our equality-loving-but-hard-pressed-to-fully-realize democracy. Sexism and misogyny are grist for the patriarchal mill.

— T. DENEAN SHARPLEY-WHITING, BLACK SCHOLAR

182 At the bottom, feminism is not widely understood as a movement to end sexism, racism, and/or male privilege, but as a predominantly and unalterably white move to unseat aspiring black men.

— T. DENEAN SHARPLEY-WHITING, BLACK SCHOLAR

183 We, black women, have always been supportive of black men in the struggle against racism, even while we were being raped. Even while rape and assault has been going on in our communities. This is important because so many react as if talking about rape and assault in our communities is somehow not being supportive of black men, or as if it were not being loyal to black men.

— AISHAH SHAHIDAH SIMMONS, BLACK FILMMAKER

184 The reason racism is a feminist issue is easily explained by the inherent definition of feminism. Feminism is the political theory and practice to free all women: women of color, working-class women, poor women, physically challenged women, lesbians, old women, as well as white economically privileged heterosexual women. Anything else than this is not feminism, but merely female self-aggrandizement.

— BARBARA SMITH, BLACK ACTIVIST

185 Every time I get a new girlfriend, I have to introduce her as my best friend to my parents. They think I'm very social.

— KHALIDA SAED, IRANIAN AMERICAN ACTIVIST

186 To the degree that we are traditionally coupled off or safely sexless, our presence is increasingly tolerated; to be simultaneously single and sexual is a far less appropriate thing. From schools to popular media to even most gay community organizing, gay sexuality itself is rarely discussed outside of the confines of the diseases it can breed. Its associated risks increasingly define it.

— KAI WRIGHT, BLACK JOURNALIST

187   Sexuality is considered a private matter; yet it has a powerful and volatile public social life.

—TRICIA ROSE, BLACK SCHOLAR

188   What we're about is drawing on our traditions, regaining our strength as women in the ways handed down to us by our grandmothers and their grandmothers before them. Our creation of an Indian women's organization is not a criticism or division from our men. Only in this way can we organize ourselves as Indian women to meet our responsibilities, to be fully supportive of the men, to work in tandem with them as partners in a common struggle for the liberation of our people and our land. So, instead of dividing away from the men, what we are doing is building strength and unity in a traditional way.

—PHYLLIS YOUNG, AMERICAN INDIAN ACTIVIST

Wisdom

189   The function of freedom is to free someone else.

—TONI MORRISON, BLACK NOVELIST

190   One must view the world through the eye in one's heart rather than just trust the eyes in one's head.

—MARY CROW DOG, AMERICAN INDIAN ACTIVIST

191   Sometimes a lie makes life more bearable.

—WALTER MOSLEY, BLACK NOVELIST

192   Telling the truth allows others to see who we really are, makes them treat us according to our declarations, and, therefore, places us in a position closer to our emotions. Telling the truth will open dialogues.

—WALTER MOSLEY, BLACK NOVELIST

193   There's a world of difference between truth and facts. Facts can obscure the truth.

—MAYA ANGELOU, BLACK POET

194   Life seems to love the liver of it.

—MAYA ANGELOU, BLACK POET

195   Reality has changed chameleon-like before my eyes so many times that I have learned, or am learning, to trust almost anything except what appears to be so.

—MAYA ANGELOU, BLACK POET

196   There's a period of life when we swallow a knowledge of ourselves, and it becomes either good or sour inside.

—PEARL BAILEY, BLACK SINGER

197   Hatred, which could destroy so much, never failed to destroy the man who hated and this was an immutable law.

—JAMES BALDWIN, BLACK WRITER

198   I imagine one of the reasons people cling to their hates so stubbornly is because they sense, once hate is gone, they will be forced to deal with pain.

—JAMES BALDWIN, BLACK WRITER

199   I think that failure is just as important as success. In a way, failure is a kind of success if you can look at it in the right way, if you can accept it and enjoy it in the right way.

—Margaret Cho, Asian American comedian

200   It is better to concentrate on what can be done than to despair about what cannot be done.

—Ella Baker, Black civil rights leader

201   Any place is beautiful: if you treat it as the answer to a question you're asking yourself every day, just by being there.

—Nam Le, Vietnamese writer

202   We start with gifts. Merit comes from what we make of them.

—Jean Toomer, Black novelist

203   There are so few truth-speaking traditions in this society in which the myth of "Western civilization" has claimed the allegiance of so many. We have rarely been encouraged and equipped to appreciate the fact that the truth works, that it releases the Spirit and that it is a joyous thing.

—Toni Cade Bambara, Black writer

204   All paths are the same: they lead nowhere...They are paths going through the bush, or into the bush. In my own life I could say I have traversed long, long paths but I am not anywhere. My benefactor's question has meaning now. Does this path have a heart? If it does, the path is good; if it doesn't, it is of no use. Both paths lead nowhere; but one has a heart, the other doesn't. One makes for a joyful journey; as long as you follow it, you are one with it. The other will make you curse your life. One makes you strong; the other weakens you.

—Carlos Castaneda, Latino writer

2 0 5 The world becomes a stream of tremendously rapid, unique events. So you must trim your body to make it a good receptor. The body is an awareness; and it must be treated impeccably.

—CARLOS CASTANEDA, LATINO WRITER

2 0 6 The being alone is better. That is what one has to learn ultimately. It really is better to be alone; it is horrible—but it is better.

—LORRAINE HANSBERRY, BLACK PLAYWRIGHT

2 0 7 Every human being is in enormous conflict about something, even if it's how to get to work in the morning and all of that.

—LORRAINE HANSBERRY, BLACK PLAYWRIGHT

2 0 8 Blessings flow in the space of gratitude. Everything in your life is happening to teach you more about yourself so even in a crisis, be grateful. When disappointed, be grateful. When things aren't going the way you want them to, be grateful that you have sense enough to turn it around.

—OPRAH WINFREY,
BLACK TALK SHOW HOST AND PHILANTHROPIST

2 0 9 All you need to do is know who you are.

—OPRAH WINFREY,
BLACK TALK SHOW HOST AND PHILANTHROPIST

2 1 0 Whenever there is chaos, it creates wonderful thinking. I consider chaos a gift.

—SEPTIMA CLARK, BLACK CIVIL RIGHTS ACTIVIST

211   Many of the old wisdom keepers died without passing on what they knew because my generation and my parents' generation were being pressured to assimilate, to turn our backs on the old beliefs.

—ELENA AVILA, LATINA CURANDERA

212   Innocence involves an unseeing acceptance of things at face value, an ignorance of the area below the surface...One cannot have both compassion and innocence.

—EUGENIA W. COLLIER, BLACK POET

213   Life is like a circle. You walk and walk only to find yourself at the place you started from.

—HENRY CROW DOG, AMERICAN INDIAN ACTIVIST

214   That's what being young is all about. You have the courage and the daring to think that you can make a difference. You're not prone to measure your energies in time. You're not likely to live by equations.

—RUBY DEE, BLACK ACTOR

215   The kind of beauty I want most is the hard-to-get kind that comes from within—strength, courage, dignity.

—RUBY DEE, BLACK ACTOR

216   To allow our ancestors to dwell among us and to invite their wisdom to enter us is powerful. We are nurtured by their presence. This truth has been passed through generations.

—BELL HOOKS, BLACK SCHOLAR

2 1 7   Living simply is often the price one pays for choosing to be different.

— BELL HOOKS, BLACK SCHOLAR

2 1 8   I'm a hundred-and-one years old and at my age, honey, I can say what I want!

— ANNIE ELIZABETH "BESSIE" DELANY, BLACK DENTIST

2 1 9   There's no simplicity of truth at all. People are forced because of circumstance to live lives of hypocrisy, of gaps, of fears—not whole lives; and yet we as humans tend to hope for simplicity of truth.

— KIRAN DESAI, SOUTH ASIAN NOVELIST

2 2 0   Danger has been a part of my life ever since I picked up a pen and wrote. Nothing is more perilous than truth in a world that lies. Nothing is more perilous than knowledge in a world that has considered knowledge a sin since Adam and Eve ... There is no power in the world that can strip my writings from me.

— NAWAL EL SAADWI, ARAB WRITER

2 2 1   In the process of telling the truth about what you feel or what you see, each of us has to get in touch with himself or herself in a really deep, serious way. Our culture does not encourage us to undertake that attunement. Consequently, most of us really exist at the mercy of other people's formulations of what's important.

— JUNE JORDAN, BLACK POET

2 2 2   Your life feels different on you, once you greet death and understand your heart's position. You wear your life like a garment from the mission bundle sale ever after—lightly because you realize you never paid nothing for it, cherishing because you know you won't ever come by such a bargain again.

— LOUISE ERDRICH, AMERICAN INDIAN NOVELIST

223   Imagination, like memory, can transform lies to truths.

—Cristina Garcia, Latina writer

224   Memory is a skilled seducer.

—Cristina Garcia, Latina writer

225   It is the habit of most generations to see themselves in crisis, and to imagine that their experience is without precedent in history.

—Bayard Rustin, Black civil rights activist

226   Death is a slave's freedom.

—Nikki Giovanni, Black poet

227   Facts are only tools to gain control over yourself and other people.

—Nikki Giovanni, Black poet

228   i move on feeling and have learned to distrust those who don't.

—Nikki Giovanni, Black poet

229   Confronting chronic emotional pain in black life is the terrain of political resistance we must now explore, the new revolutionary frontier—mental health—emotional well being. When we can frankly, boldly, courageously acknowledge the ongoing suffering, we will make triumphant well-being a norm for all black people.

—bell hooks, Black scholar

230   Old memories are so empty when they cannot be shared.

—Jewelle Gomez, Black poet

231   Wise women and men admit that life is a mystery.

—BARBARA HOLMES, BLACK THEOLOGIAN

232   We are seekers of light and life, bearers of shadows and burden. We are struggling to journey together toward moral fulfillment.

—BARBARA HOLMES, BLACK THEOLOGIAN

233   It is time to awaken to self, society, and the cosmos. For none of us has the luxury of sleepwalking through impending cultural and scientific revolutions.

—BARBARA HOLMES, BLACK THEOLOGIAN

234   We function in a world that seems familiar until sleep, disaster, death, or wonder causes us to shift our gaze. On those occasions we glimpse a spectrum of realities that defies the limits of our language.

—BARBARA HOLMES, BLACK THEOLOGIAN

235   Liberation is initiation into our fullest humanity, including those aspects of our flawed self and crazy world that we would rather deny.

—JOE PEREZ, LATINO WRITER

236   To a haughty belly, kindness is hard to swallow and harder to digest.

—ZORA NEALE HURSTON, BLACK WRITER

237   Folklore is the boiled-down juice, or pot-likker, of human living.

—ZORA NEALE HURSTON, BLACK WRITER

238   I want a busy life, a just mind and a timely death.

—Zora Neale Hurston, Black writer

239   Nostalgia is corrosive.

—Gerald Torres, Latino scholar

240   That is the way with people . . . If they do you wrong, they invent a bad name for you, a good name for their acts and then destroy you in the name of virtue.

—Zora Neale Hurston, Black writer

241   The present was an egg laid by the past that held the future inside its shell.

—Zora Neale Hurston, Black writer

242   We're here to transform who we are as human beings, from a place of wisdom, not desperation.

—Dafina Kuficha, Black healer

243   There is nothing to make you like other human beings so much as doing things for them.

—Zora Neale Hurston, Black writer

244   Silence is all the genius a fool has.

—Zora Neale Hurston, Black writer

245 There is no agony like bearing an untold story inside you.

—ZORA NEALE HURSTON, BLACK WRITER

246 Once you wake up thought in a man, you can never put it to sleep again.

—ZORA NEALE HURSTON, BLACK WRITER

247 I am not at all interested in the pursuit of happiness. I am interested in pursuing a truth, and the truth often seems to be not happiness but its opposite.

—JAMAICA KINCAID, BLACK WRITER

248 Proverbs are short sayings made out of long experience.

—ZORA NEALE HURSTON, BLACK WRITER

249 I don't want to seem morbid, but it feels to me that the process of dying is actually dying into a greater presence. It isn't lessening, it's actually more. And we die into greater awe, greater splendor, greater terror, and greater presence.

—LI-YOUNG LEE, ASIAN AMERICAN POET

250 For we have been socialized to respect fear more than our own needs for language and definition, and while we wait in silence for that final luxury of fearlessness, the weight of that silence will choke us.

—AUDRE LORDE, BLACK WRITER

251 To act is to be committed, and to be committed is to be in danger.

—JAMES BALDWIN, BLACK WRITER

252   It ain't nothing to find no starting place in the world. You just start from where you find yourself.

—AUGUST WILSON, BLACK PLAYWRIGHT

253   One isn't necessarily born with courage, but one is born with potential. Without courage, we cannot practice any other virtue with consistency.

—MAYA ANGELOU, BLACK POET

254   Defeat is not bitter unless you swallow it.

—JOE CLARK, BLACK EDUCATOR

255   Human salvation lies in the hands of the creatively maladjusted.

—MARTIN LUTHER KING, JR., BLACK CIVIL RIGHTS ACTIVIST

256   To be afraid is to behave as if the truth were not true.

—BAYARD RUSTIN, BLACK CIVIL RIGHTS ACTIVIST

257   Whatever is bringing you down, get rid of it, because you'll find that when you're free, your true creativity, your true self comes out.

—TINA TURNER, BLACK SINGER

258   It is by studying the goals, dreams, and aspirations we spend our lives and energies securing that a society is judged.

—MARCO PORTALES, LATINO SCHOLAR

259 I think it is time to reintroduce what is desirable, especially when we endeavor to provide students of life with clearer purposes, purposes other than simply making money. Too long have people labored and lived without voicing ideas that might change lives, without motivating true leaders, leaving all of us to settle for what we see, for what is everywhere around us.

—MARCO PORTALES, LATINO SCHOLAR

260 People ought always to be considered first and foremost, not products and not profits.

—MARCO PORTALES, LATINO SCHOLAR

261 We humans are similar to each other, but like fingerprints and cultures, not quite the same, so viva la diferencia and let's get to know one another, born of respect.

—PIRI THOMAS, LATINO WRITER

262 Humor is laughing at what you haven't got when you ought to have it.

—LANGSTON HUGHES, BLACK POET

263 You're born naked, the rest is drag.

—RUPAUL CHARLES, BLACK ENTERTAINER

264 Hope is delicate suffering.

—AMIRI BARAKA, BLACK POET

265 When I care to be powerful—to use my strength in the service of my vision—then it becomes less and less important whether I am afraid.

—AUDRE LORDE, BLACK WRITER

266   We are what we imagine. Our very existence consists in our imagination of ourselves. The greatest tragedy that can befall us is to go unimagined.

—N. Scott Momaday, American Indian writer

267   We each have a purpose and some people go their whole lives without finding theirs. My purpose is to bring people's emotions to the top through my music.

—Mary J. Blige, Black singer

268   There is something about democratic individuality which is very different from rugged, ragged, rapacious individualism.

—Cornel West, Black scholar

269   A man without ambition is dead. A man with ambition but no love is dead. A man with ambition and love for his blessings here on earth is ever so alive.

—Pearl Bailey, Black singer

270   I don't believe that life is supposed to make you feel good, or to make you feel miserable either. Life is just supposed to make you feel.

—Gloria Naylor, Black writer

271   My soul is full of concern and love, and I understand the meaning of my own life and the lives of others.

—Betty Shabazz, Black educator

272   Every intersection in the road of life is an opportunity to make a decision.

—Duke Ellington, Black musician

273 You cannot belong to anyone else until you belong to yourself.

—PEARL BAILEY, BLACK SINGER

274 If you escape from people too often, you wind up escaping from yourself.

—MARVIN GAYE, BLACK SINGER

275 I do not deal in happiness. I deal in meaning.

—RICHARD WRIGHT, BLACK NOVELIST

276 This life is not real. I conquered the world and it did not bring me satisfaction.

—MUHAMMAD ALI, BLACK BOXER

277 We think that life is all real—all of it. The personal, the spiritual, the supernatural, the "cosmic," the political, the economic, the sacred, the profane, the tragic, the comic, the ordinary, the boring, the annoying, the infuriating.

—PAULA GUNN ALLEN, AMERICAN INDIAN WRITER, EDUCATOR

278 Soul is a way of life, but it is always the hard way.

—RAY CHARLES, BLACK MUSICIAN

279 We must change in order to survive.

—PEARL BAILEY, BLACK SINGER

280 When I see trouble coming, I go on up ahead to meet it.

—BERNICE JOHNSON REAGON, BLACK SINGER

281   You think dark is just one color, but it ain't. There're five or six kinds of black. Some silky, some woolly. Some just empty. Some like fingers. And it don't stay still. It moves and changes from one kind of black to another. Saying something is pitch black is like saying something is green. What kind of green? Green like my bottles? Green like a grasshopper? Green like a cucumber, lettuce, or green like the sky just before it breaks loose to storm? Well, night black is the same way. Might as well be a rainbow.

—Toni Morrison, Black novelist

282   What difference do it make if the thing you scared of is real or not?

—Toni Morrison, Black novelist

283   A free society has room for motion—and when the hearts and minds of a free society are given space to breathe and think—then that society will always breathe and think.

—Jackie Robinson, Black athlete

284   We die. That may be the meaning of life. But we do language. That may be the measure of our lives.

—Toni Morrison, Black novelist

285   There is really nothing more to say—except *why*. But since *why* is difficult to handle, one must take refuge in *how*.

—Toni Morrison, Black novelist

286   All the facts are lies.

—Willie Perdomo, Latino poet

287 Each of us must make his own true way, and when we do, that way will express the universal way.

—Shunryu Suzuki Roshi, Japanese Buddhist teacher

288 Most people are so hard to please that if they met God, they'd probably say yes, she's great, but...

—Diana Ross, Black singer

289 These moments, and moments like these in life, I realized, mean something more than what they are, than how they are experienced as mere minutes. They are the substance of human happiness.

—Arundhati Roy, Indian writer

290 We recognize that we are the products of many cultures, traditions and memories; that mutual respect allows us to study and learn from other cultures; and that we gain strength by combining the foreign with the familiar.

—Kofi Annan, Black diplomat

291 Our society allows people to be absolutely neurotic and totally out of touch with their feelings and everyone else's feelings, and yet be very respectable.

—Ntozake Shange, Black poet

292 in our ordinaryness we are most bizarre.

—Ntozake Shange, Black poet

293 It's a long old road, but I know I'm gonna find the end.

—Bessie Smith, Black singer

294   Freedom begets creativity. Passion is a MUST to pursue dreams. Intelligence is the ability to adapt, and once again to adapt allows freedom.

—KINNIE STAR, AMERICAN INDIAN MUSICIAN

295   There had been so many moments in the past, during the dark days of apartheid's vicious awfulness, that we had preached, "This is God's world and God is in charge!" Sometimes, when evil seemed to be on the rampage and about to overwhelm goodness, one had held on to this article of faith by the skin of one's teeth.

—DESMOND TUTU, BLACK ARCHBISHOP

296   How can you say luck and chance are the same thing? Chance is the first step you take, luck is what comes afterwards.

—AMY TAN, ASIAN AMERICAN WRITER

297   Humor may not be laughter, it may not even be a smile; it is a point of view, an attitude toward experience.

—HOWARD THURMAN, BLACK THEOLOGIAN

298   To love life is to be whole in all one's parts; and to be whole in all one's parts is to be free and unafraid.

—HOWARD THURMAN, BLACK THEOLOGIAN

299   Our lot on this earth is to seek and to search. Now and again we find just enough to enable us to carry on. I doubt that any of us will completely find and be found in this life.

—JEAN TOOMER, BLACK NOVELIST

300 But what's the truth? The truth speaks in tongues.

— GARY DELGADO, BLACK ORGANIZER

301 The complexities of life situations are really not as complicated as we tend to experience them.

— CHOGYAM TRUNGPA, TIBETAN BUDDHIST TEACHER

302 There is no right choice, no having it all, no getting through this world unscathed.

— TRICIA ROSE, BLACK SCHOLAR

303 Expect nothing. Live frugally / On surprise.

— ALICE WALKER, BLACK WRITER

304 Not everyone's life is what they make it. Some people's life is what other people make it.

— ALICE WALKER, BLACK WRITER

305 Yes, Mother…I can see you are flawed. You have not hidden it. That is your greatest gift to me.

— ALICE WALKER, BLACK WRITER

306 Nobody is as powerful as we make them out to be.

— ALICE WALKER, BLACK WRITER

307   People tend to think that life really does progress for everyone eventually, that people progress, but actually only some people progress. The rest of the people don't.

— ALICE WALKER, BLACK WRITER

308   Resistance is the secret of joy!

— ALICE WALKER, BLACK WRITER

309   I was taught that we're given a mind and a heart, and when we start to use the mind too much we get out of balance. We have to maintain a balance. Anytime I put prayer aside and try to do paperwork or do politics too much, I get myself in trouble.

— TOM GOLDTOOTH, AMERICAN INDIAN ACTIVIST

310   I learned early in life not to judge others. We outcasts are very happy and content to leave that job to our social superiors.

— ETHEL WATERS, BLACK SINGER

311   Laughter has its limits, its risks. It can be a screen, a blinder, a way to avoid putting a bold eye on an uncomfortable reality.

— TONI CADE BAMBARA, BLACK WRITER

312   Man does possess the capability to learn from his previous mistakes, as egregious as they may be. I hope that in the future we heed the words of the prophets and cries of the estranged.

— YVONNE BRATHWAITE BURKE, BLACK POLITICIAN

3 1 3   Human beings are equipped with divinely planted yearnings and long-ings. That's what the Constitution means by "certain inalienable rights."

—NANNIE BURROUGHS, BLACK EDUCATOR

3 1 4   If people could make me angry they could control me. Why should I give someone else such power over my life?

—BENJAMIN CARSON, BLACK SURGEON

3 1 5   How far you go in life depends on your being tender with the young, compassionate with the aged, sympathetic with the striving, and tolerant of the weak and the strong. Because someday in life you will have been all of these.

—GEORGE WASHINGTON CARVER, BLACK SCIENTIST

3 1 6   Where I come from, the words most highly valued are those spoken from the heart, unpremeditated and unrehearsed.

—LESLIE MARMON SILKO, AMERICAN INDIAN WRITER

3 1 7   It is only by closing the ears of the soul, or by listening too intently to the clamors of the senses, that we become oblivious of their utterances.

—ALEXANDER CRUMMELL, BLACK ABOLITIONIST

3 1 8   Herein lies the tragedy of the age: not that men are poor—all men know something of poverty; not that men are wicked—who is good? Not that men are ignorant—what is truth? Nay, but that men know so little of men.

—W.E.B. DU BOIS, BLACK SCHOLAR AND ACTIVIST

3 1 9   Freedom from hate unconditionally, freedom from self pity. Freedom from the fear of doing something that would help someone else more than me. Freedom from the kind of pride that makes me feel I am better than my brother.

—DUKE ELLINGTON, BLACK MUSICIAN

3 2 0   Memory is a funny thing. If you want to bury it, it will be bottled up deeply inside. But if you decide to unleash it, it will open a floodgate and take over everything else.

—KIEN NGUYEN, ASIAN AMERICAN DENTIST

3 2 1   The most rewarding freedom is freedom of the mind.

—AMY JACQUES GARVEY, BLACK ACTIVIST AND JOURNALIST

3 2 2   In order to free ourselves we cannot ignore our bonds, pretending that they don't exist as we have for so long. We must consider the nature of these chains. Understanding something of the process that forged these links might allow us the slack we need to slip away—carrying only our personal loads, our children and our humanity, toward their full potentials.

—WALTER MOSLEY, BLACK NOVELIST

3 2 3   Death must become one's best friend in order to teach us what is important in life.

—SAMINA ALI, SOUTH ASIAN WRITER

3 2 4   Power comes not from the barrel of a gun, but from one's awareness of his or her own cultural strength and the unlimited capacity to empathize with, feel for, care, and love one's brothers and sisters.

—ADDISON GAYLE, JR., BLACK CRITIC

3 2 5   Truth is the baby of the world, it never gets old.

—DICK GREGORY, BLACK COMEDIAN

3 2 6   When you start measuring somebody, measure him right, child, measure him right. Make sure you done taken into account what hills and valleys he come through before he got to wherever he is.

—LORRAINE HANSBERRY, BLACK PLAYWRIGHT

3 2 7   The possibilities of man are infinite. So indeed is his cruelty and backwardness and it is a long march about.

—LORRAINE HANSBERRY, BLACK PLAYWRIGHT

3 2 8   Sometimes it's worse to win a fight than to lose.

—BILLIE HOLIDAY, BLACK SINGER

3 2 9   You've got to have something to eat and a little love in your life. Everything goes smack back to that.

—BILLIE HOLIDAY, BLACK SINGER

3 3 0   Everybody has some special road of thought along which they travel when they are alone to themselves. And his road of thought is what makes every man what he is.

—ZORA NEALE HURSTON, BLACK WRITER

3 3 1   I know the beast will go down, but sometimes I see a growing baby beast that will replace it, and that worries me. I don't want revolution, I want evolution.

—NILAK BUTLER, AMERICAN INDIAN ACTIVIST

332 When a man is despised and hated by other men and all around are the instruments of violence in behalf of such attitudes, then he may find himself resorting to hatred as a means of salvaging a sense of self, however fragmented.

—HOWARD THURMAN, BLACK THEOLOGIAN

333 It's hard to be a human being and deeply painful to be conscious.

—INÉS HERNÁNDEZ-ÁVILA,
NATIVE-CHICANA WRITER AND SCHOLAR

334 Language, belief, perception, and action are all intimately interrelated. The words we use shape what we perceive, which in turn shapes how we act. Language's creative power requires that I think carefully and thoroughly about the possible effects my words might have and the effects I desire.

—ANALOUISE KEATING, LATINA SCHOLAR

335 Our society rarely teaches us about the strength or power of peace and nonviolence. I adopted a less warlike approach, searching for the courage and faith to walk the same path as those who once looked like enemies.

—RENÉE M. MARTÍNEZ, LATINA EDUCATOR

336 Avoid clichés, avoid generalizations, find your own voice, show compassion, and ask the important questions.

—AMY TAN, ASIAN AMERICAN NOVELIST

337 Your thoughts, your evolving answers to the important questions, are what will give you interesting lives, make you interesting people capable of changing the world.

—AMY TAN, ASIAN AMERICAN NOVELIST

338   Heroes are important. In their courage and selflessness, they give us ordinary folks higher standards to aspire to.

—NATHAN MCCALL, BLACK JOURNALIST

339   I believed with all my heart something that many people seem unable to comprehend: that it's entirely possible for folks who are basically good at heart to do bad things.

—NATHAN MCCALL, BLACK JOURNALIST

340   Unfocused anger has self-destructive properties. Destruction may purge and even on some levels purify, but I'm no longer convinced it facilitates healing—perhaps even the opposite. Our answers somehow lie in building and creating, moving forward and beyond, allowing wounds to heal and scars to fade gracefully. Not to forget or deny pain, but to embrace it and move on.

—RENÉE M. MARTÍNEZ, LATINA EDUCATOR

341   Wisdom is not a fixed quality. It circulates among us.

—SISTER SOULJAH, BLACK HIP-HOP ARTIST

342   If there is any philosophy, it's that those who have walked a certain path should know some things, should remember some things that they can pass on, that others can use to walk the path a little better.

—ELLA BAKER, BLACK CIVIL RIGHTS ACTIVIST

CHAPTER 3

Relationship

Love

1 I had not loved enough. I'd been busy, busy, so busy, preparing for life, while life floated by me, quiet and swift as a regatta.

—Lorene Cary, Black writer

2 Through a love experience I discovered the reality of the soul.

—Jean Toomer, Black novelist

3 To love someone is to believe in her or him. To believe in someone is to expect the highest standard of her or his humanity. If we can achieve this kind of love, we can do anything.

—Walter Mosley, Black novelist

4 I can fall in love with the sound of a voice.

—Inés Hernández-Ávila,
Native-Chicana writer and scholar

5   Love does not begin and end the way we seem to think it does. Love is a battle, love is a war; love is growing up.

—JAMES BALDWIN, BLACK WRITER

6   If I order entrees, it would be more than one, because I deserve to eat what I like. I never eat leftovers. I never take anything home. I never eat anything that doesn't taste heavenly. I never eat when I am not hungry. I never let myself get too hungry. I never deny myself a fucking thing because I have denied myself enough for 1000 lifetimes and there is no more denial for me in the way that I live. I deserve all the mozzarella sticks, all the fucking chocolate, all the fucking pizza, all the chicken à la king, and I deserve to leave what I don't finish on the plate.

So there you go. Big secret diet. Love. Love and the audacity to actually waste food.

—MARGARET CHO, ASIAN AMERICAN COMEDIAN

7   For most of our lives the lesson is to love ourselves even more deeply, especially because we are the survivors of colonization.

—PATRISIA GONZALES, LATINA WRITER

8   It matters when the feather of a kiss at your nape stuns fate into destiny or sorrow at the gate gives up—a simple matter to matter as you mean to me.

—LORNA DEE CERVANTES, LATINA POET

9   I wear you like a love that is really a sweater. I love you like the filling of slough. I don't know where to take off above the barren ghost trees at the heart of your river or if my wings would hold more wind than a sleeve.

—LORNA DEE CERVANTES, LATINA POET

10   So, like most ghetto girls who haven't yet been turned into money-hungry heartless bitches by a godless money-centered world, I have a problem: I love hard. Maybe too hard. Or maybe it's too hard for a people without structure—structure in the sense of knowing what African womanhood is.

—SISTER SOULJAH, BLACK HIP-HOP ARTIST

11   To love myself, to understand my value and my power, to please God, I must add to the good in the world and not the evil.

—SISTER SOULJAH, BLACK HIP-HOP ARTIST

12   Too many of us are in pain; too many of us are lonely. Sex is everywhere while true love falls victim to the turmoil of our fight merely to survive.

—SISTER SOULJAH, BLACK HIP-HOP ARTIST

13   He said he would love me like a revolution, like a religion.

—SANDRA CISNEROS, LATINA WRITER

14   I didn't want it like that. Not against the bricks or hunkering in somebody's car. I wanted it to come undone like a gold thread, like a tent full of birds.

—SANDRA CISNEROS, LATINA WRITER

15   Love is an active verb and I have many loving tools in the service of loving myself.

—AYA DE LEON, LATINA PERFORMER

16   It takes a long time to really be married. One marries many times at many levels within a marriage. If you have more marriages than you have divorces within a marriage, you're lucky and you stick it out.

—RUBY DEE, BLACK ACTOR

17 Love is the only thing—I don't want to say that "makes it bearable"— but I feel like without the possibility of love, this place would just devour us. Honestly, connecting once at the deepest level with someone, you know, once you've done that, even if your life goes to hell, man, it was really worth living.

—JUNOT DIAZ, LATINO WRITER

18 "Here," she said, "in this here place, we flesh; flesh that weeps, laughs; flesh that dances on bare feet in grass. Love it. Love it hard. Yonder they do not love your flesh. They despise it. They don't love your eyes; they'd just as soon pick em out. No more do they love the skin on your back. Yonder they flay it. And O my people they do not love your hands. Those they only use, tie, bind, chop off and leave empty. Love your hands! Love them. Raise them up and kiss them. Touch others with them, pat them together, stroke them on your face 'cause they don't love that either. You got to love it, you!...More than your life-holding womb and your life-giving private parts, hear me now, love your heart. For this is the prize."

—TONI MORRISON, BLACK NOVELIST

19 You see I thought love got easier over the years so it didn't hurt so bad when it hurt, or feel so good when it felt good. I thought it smoothed out and old people hardly noticed it. I thought it curled up and died, I guess. Now I saw it rear up like a whip lash.

—LOUISE ERDRICH, AMERICAN INDIAN NOVELIST

20 I want to lean into her the way wheat leans into wind.

—LOUISE ERDRICH, AMERICAN INDIAN NOVELIST

21 The brother that gets me is going to get one hell of a fabulous woman.

—ARETHA FRANKLIN, BLACK SINGER

2 2   We were all trying to understand the history that brought us to where we are, responding to the atmosphere of panic, fear, and shameful intolerance that followed in this country, and ultimately trying to get back to the experience of love in spite of it all.

—VIJAY IYER, SOUTH ASIAN MUSICIAN

2 3   In Spanish you'd never say, "I think I love you"... You'd say, "I feel love for you so deeply that when I just think of you, I start to tremble and feel my heart flutter."

—VICTOR VILLASEÑOR, LATINO WRITER

2 4   We love because it's the only true adventure.

—NIKKI GIOVANNI, BLACK POET

2 5   The more you love someone the more he wants from you and the less you have to give since you've already given him your love.

—NIKKI GIOVANNI, BLACK POET

2 6   Black love is a powerful force. The Black community has a way of coming together and rescuing each other and lifting each other up when someone has been attacked, undermined, or otherwise disenfranchised.

—TAVIS SMILEY, BLACK TALK SHOW HOST

2 7   My problem was that I was not only physically handicapped, small, and short, but worse, I also wore glasses and was smarter than all the boys I knew! Alas, an insurmountable combination. Yet somehow I have managed to have intimate relationships, all of them with extraordinary men.

—SUCHENG CHAN, ASIAN AMERICAN SCHOLAR

28 Dialogue makes love possible. I want to think critically about intellectual partnership, about the ways black women and men resist by creating a world where we can talk with one another, where we can work together.

—BELL HOOKS, BLACK SCHOLAR

29 When one is too old for love, one finds great comfort in good dinners.

—ZORA NEALE HURSTON, BLACK WRITER

30 Love, I find, is like singing. Everybody can do enough to satisfy themselves, though it may not impress the neighbors as being very much.

—ZORA NEALE HURSTON, BLACK WRITER

31 I love myself when I am laughing. And then again when I am looking mean and impressive.

—ZORA NEALE HURSTON, BLACK WRITER

32 I have a strong suspicion, but I can't be sure, that much that passes for constant love is a golded-up moment walking in its sleep. Some people know that it is the walk of the dead, but in desperation and desolation, they have staked everything on life after death and the resurrection, so they haunt the graveyard. They build an altar on the tomb and wait there like faithful Mary for the stone to roll away. So the moment has authority over all of their lives. They pray constantly for the miracle of the moment to burst its bond and spread out over time.

—ZORA NEALE HURSTON, BLACK WRITER

33 A sanctified relationship is one in which neither party silences or sacrifices, and each is responsible for expressing his or her strength and vulnerability. Real closeness, I now know, cannot be pursued or demanded. Love is the passion of two people clarifying their beliefs and values through each other.

—PHOEBE ENG, ASIAN AMERICAN LECTURER

34   To love is to make of one's heart a swinging door.

—HOWARD THURMAN, BLACK THEOLOGIAN

35   Rain knows the earth and loves it well, for rain is the passion of the earth.

—ESTELA PORTILLO TRAMBLEY, LATINA WRITER

36   The long-term accommodation that protects marriage and other such relationships is . . . forgetfulness.

—ALICE WALKER, BLACK WRITER

37   Love—that arbitrary and inexorable tyrant.

—HARRIET E. WILSON, BLACK WRITER

38   Pity and love know little about severance. One attends the other.

—HARRIET E. WILSON, BLACK WRITER

39   You can have the number-one album, number-one-selling automobile, or whatever, but if you don't have somebody to run home to and jump up and down about it, then it's really empty.

—ANITA BAKER, BLACK SINGER

40   Unconditional love not only means I am with you, but also I am for you, all the way, right or wrong . . . Love is indescribable and unconditional. I could tell you a thousand things that it is not, but not one that it is. Either you have it or you haven't, there's no proof of it.

—DUKE ELLINGTON, BLACK MUSICIAN

41   Most of us love from our need to love, not because we find someone deserving.

—NIKKI GIOVANNI, BLACK POET

42   Love makes your soul crawl out from its hiding place.

—ZORA NEALE HURSTON, BLACK WRITER

43   Nonviolence is the answer to the crucial political and moral questions of our time; the need for man to overcome oppression and violence without resorting to oppression and violence.... Man must evolve for all human conflict a method which rejects revenge, aggression and retaliation. The foundation of such a method is love.

—MARTIN LUTHER KING, JR., BLACK CIVIL RIGHTS ACTIVIST

44   Most people have a harder time letting themselves love than finding someone to love them.

—BILL RUSSELL, BLACK ATHLETE

45   The people to whom we are attracted often reveal larger life themes.

—PHOEBE ENG, ASIAN AMERICAN LECTURER

46   Fairy tales about women, love, and romance almost always revolve around rescue and an imaginary future with a perfect love where loss, pain, and scarring cannot follow.

—TRICIA ROSE, BLACK SCHOLAR

47   Knotted with love / the quilts sing on.

—TERESA ACOSTA, LATINA POET

Family and Friendship

48   I say that if the nuclear family is what morality is, then I don't want to be moral.

—MIA ANDERSON, BLACK DRAMATIST

49   Looking at people who belong to us, we see the past, present, and future.

—GAIL LUMET BUCKLEY, BLACK WRITER

50   Home is for me not a place, it is *la familia*—a feeling of having an inside joke with your immediate family and community... That feeling connects us like a thread and it tells you that you belong.

—CECILIA BETANCOURT CORRAL, LATINA WRITER

51   It is the family that gives us a deep private sense of belonging. Here we first begin to have our self defined for us.

—HOWARD THURMAN, BLACK THEOLOGIAN

52   A man must be at home somewhere before he can feel at home everywhere.

—HOWARD THURMAN, BLACK THEOLOGIAN

53   Life, they say, is what you make it. For me, it is also where you make it.

—BARBARA HELEN HILL, AMERICAN INDIAN WRITER, ARTIST

54   Over the years, I've talked with my parents many times, but we've never really communicated. When we talk, it sounds like baby talk—at least my side of it...I don't know half the words I need; I either never learned them, or I heard but forgot them.

—BEN FONG-TORRES, ASIAN AMERICAN JOURNALIST

55   We were torn between obligations to the family and the freedom we naturally wanted.

—BEN FONG-TORRES, ASIAN AMERICAN JOURNALIST

56   I was the site of connection in their desperate lives, the site of belonging. I was expected to give meaning to their lives. I was to fulfill my mother's bourgeois aspirations, I was to actualize father's working-class dreams.

—YVETTE GISELE FLORES-ORTIZ, LATINA PSYCHOLOGIST

57   Children's talent to endure stems from their ignorance of alternatives.

—MAYA ANGELOU, BLACK POET

58   Blacks concede that hurrawing, jibing, jiving, signifying, disrespecting, cursing, even outright insults might be acceptable under particular conditions, but aspersions cast against one's family call for immediate attack.

—MAYA ANGELOU, BLACK POET

59   You can never go home again, but the truth is you can never leave home, so it's all right.

—MAYA ANGELOU, BLACK POET

60   The revolution begins at home.

—GLORIA ANZALDÚA, LATINA WRITER

61   Sometimes being a friend means mastering the art of timing. There is a time for silence. A time to let go and allow people to hurl themselves into their own destiny. And a time to prepare to pick up the pieces when it's all over.

—OCTAVIA BUTLER, BLACK WRITER

62   How do we negotiate between American individualism on one hand and Asian family communalism on the other? How do we celebrate our individuality while still preserving connections to the family group?

—PHOEBE ENG, ASIAN AMERICAN LECTURER

63   Filial piety cannot become a cultural excuse that absolves us from having to determine who we are and what our lives stand for.

—PHOEBE ENG, ASIAN AMERICAN LECTURER

64   There comes a day when daughter breaks from mother and becomes a woman. And as it was our duty to listen and learn when we were young, so it becomes our duty to catch the wind and fly out on our own. Our lives are ours to learn from.

—PHOEBE ENG, ASIAN AMERICAN LECTURER

65   It is as if since the last time we spoke with each other we have been holding our breath, and only with each other do we have a proper place to let it go. We desperately need to hear and tell. We are always surprised at how similar some of our intimate circumstances are and hang on each other's every word to find out how the other has handled it.

—TRICIA ROSE, BLACK SCHOLAR

66 Few things are as gratifying as a good conversation with trusted women friends.

—TRICIA ROSE, BLACK SCHOLAR

67 Power travels in the bloodlines, handed out before birth.

—LOUISE ERDRICH, AMERICAN INDIAN NOVELIST

68 My father...lived as if he were poured from iron, and loved his family with a vulnerability that was touching.

—MARI E. EVANS, BLACK POET

69 Family is forever in the backdrop, hurting or being hurt, taunting or being taunted, accusing and being accused, disappointing or being disappointed.

—GARY SOTO, LATINO POET

70 My disaffection from middle-class values had something to do with the familiar constrictions of an immigrant's life—the fact that my parents, who were working constantly to secure our family's future, ironically had little time left for me.

—VIET THANH NGUYEN, ASIAN AMERICAN SCHOLAR

71 If we are to save our children then we must become people they will look up to. Children need heroes now more than ever because the poor children of this nation live with monsters every day.

—GEOFFREY CANADA, BLACK EDUCATOR AND ACTIVIST

7 2   Our people have always been known for their strong family ties, for people within one family group caring for each other, for the "helpless ones," the old folks and especially the children, the coming generation.

—MARY CROW DOG, AMERICAN INDIAN ACTIVIST

7 3   Like most reservation kids we wound up with our grandparents. We were lucky. Many Indian children are placed in foster homes. This happens even in some cases where parents or grandparents are willing and able to take care of them, but where the social workers say their homes are substandard, or where there are outhouses instead of flush toilets, or where the family is simply "too poor." A flush toilet to a white social worker is more important than a good grandmother.

—MARY CROW DOG, AMERICAN INDIAN ACTIVIST

7 4   It seems to me that trying to live without friends is like milking a bear to get cream for your morning coffee. It is a whole lot of trouble, and then not worth much after you get it.

—ZORA NEALE HURSTON, BLACK WRITER

7 5   If you wanted help, and self-respect, you looked to black folk. You don't have to bow your head to a brother. He helps you because it's right. He helps you because he understands what you need, and he knows that he's only a slender breath away from the same need. He knows that he may have to come calling for help before long.

—WALTER MOSLEY, BLACK NOVELIST

7 6   We are not complete. Right now, the black American family in America is incomplete and displaced.

—CHUCK D, BLACK RAPPER

77   Before we can leave our parents, they stuff our heads like the suitcases which they jam-pack with homemade underwear.

—MAXINE HONG KINGSTON, ASIAN AMERICAN NOVELIST

78   My mother is not smiling, Chinese do not smile for photographs. Their faces command relatives in foreign lands—"Send money"—and posterity forever—"Put food in front of the picture."

—MAXINE HONG KINGSTON, ASIAN AMERICAN NOVELIST

79   Everywhere, everywhere, children are the scorned people of the earth.

—TONI MORRISON, BLACK NOVELIST

80   Soon after Pearl Harbor my father was the first man to be picked up by the local authorities and taken to jail in Petersburg, Alaska. When I used to go home from school, I walked by the jailhouse and there was a little barred window from which my dad used to call and wave to me. I am ashamed now to say that I would take another route home because it was too embarrassing for me. I am left with terrible guilt about avoiding him.

—JUNE OYAMA TAKAHASHI, ASIAN AMERICAN ACTIVIST

81   I sometimes wonder if we were better off when we had fewer rights, but more revolution. I'm asking because after seeing my family fall apart, seeing the Movement fall apart, I know real revolution was at home.

—EISA NEFERTARI ULEN, BLACK WRITER

82   Few states make a distinction between parents who *choose* to neglect their children and parents who can't afford food, clothing, and shelter. Essentially, a state can take someone's child because they are too poor.

—AKIBA SOLOMON, BLACK JOURNALIST

83   The campaign to increase adoptions has hinged on the denigration of foster children's parents, the speedy destruction of their family bonds, and the rejection of family preservation as an important goal of child welfare practice.

— Dorothy Roberts, Black scholar

84   In spite of everything, we never gave up. The more we were despised, the harder we worked. We always had hope that some day things would be better. If not for us, then for our children.

— Yoshiko Uchida, Asian American writer

85   Here is what I believe: we forgive any sacrifice by our parents so long as it is not made in our name.

— Nam Le, Vietnamese writer

86   No song or poem will bear my mother's name. Yet so many of the stories that I write, that we all write, are my mother's stories.

— Alice Walker, Black writer

87   In search of my mother's garden, I found my own.

— Alice Walker, Black writer

88   Our working-class lives and *cultura* meant that we relied on each other for the cleaning, the shopping, and the respite of a good *chisme*. *Familia* was not a cliché but something I smelled when the house was crowded with aunties wearing Ben-Gay for their *Dolores*.

— Daisy Hernandez, Latina writer

89   Friends and good manners will carry you where money won't go.

— Margaret Walker, Black educator

90   I feel like I know a few things, and one that's important is that we have to be strong enough to continue to love and care about the generations to come in the way our ancestors have done for us.

—LAURIE WEAHKEE, AMERICAN INDIAN ACTIVIST

91   I cannot forget my mother. Though not as sturdy as others, she is my bridge. When I needed to get across, she steadied herself long enough for me to run across safely.

—RENITA WEEMS, BLACK WRITER

92   The truth is that no matter how we fix our hair, our greens, or ourselves, we will never "fix" what's really ailing our families until we turn outward and collectively address the ever-growing consequences of our oppression.

—MAKANI THEMBA-NIXON, BLACK ACTIVIST

93   When I work with parents, I tell them, you know, "I'm just a lawyer. These are your kids, they're not my kids. No one knows your kids better than you do, no one loves them better than you do." They have to develop their own leadership ability. And they can. I've seen over and over that they can.

—DEBORAH ESCOBEDO, LATINA LEGAL ADVOCATE

94   We are—with, of course, the inevitable exceptions—ardently family-oriented and prefer to live near as many relatives as possible. We don't—under any circumstances—put our parents into nursing or retirement homes.

—STEVEN SALAITA, ARAB AMERICAN SCHOLAR

95   Parents are the most influential people on the planet.

—SISTER SOULJAH, BLACK HIP-HOP ARTIST

96   All of this ugliness and emptiness can be washed away by connecting. We can heal each other through nurturing and sitting in that circle with our relatives and just to hear the word "relative" and know it means you.

—SANDRA WHITE HAWK, AMERICAN INDIAN ACTIVIST

97   She is a friend of my mind. She gather me, man. The pieces I am, she gather them and give them back to me in all the right order.

—TONI MORRISON, BLACK NOVELIST

98   As Indian people, the number one priority has always been our children. We're the kind of people that say: "Do whatever you want to me, I'll endure. But mess with my child, then I'll have to kick the shit out of you."

—JANET ROBIDEAU, AMERICAN INDIAN ACTIVIST

99   The person who brings children into the world is highly honored. You are performing a divine duty and responsibility...You cannot always determine what they will do, but you can do your best to imbue certain ideas that will be guideposts and warnings and stops in their lives.

—CLARENCE L. FRANKLIN, BLACK MINISTER

100   Too many families are wrenched apart, as even children are forced to supplement meager incomes. Family can only really exist among those who can afford one. In an increasing number of homeless, poor, and working poor families, the things that people must do to survive undermines most family structures.

—LUIS J. RODRIGUEZ, LATINO WRITER

101   The dissolution of the family unit is more than just a minority problem. Every family needs the love and input from grandma, grandpa, and mom and dad—and these homeless kids need the attention, love, and consistency only a family can bring.

—LOUIS GOSSETT, JR., BLACK ACTOR

102 Reunions are the conveyor belts of our individual histories. They reaffirm the thread of continuity, establish pride in self and kin, and transmit a family's awareness of itself, from the youngest to the oldest. Reunions are a means of communicating with our living kin and that in turn is testament to our heritage. Reunions are nothing less than a family's roots brought to the surface.

— ALEX HALEY, BLACK WRITER

103 I can say to my children: There is a chance for you. No guarantee, but a chance.

— JACKIE ROBINSON, BLACK ATHLETE

104 At the time of the child's birth it is greeted by its family and is identified with the events that occur in the natural world at the time of its emergence from its mother's womb. At the breasts of women, the generations are nourished. From the bodies of women flows the relationship of those generations both to society and to the natural world. In this way the earth is our mother, grandma says. In this way, we as women are earth.

— KATSI COOK, AMERICAN INDIAN MIDWIFE

105 Slavery's requirement that we have no families, with men used solely as sources of seed and children sold away from their mothers, hovers over us even today.

— CAMILLE COSBY, BLACK PHILANTHROPIST

106 Part of *la familia* and also my own person, that full and impossible combination! Isn't that what we all want—to put it all together and become that bigger version of our selves *and* still be loved by those who have only partially known us?

— JULIA ALVAREZ, LATINA WRITER

107   Finally, brothers and sisters, it is beauty, security, health, love, enlightenment, and happiness we seek. We can find such music only in a functioning social family-hood whose members are aware of its source, soil, and soul, and who come as studious searchers for spiritual strength to a space that is devoid of stress, staleness, and the sameness that produces silliness without stop-time.

—HAKI MADHUBUTI, BLACK POET

108   From the houses and apartments in which I lived, I remember most of all the doors and how they opened for me...I remember coming and going, going and coming. That, for me, was home.

—REBECCA WALKER, BLACK ACTIVIST

109   The important thing is to sit down at the table and talk. Some things are just easier to say across the remains of a shared meal.

—JESSICA B. HARRIS, BLACK COOKBOOK AUTHOR

Community

110   Nobody, but nobody / Can make it out here alone.

—MAYA ANGELOU, BLACK POET

111   Our relations to each other, our prayers whispered across generations to our relatives, are what bind our cultures together.

—WINONA LADUKE, AMERICAN INDIAN ACTIVIST

112 As connected as we are—to friends, to family, to each other—we often feel we are ultimately on our own as we make our way through life, and that can be a frightening prospect. We can overcome this fear only by reaching out to one another, and in our shared courage, we will learn.

—PHOEBE ENG, ASIAN AMERICAN LECTURER

113 The idea that happiness can insulate us against the results of our environmental madness is a rumor circulated by our enemies to destroy us.

—AUDRE LORDE, BLACK WRITER

114 The fact that we are here and that I speak now these words is an attempt to break that silence and bridge some of those differences between us, for it is not difference which immobilizes us, but silence. And there are so many silences to be broken.

—AUDRE LORDE, BLACK WRITER

115 We understand our community's problems from the inside. Our work directly reflects the history, experience, culture, and wishes of the unique people and community that it serves. We are concerned first and foremost with the continuation and well-being of our tribe and our community.

—GAIL SMALL, AMERICAN INDIAN ACTIVIST

116 To work effectively as an agent of change in a pluralistic society, it is necessary to be able to connect with people different from oneself.

—BEVERLY DANIEL TATUM, BLACK EDUCATOR

117 We all need community to give us energy, to strengthen our voices, and to offer constructive criticism when we stray off course.

—BEVERLY DANIEL TATUM, BLACK EDUCATOR

118   Indian time conveys an old grasp of time and life, perceived and experienced collectively by Indian people.

—Anna Lee Walters, American Indian writer

119   I am actually dying on my feet because I am giving every moment, almost night and day—every little crevice I can get into, every opportunity I can get to whisper into the ear of an upper official, I am trying to breathe my soul, a spiritual something, into the needs of our people.

—Mary McLeod Bethune, Black educator

120   The stories are always bringing us together, keeping this whole together, keeping this family together, keeping this clan together. "Don't go away, don't isolate yourself, but come here, because we have all had these kinds of experiences." And so there is this constant pulling together to resist the tendency to run or hide or separate oneself during a traumatic emotional experience. This separation not only endangers the group but the individual as well—one does not recover by oneself.

—Leslie Marmon Silko, American Indian writer

121   To share one's food is to demonstrate one's humanity.

—Leslie Marmon Silko, American Indian writer

122   Food is just another way of being able to talk about our life journeys to each other.

—Faye Bush, Black community organizer

123   Eating alone and cooking fast meals is an assimilating practice forced by circumstance on immigrants. People just don't have time to cook.

—Mayron Payes, Latino organizer

124 It's about nourishing ourselves, having fun, and acknowledging that, even with all the rending experiences we've gone through, we are whole people. Food nourishes the whole.

—GRACE KONG, ASIAN AMERICAN ORGANIZER

125 No matter what accomplishments you make, somebody helps you.

—ALTHEA GIBSON, BLACK ATHLETE

126 Each community has its own spirit and that has to be honored and respected.

—NILAK BUTLER, AMERICAN INDIAN ACTIVIST

127 If Paul Robeson had not been there, I would not be here. And so it is with the youth of today. The stand you took will help us with a stand in the days, weeks, months, and years ahead, for peace, for the rights and needs of the people.

—SIDNEY POITIER, BLACK ACTOR

128 Idealization of a group is a natural consequence of separation from the group; in other worlds, it is a by-product of alienation.

—PAULA GUNN ALLEN, AMERICAN INDIAN SCHOLAR

129 When one is a Native lesbian, the desire to connect all becomes an urgent longing. Faced with homophobia from our own communities, faced with racism and homophobia from the outsiders who hold semblances of power over us, we feel that desire to connect in a primal way.

—BETH BRANT, AMERICAN INDIAN WRITER

130   In the telling and retelling of their stories, they create communities of memory.

—RONALD TAKAKI, ASIAN AMERICAN SCHOLAR

131   People appear to always be in a hurry. Everyone seems to be a stranger. They pray once a week while in church and they pretend to have no relatives . . . Seeing all of this makes me feel sorry for non-Native people. I walk a fine line and keep one foot in each world. That is how it is for me.

—WILEY STEVE THORNTON, AMERICAN INDIAN WRITER

132   We didn't have a generation gap, we had a generation Grand Canyon.

—MARY CROW DOG, AMERICAN INDIAN ACTIVIST

133   Today's black athlete is very different. Their identity is different; they live in a rich, largely white world—a world where black individuality is tolerated so long as it is without reference to the black community.

—HARRY EDWARDS, BLACK EDUCATOR

134   Self-autonomy is the key to autonomy as peoples, as communities, and as communities in solidarity. How is a people, a community, free? When each individual realizes freedom from within, and thereby recognizes everyone else's right to it.

—INÉS HERNÁNDEZ-ÁVILA,
NATIVE-CHICANA WRITER AND SCHOLAR

135   Without community, there is no liberation, only the most vulnerable and temporary armistice between an individual and her oppression. But community must not mean a shedding of our differences, nor the pathetic pretense that these differences do not exist.

—AUDRE LORDE, BLACK WRITER

136 This work is about the "long run," not just for today, for any possible accolades or to meet funding deadlines—but for the adequate and full protection, health and balance, as Native elders say, of our young people seven generations from now.

—Luis J. Rodriguez, Latino writer

137 All communities are sites of collective imagination, social processes rather than mere locations for living and work.

—Manning Marable, Black scholar

138 These cultural celebrations are also about building community in a new land. Lifted out of the context of our home cultures, traditions like the quinceanera become malleable; they mix with the traditions of other cultures that we encounter here; they become exquisite performances of our ethnicities within the larger host culture while at the same time reaffirming that we are not "them" by connecting us if only in spirit to our root cultures.

—Julia Alvarez, Latina writer

139 Remember you live in community. You have a responsibility to be accountable to your family and your community as well as yourself.

—Cherríe Moraga, Latina writer

140 We don't know enough about each other's cultures, histories and struggles in general to truly respect and understand each other as people. I believe that part of my mission in this life is to be a bridge between communities, to bring people together so we can see each other's common humanity, respect each other's struggles, and come together to make life as bearable for each other in this country as we can.

—Ishle Yi Park, Asian American poet

141   Community organizations are frequently the sites where many working-class and low-income black, Asian, and Latina women become actively engaged in day-to-day resistance. These neighborhood struggles led by women greatly enrich our understanding of the possibilities for change within the entire society and we should support them and learn from them.

—MANNING MARABLE, BLACK SCHOLAR

142   In this country, lesbianism is a poverty—as is being brown, as is being a woman, as is being just plain poor. The danger lies in ranking the oppressions. The danger lies in failing to acknowledge the specificity of the oppression. The danger lies in attempting to deal with oppression purely from a theoretical base. Without an emotional, heartfelt grappling with the source of our own oppression, without naming the enemy within ourselves and outside of us, no authentic, non-hierarchical connection among oppressed groups can take place.

—CHERRÍE MORAGA, LATINA WRITER

143   Women are demanding that the quality of our experience be a marker by which our communities are judged.

—BERNICE JOHNSON REAGON, BLACK SINGER

144   This is how my parents' community works. They don't have endless meetings and minutes. When there is a birth, the aunties know immediately. When someone dies, it doesn't take long for the food rotation to be set up.

—BUSHRA REHMAN, SOUTH ASIAN WRITER

145   You must first have a community, one that you share joy with as well as suffering.

—BUSHRA REHMAN, SOUTH ASIAN WRITER

146 Perhaps the most striking lesson for me in more than a decade of doing this work is the extent to which so many people of so many backgrounds share a common dream of community. Through leading trainings, I've had the chance to have small-group, intensive interaction with about 10,000 people. Often, we ask participants to draw pictures of their ideal world. It doesn't matter what race they are or how much money they have, whether they came in a Lexus or they came in a bus—their pictures look much the same. The world is green. Their communities are circular. They are villages with few cars and lots of space.

—MAKANI THEMBA-NIXON, BLACK ACTIVIST

147 Having a history—a connection over time—with the people around you deepens and enriches any interaction. Of course, this connection comes, in part, from being settled down in a place, but a lot also depends on the openness and attitude of the people you find there.

—JULIA ALVAREZ, LATINA WRITER

148 We have to change our own mind...We've got to change our own minds about each other. We have to see each other with new eyes. We have to come together with warmth.

—MALCOLM X, BLACK ACTIVIST

CHAPTER 4

Work and Play

Labor

1   The fight for unionization concerns the businessman, the doctor, the lawyer and other professional folk, because their fate is tied up directly with the fate of the working man. They cannot exist except with the money made by the working man.

— ELLA BAKER, BLACK CIVIL RIGHTS LEADER

2   Our labor is designed to maintain the values of our economy…Not human values but the values of the system that rules us.

— WALTER MOSLEY, BLACK NOVELIST

3   I cannot conceive of an effective and progressive coalition which does not include the labor movement.

— BAYARD RUSTIN, BLACK CIVIL RIGHTS ACTIVIST

4   The young people saw the situation—no time with their mothers because of long hours, their mothers complaining of injuries, having to get part-time jobs themselves. They saw connections between their experiences and their mothers' experiences.

— STACY KONO, ASIAN AMERICAN ORGANIZER

5   Our labor has become more important than our silence.

—AUDRE LORDE, BLACK WRITER

6   The ability to take pride in your own work is one of the hallmarks of sanity. Take away the ability to both work and be proud of it and you can drive anyone insane.

—NIKKI GIOVANNI, BLACK POET

7   We are more than workers and consumers; indeed, we are more than bodies in need of food, clothes, shelter. We are humanity, complex and multi-, the victims and shapers of the world we inhabit.

—ROBIN D.G. KELLEY, BLACK SCHOLAR

8   The sweat of hard work is not to be displayed. It is much more graceful to appear favored by the gods.

—MAXINE HONG KINGSTON, ASIAN AMERICAN NOVELIST

9   By diversifying, I make it much more possible to survive. I do cross boundaries. I do innovative things that other people don't do, but I don't consider it risk-taking; I think I am galvanizing my career.

—WALTER MOSLEY, BLACK WRITER

10   We strongly feel that worker organizing should not be categorized as just an economic justice issue. It's not. It's the most effective way for workers to build racial unity.

—ROY HONG, ASIAN AMERICAN ACTIVIST

1 1   Spend one day working out in the fields picking oranges or tomatoes at piece rate and see how much money you make at the end of the day. That is, if you can make it until the end of the day.

—TIRSO MORENO, LATINO ORGANIZER

1 2   The inattention to the crisis of low-wage jobs reflects the invisibility of the Black working poor. This invisibility is startling given that every day Blacks go to work. They drive buses throughout U.S. cities. They work in schools as teachers, clerical staff and maintenance workers. They care for small children, disabled adults and the elderly. Some Blacks repair electrical lines or work in hospitals. Blacks unload the ships at our ports and move containers to inland warehouses. Others drive trucks carrying goods from these warehouses to the stores in which we shop. Some Blacks ring up sales in these stores while others provide security at these stores and office buildings. Black people work.

—STEPHEN PITTS, BLACK ECONOMIST

1 3   Workers, by fighting and struggling together, get a little more here, a little more there.

—PHILIP VERA CRUZ,
ASIAN AMERICAN LABOR ORGANIZER

1 4   Well, it's easy to see that the rich are just goddamn parasites whose only work is to count the money they have from the workers. But I think in the long run the system will change. It has to because as the corporations get bigger and expand all over the world, and the masses of workers become more and more the victims of unemployment and starvation wages, then the pressure from the bottom, from these workers, for some major change has to increase.

—PHILIP VERA CRUZ,
ASIAN AMERICAN LABOR ORGANIZER

15 Not surprisingly, to be pushed out first were those who are quickly becoming irrelevant to the productive process—the uneducated young, the useless aged, and many of those whose skins are dark.

—JULIAN BOND, BLACK CIVIL RIGHTS LEADER

16 Unlike the gentle rain, unemployment does not fall on everyone equally. It falls first on the poor, longest on the Black, and hardest on Black youth.

—JOHN CONYERS, BLACK POLITICIAN

17 It is ironic that in a society based upon the work ethic, the worth of an individual is often confused with the work that he or she performs.

—JOHN CONYERS, BLACK POLITICIAN

18 You can give a man some food and he'll eat it. Then he'll only get hungry again. But give a man some ground of his own and a hoe, and he'll never go hungry again.

—FANNIE LOU HAMER, BLACK ACTIVIST

19 Without the dynamism of the social movements, such as the anti-racist struggle, feminism, the gay and lesbian movement, the disability movement, the basic needs struggles, and the human rights campaigns, among others, the unions will slump back into the politically ineffective strategy of the bottom line. If unions do not take up the issues of the people, they will be unable to fight beyond the narrow confines of the workplace and they will not be able to fashion a program for widespread social change.

—VIJAY PRASHAD, SOUTH ASIAN SCHOLAR

20 I'm into a world where people are judged by the wealth of their soul, not their pockets. You know what I mean? I want each person to have what they've earned *by right of consciousness*, you see. The basis of it is what you can conceive mentally—the infinite power will give you the substance to create it, you see. There has been entirely too much rip off for me. There have been too many people who have tilled the soil and not eaten the fruit. There have been too many people that have written the poems and not gotten the praise. There have been too many people that have created the invention and then been used by the machine. That has to stop.

—LUISAH TEISH, BLACK PERFORMER

Economic Justice

21   The fact is, we do not have a free-market economy and never completely had a free-market economy. Many of the problems minority workers and students face, and many of the benefits white workers and students receive, are not merely the product of thrift and hard work in a free-market economy but outcomes determined largely by government policy.

—ROBIN D.G. KELLEY, BLACK SCHOLAR

22   In 1962 I became a single mother with five children and went on welfare. When I took my oldest to the doctor, he said the governor was going to cut off Medi-Cal and told me about a demonstration. I went, we stopped the cuts and a movement of the poorest was born.

—ALICIA ESCALANTE, LATINA ACTIVIST

23   Standing in the eye of the storm are the new multiracial, urban working classes. It is they, not the Democratic Party, not a bunch of smart policy analysts, not corporate benevolence, who hold the key to transforming the city and the nation.

—ROBIN D.G. KELLEY, BLACK SCHOLAR

24   I am suggesting that the only way to implement changes, whether at a policy level, a personal level, or a broad cultural level, is through collective struggle. And at the heart of this movement must be working people and the jobless poor.

—ROBIN D.G. KELLEY, BLACK SCHOLAR

25   Everywhere men sought wealth and especially in America there was extravagant living; everywhere the poor planned to be rich and the rich planned to be richer.

—W.E.B. DU BOIS, BLACK SCHOLAR AND ACTIVIST

26   Sadly, the real culprit is, and has always been, a breed named greed.

—PIRI THOMAS, LATINO WRITER

27   This economy continually generates extremes of wealth and poverty, and whenever you have large numbers of people who have been kept from meaningful labor, those in power are not interested in educating them. Why do they want to have highly educated, unemployed angry people?

—RICHIE PEREZ, LATINO ACTIVIST

28   Today cities represent economic activity, the chance to enter the great race and achieve prosperity—at least prosperity of the moment.

—VINE DELORIA, JR., AMERICAN INDIAN WRITER

29   There is something about poverty that smells like death. Dead dreams dropping off the heart like leaves in a dry season and rotting around the feet; impulses smothered too long in the fetid air of underground caves.

—ZORA NEALE HURSTON, BLACK WRITER

30   Dignity and self-respect are not abstract virtues that can be cultivated in a vacuum. They are related to one's job, education, residence, mobility, family responsibilities, and other circumstances that are determined by one's economic and social status in the society.

—Bayard Rustin, Black civil rights activist

31   I am entirely in favor of Negroes running grocery stores, as long as they realize the danger that they will be out of business the moment the A and P decides to open a supermarket around the corner. But beyond that, it seems to me highly questionable to speak of black capitalism when 95 percent of Negroes are workers and hundreds of thousands of them are unemployed. To talk to Negroes about becoming capitalists when masses of them are barely surviving in the *lumpenproletariat* is to substitute a mirage for social analysis.

—Bayard Rustin, Black civil rights activist

32   It's going to take an act of Congress to deal with poverty...We have the resources but we don't have the will.

—Coretta Scott King, Black civil rights leader

33   I'm fulfilled in what I do...I never thought that a lot of money or fine clothes—the finer things of life—would make you happy. My concept of happiness is to be fulfilled in a spiritual sense.

—Coretta Scott King, Black civil rights leader

34   I may drive a twenty year old car, and I may live in a crappy neighborhood, but I feel like I'm one of the richest persons around, and nobody can take that away from me, because when you have that foundation and that sense of who you are and what you can do, even if everything's stripped away from you, your spirit, and your love, and your drive simply cannot be taken away.

—Kalani Queypo, Native Hawaiian actor

35 Any movement that comes up is usually on some sort of a self-pride thing, which doesn't have anything to do with people paying the bills and bettering their quality of life.

— BOOTS RILEY, BLACK HIP-HOP ARTIST

36 By buying and wearing many products, we are validating many of these corporations, so we should think twice.

— HANK WILLIS THOMAS, BLACK ARTIST

37 In essence I am being asked what social class I belong to. What kind of Latino I am. Now, we spend a lot of energy in this country talking about race and not enough talking about class, but is this the way to start that much-needed discussion? I have come to feel I am disappointing certain people when I say I grew up in the suburbs. That I didn't want for much. That, though we were never ostentatious, we never had serious money problems. We always had food to eat, had safety and comfort and good schooling. These are facts: I grew up comfortably, in an American sense—which means, of course, that in a macro-global sense, I am filthy fucking rich.

— DANIEL ALARCON, LATINO WRITER

38 People of color (including Asians) are the first to get hurt by shifts in the economy and the last to recover when times are better. People of color have always been victims of changes in the economy. However, rapid changes mean more suffering and more often.

— MAKANI THEMBA-NIXON, BLACK ACTIVIST

39 In communities of color, policies designed to control and incarcerate the increasing numbers of unemployed or marginally employed are proliferating. It feels like there is a chute from high school to prison in many of our communities—and it's increasingly difficult to tell the difference between the two.

— MAKANI THEMBA-NIXON, BLACK ACTIVIST

40   The rich rob the poor, and the poor rob one another.

—SOJOURNER TRUTH, BLACK ABOLITIONIST

41   What I have here is a complete indictment of our present-day society, our whole world. What's wrong with it is money, honey, money.

—MARGARET WALKER, BLACK EDUCATOR

42   Money, it turned out, was exactly like sex, you thought of nothing else if you didn't have it and thought of other things if you did.

—JAMES BALDWIN, BLACK WRITER

43   If you and I don't build a bridge back, throw out some strong lifelines to our children, youth and families whom poverty, unemployment are engulfing, they're going to drown, pull many of us down with them and undermine the future our forebears dreamed, struggled, and died for.

—MARIAN WRIGHT EDELMAN, BLACK ACTIVIST

44   Poverty is a hellish state to be in. It is no virtue. It is a crime.

—MARCUS GARVEY, BLACK ACTIVIST

45   Neoliberal economists have a dogma that the free market is inherently good, and an almost religious belief that under it, all things will be more efficient. These are beliefs. The rich and those in power benefit from this, because they created the rules of the game. They don't believe the myths, but it helps them that the rest of us believe.

—PANCHO ARGUELLES, LATINO ORGANIZER

46   We also don't have to accept the dictatorship of the global economy. Most people assume that free trade and the world market are as sacred and unquestionable as motherhood and apple pie. But why should human beings be cannon fodder for global economic war? Instead of producing for export, instead of importing our food and clothing, why can't we begin producing for our own needs, thus creating a safer, healthier, more self-reliant society?

—GRACE LEE BOGGS, ASIAN AMERICAN ACTIVIST

47   Understanding money means understanding America. The revolution needs accountants.

—FARAI CHIDEYA, BLACK JOURNALIST

48   One of the most revolutionary things artists and activists could do is conduct their lives not as poverty crusades, all sackcloth and ashes, but as crusades to end poverty, including our own. Learning how to manage money—and sharing that information with others—is transformative.

—FARAI CHIDEYA, BLACK JOURNALIST

49   Now, who creates wealth? In my view, it's workers who create wealth. It's women working away in the factories in the U.S. who create wealth; women peasants in India who create wealth. But who is creating wealth in the racist worldview? The corporations who steal from us and those young white fellows on Wall Street who speculate on currencies.

—VANDANA SHIVA, SOUTH ASIAN SCIENTIST

50   Accumulating wealth—as distinct from making a big income—is key to your financial independence. It gives you control over assets, power to shape the corporate and political landscape, and the ability to ensure a prosperous future for your children and their heirs . . . Wealth is used not just to pay the rent or buy groceries, but to create opportunities, to free you to pursue your dreams.

—JESSE JACKSON, BLACK POLITICIAN

5 1   Although they sport the trappings of prosperity, they don't seem happy. They look hurried and harried, tense—as uptight as the white people they emulate.

—NATHAN MCCALL, BLACK JOURNALIST

5 2   Beyond the quest for financial security and personal comfort, what, if anything, are we committed to?

—NATHAN MCCALL, BLACK JOURNALIST

5 3   Everywhere I look I see chains, from the planned obsolescence that binds us to an endless line of ever more useless machines to captivating television shows *about nothing* to the value of the dollar bills insecurely nestled at the bottom of my pocket.

—WALTER MOSLEY, BLACK NOVELIST

5 4   We have accepted the blinding lights of popular culture as the true vision of our world. After all, aren't the movie stars and football players multimillionaires? Isn't that what we all really want to be?

—WALTER MOSLEY, BLACK NOVELIST

5 5   The obsession with the margin of profit grinds all that is good about us into sausage, into synthetic cases filled with an amorphous blob of meat byproducts that are sold by the pound and forgotten.

—WALTER MOSLEY, BLACK NOVELIST

5 6   The American myth that anyone who works hard will get ahead, and that wealth accumulation is a product of individual effort and merit, is no longer sustainable.

—MANNING MARABLE, BLACK SCHOLAR

57   It is very difficult for people who have been peripheralized to suddenly decide to take economic control, because we live in an era of self-sufficiency, not collective sufficiency.

—JULIANNE MALVEAUX, BLACK ECONOMIST

58   We really need to demystify poverty and demonstrate that it is a failure of the system and not a failure of individuals. We need to talk about it and deconstruct these lies. People who aspire to grab public attention can do an awful lot to show what it means to be poor—that it does not mean that one is morally lax or somehow deficient; that what it means is that you just "don't have no money." That is what poverty is: "you don't have no money." It is not a magical, mystical state of being, as if somebody threw some magic dust on you and you became a lowlife. We have to keep talking about that, placing that idea out there.

—JULIANNE MALVEAUX, BLACK ECONOMIST

59   I am a big advocate of writing down every penny that you spend during an entire month, so that you can see where your income goes. Even if your monthly income is only twenty-five dollars, look at what you are doing with that. Start telling yourself that you do not need something to be happy, and see if it does not work.

—BELL HOOKS, BLACK SCHOLAR

60   We as a country have been too willing to take from our weakest when times get hard. People who allow this to happen must be educated, must be challenged, must be turned around.

—GEOFFREY CANADA, BLACK EDUCATOR AND ACTIVIST

61   I could have accepted our flimsy shack, our smelly outhouse, and our poverty—but only on my terms. Yes, I would have accepted poverty, dignified, uninterfered-with poverty, but not the drunken, degrading, and humiliating poverty we had to endure.

—MARY CROW DOG, AMERICAN INDIAN ACTIVIST

62   Those who live in relative deprivation, in the shadow of the American Dream, cannot be found easily. Their neighborhoods are often segregated by racism as much as by class inequality, or else by the urban disregard of the full-time rural dwellers (as opposed to those who go to the "country" for the weekend). Their existence is frequently denied, or else if they are acknowledged, it is only to be criticized for one or another personal failing of those who cannot make it in this country of opportunity.

—Vijay Prashad, South Asian scholar

63   To combat debt is not simply to demand its forgiveness, but principally to change the conditions that produce inequality. To fight inequality is not simply to bargain for higher wages, but principally to change the way power is held in our society, to fight to radically alter the institutions and attitudes that shape accumulation and dignity.

—Vijay Prashad, South Asian scholar

64   The "ownership" of the rich is based on the "dispossession" of the poor—it is the common, public resources of the poor which are privatized, and the poor who are disowned economically, politically, and culturally.

—Vandana Shiva, South Asian scientist

65   You know what a trillion dollars is? It's just a whole pile of pennies, y'all. That's all it is. It's just a pile of pennies.

—Melvin Van Peebles, Black filmmaker

66   I have really, really tried to understand the genesis of our economic plight. Part of that genesis, I believe, is justice. People want to believe in justice, or people want justice. This creates an oxymoron: justice, capitalism, and colored folks.

—Melvin Van Peebles, Black filmmaker

Arts and Culture

67   I feel like the best political work I can do is to try to put a human face on people who are culturally erased. Rather than try to be didactic, or deliver some kind of message, I just try to go for the human element, and try to be really personal and intimate.

—Diana Abu-Jaber, Arab American novelist

68   Language as expression and perception—that is at the core of what a song is.

—Simon Ortiz, American Indian poet

69   The supreme test of technical skill and creative imagination is the depth of art it requires to render the infinite varieties of the human spirit—which invariably hangs *between* despair and joy.

—Lorraine Hansberry, Black playwright

70   When the artist achieves a force of art which is commensurate with his message—he hooks us. When he doesn't, we are bored or offended about being lectured to, and confused because we think it must be the "Message" which is out of place—or uninteresting or trivial or ridiculous because of the clumsy way he has hurled it at us.

—Lorraine Hansberry, Black playwright

71   The urge to create is essential, the same as the urge to live.

—Jessica Hagedorn, Asian American writer

7 2   Sometimes writing is the only mark of your humanity left. Sometimes the refusal to give in is the best resistance. Sometimes it is the only way to stay sane. Sometimes it is the only thing that makes sense.

—CHRIS ABANI, BLACK NOVELIST

7 3   The poem needs to be sharp, as clear and faceted as broken glass. It must pick up the multitudinous cries of the world that we are.

—MEENA ALEXANDER, SOUTH ASIAN WRITER

7 4   Everybody is influenced by somebody or something. If there is an original, who is the original?

—ERNESTINE ANDERSON, BLACK SINGER

7 5   Nobody can teach you how to sing the blues, you have to feel the blues.

—ERNESTINE ANDERSON, BLACK SINGER

7 6   Art is important as it commemorates the seasons of the soul, or a special or tragic event in the soul's journey. Art is not just for oneself, not just a marker of one's own understanding. It is also a map for those who follow after us.

—CLARISSA PINKOLA ESTÉS, LATINA PSYCHOLOGIST

7 7   Music was my refuge. I could crawl into the spaces between the notes and curl my back to loneliness.

—MAYA ANGELOU, BLACK POET

7 8   Writing is one of the few professions in which you can psychoanalyze yourself, get rid of hostilities and frustrations in public, and get paid for it.

—OCTAVIA BUTLER, BLACK WRITER

79 Art can't be the exclusive domain of the elite. It has to belong to everyone; otherwise, it will continue to divide the privileged from the underprivileged.

—ELIZABETH CATLETT, BLACK SCULPTOR

80 I don't think art can change things. But art can prepare people for change, it can be educational and persuasive to people's thinking.

—ELIZABETH CATLETT, BLACK SCULPTOR

81 One doesn't "get" an "idea" for a novel. The "idea" more or less "gets" you. It uses you as a kind of culture, the way a pearl uses an oyster.

—DIANA CHANG, ASIAN AMERICAN POET

82 There are so few recognized talents in the poetry world because of people's awe for dead, antiquated stuff.

—SAUL WILLIAMS, BLACK POET

83 Poetry has the power of getting us onto new grounds with the same stuff so it's a new approach to everyday language. With that new approach can come new understandings and new perspectives, and those are the most powerful things you can have on this planet.

—SAUL WILLIAMS, BLACK POET

84 I don't quite believe in art for art's sake. I believe there must be a higher order. What we write can change the world. That may sound a little idealistic but I feel it's very important that poetry make something happen.

—MARILYN CHIN, ASIAN AMERICAN POET

85   I see art as a hyper-truth. It's even truer than the truth, because number one, you can get people to stop and pay attention when it's art.

—ROSALIND BELL, BLACK PLAYWRIGHT

86   Although folk had trouble naming us, we were never blanks or aliens in a "black world." On the contrary, we were and are "polycultural." By "we," I'm not simply talking about my own family or even my 'hood, but all peoples in the Western world.

—ROBIN D. G. KELLEY, BLACK SCHOLAR

87   I think the term "polycultural" works a lot better than "multicultural," since the latter often implies that cultures are fixed, discrete entities that exist side by side—a kind of zoological approach to culture.

—ROBIN D.G. KELLEY, BLACK SCHOLAR

88   There is a saying that you cannot make social change by singing, but you cannot make social change without singing.

—QUIQUE CRUZ, LATINO MUSICIAN

89   I don't get a poem. It calls me and I accept it.

—LUCILLE SAYLES CLIFTON, BLACK POET

90   People wish to be poets more than they wish to write poetry, and that's a mistake. One should wish to celebrate more than one wishes to be celebrated.

—LUCILLE SAYLES CLIFTON, BLACK POET

91   Creativity is the antidote for violence and destruction. Art is our most human expression, our voice to communicate our stories, to challenge injustice and the misrepresentations of mainstream media, to expose harsh realities and engender even more powerful hope, a force to bring diverse peoples together, a tool to rebuild our communities, and a weapon to win this struggle for universal liberation.

—CLIMBING POETREE (ALIXA AND NAIMA), BLACK ARTISTS

92   If memory is a shifting mirror, then writing is an effort to keep it stilled, if only for a while, to try to find a point of focus, some sense of understanding.

—BICH MINH NGUYEN, ASIAN AMERICAN WRITER

93   I have a need to keep it real and to keep it live and spontaneous. That's what matters to me, and I think that's what matters most to my audience.

—DEBORAH COLEMAN, BLACK MUSICIAN

94   You who are journalists, writers, citizens, you have the right and duty to say to those you have elected that they must practice mindfulness, calm and deep listening, and loving speech. This is a universal thing, taught by all religions.

—THICH NHAT HANH, VIETNAMESE MONK

95   In fiction you can look through everyone's eyes, and that's where I feel most at ease.

—EDWIDGE DANTICAT, BLACK NOVELIST

96   The opportunity for expression of hope, of laughter, of joy, of working out complicated things, of satire, of social commentary, and also for the keeping of the history; all of those elements are part of the role of the artist. Those elements and roles are critical to the development of a society and the survival of a community.

—KWAME DAWES, BLACK POET

97   The truth is, when I write, I begin with a simple question: How do things happen?

—AMY TAN, ASIAN AMERICAN NOVELIST

98   The best stories change us. They help us live interesting lives.

—AMY TAN, ASIAN AMERICAN NOVELIST

99   Imagination brings you close to compassion.

—AMY TAN, ASIAN AMERICAN NOVELIST

100   Art is in the process of redefining our relationships to each other.... The creative minds are bubbling, bubbling, and I know the soup that's coming up next time is going to feed a lot more of us.

—RUBY DEE, BLACK ACTOR

101   My newfound commitment and vision is to put the eclectic, contemporary, elusive Native American image on screen. I want to see characters I've never seen before, and I want the audience to feel everything they feel for other characters: anger, love, hate.

—CHRIS EYRE, AMERICAN INDIAN FILMMAKER

102   Dr. King believed that equality, accompanied by simple justice, could transform the nation. That's why I am a journalist; I believe the search for truth and justice are not incompatible. When I started out as a journalist, I thought I could change the world. I found barriers and dark corners were still there. But shining the light that Dr. King gave us can be tremendously satisfying.

—GWEN IFILL, BLACK JOURNALIST

103 My music comes first from my heart, and then goes upstairs to my head where I check it out.

—ROBERTA FLACK, BLACK SINGER

104 A song to me is a very tangible thing. I can feel it with my hands and see it with my eyes.

—ROBERTA FLACK, BLACK SINGER

105 A lot of Asian American filmmakers come out of an organizing background where you don't see organizing, filmmaking, and art as separate entities. We see it as one big life.

—RENEE TAJIMA-PEÑA, ASIAN AMERICAN FILMMAKER

106 Black Rock means Black people exercising their democratic rights in music.

—GREG TATE, BLACK CRITIC

107 I think the most creative music is coming from people of color blending these elements of their culture and creating a fusion that makes something new.

—ALBERTO CUELLAR, LATINO MUSIC PRODUCER

108 It won't be long before hip-hop will join the ranks of formerly black music and we'll have to come up with something else.

—DON BYRON, BLACK MUSICIAN

109 Art is not for the cultivated taste. It is to cultivate a taste.

—NIKKI GIOVANNI, BLACK POET

110   Poetry is the most mistaught subject in any school because we teach poetry by form and not by content.

—NIKKI GIOVANNI, BLACK POET

111   I resent people who say writers write from experience. Writers don't write from experience, though many are hesitant to admit that they don't. I want to be clear about this. If you wrote from experience, you'd get maybe one book, maybe three poems. Writers write from empathy.

—NIKKI GIOVANNI, BLACK POET

112   All writing in one way or another is political. If you speak out against things, that's directly political, and if you don't speak out against them, then that's also political. You're making a decision not to be political.

—THOMAS GLAVE, BLACK WRITER

113   Novelists have to love humanity to write anything worthwhile. Poets have to love themselves.

—MARITA GOLDEN, BLACK WRITER

114   If a day comes that I am not writing, if writing is not fulfilling what I need, then I could dance that energy, sing that energy, make a beautiful flower arrangement because that's really what the creating energy is. The creating energy is what makes us all divine...not equal to God but part of God.

—SUHEIR HAMMAD, ARAB AMERICAN POET

115   I approach a recipe like a story. I imagine it, sometimes I have a dream about it, then I go about crafting it.

—MONIQUE TRUONG, ASIAN AMERICAN NOVELIST

116   Blues, jazz, rap, tap, slang, style, and that impenetrable visage put on to protect what little freedom of personality we have managed to maintain—these attributes represent a mountain of gold that others have mined and stolen.

—Walter Mosley, Black novelist

117   A single painting cannot save anyone but can serve as a catalyst to evoke a change in someone to begin the work that can indeed save us.

—Yasmin Hernandez, Latina artist

118   The stuff I need for singing by whatever means is garnered from every thought, every heart that ever pounded the earth, the intelligence that directs the stars. The shapes of mountains, cities, a whistle leaf of grass, or a human bent with loss will revise the pattern of the story, the song. I take it from there, write or play through the heartbreak of the tenderness of being until I am the sky, the earth, the song and the singer.

—Joy Harjo, American Indian poet

119   I can't stand to sing the same song the same way two nights in succession, let alone two years or ten years. If you can, then it ain't music, it's close-order drill or exercise or yodeling or something, not music.

—Billie Holiday, Black singer

120   We are here to carve a boothole in Corporate America. We will carve the boothole bigger and bigger and bigger until all of our brothers and sisters can fit there. And it is going to be painful. But they will like it.

—Hong Kong Fever, Asian American hip-hop artist

1 2 1   I broke through some aesthetic, political and generational silences, and I felt like I had written something from the story of my people, telling the tale of the tribe, speaking from a mystery and a great unsaid, speaking from the ancestors and giving them a voice.

—Garrett Hongo, Asian American writer

1 2 2   I think acts of imagination are precisely what *enable* just politics... Though art cannot itself bring justice about, yet it calls for justice to be done.

—Garrett Hongo, Asian American writer

1 2 3   There is no politically neutral art.

—bell hooks, Black scholar

1 2 4   Maybe if we reconceptualized a group's culture, or recognized it as a group's story about resisting subordination, culture may serve to strengthen bonds among racial groups rather than create barriers between them.

—Chris Iijima, law professor and Asian American singer,
and Joanne Nobuko Miyamoto, Asian American singer

1 2 5   In my heritage, there is a saying *cultura cura*, culture cures. If the culture is a healer, the families learn how to heal; they will struggle less, be more reparative, far less wounding, far more graceful and loving. In a culture where the predator rules, all new life needing to be born, all old life needing to be gone, is unable to move and the soul-lives of its citizenry are paralyzed with both fear and spiritual famine.

—Clarissa Pinkola Estés, Latina psychologist

1 2 6   The struggle to remake culture itself, to develop new ideas, new relationships, and new values that place mutuality over materialism and collective responsibility over "personal responsibility," and place greater emphasis on ending all forms of oppression rather than striving to become an oppressor, cannot be limited to either home or work.

—ROBIN D.G. KELLEY, BLACK SCHOLAR

127 The way I see it, music is coming together with the people. People are growing, getting educated, standing up for their rights. Music is the heartbeat of that, it's medicine for the people.

—RAVEN KANATAKTA, AMERICAN INDIAN MUSICIAN

128 There is freedom when you're singing and dancing, just dance, dance, dance this oppression away.

—RAVEN KANATAKTA, AMERICAN INDIAN MUSICIAN

129 But what we fought for is a crucial part of the overall story; the terrain was often cultural, centering on identity, dignity, and fun.

—ROBIN D.G. KELLEY, BLACK HISTORIAN

130 I have the sense that the world around us, the whole universe in fact, is saturated with presence: terror, wonder, splendor, and death. Sometimes we do all we can to create illusions that it's not. Art comes along and disillusions us in order to uncover this original saturated condition.

—LI-YOUNG LEE, ASIAN AMERICAN POET

131 Culture is always tied to material movements. You're not gonna create a revolution through culture.

—BOOTS RILEY, BLACK HIP-HOP ARTIST

132 I got to the point of saying, do I want to interpret reality or create reality?

— BOOTS RILEY, BLACK HIP-HOP ARTIST

133 Big Brother is watching us, and now he has so many more tools to do it with. We need art to teach us the history of oppression so we can begin to fight it.

— ROB LOK, ASIAN AMERICAN PERFORMER

134 For those of us who write, it is necessary to scrutinize not only the truth of what we speak, but the truth of that language by which we speak it.

— AUDRE LORDE, BLACK WRITER

135 This is a power of music and the arts, to create an occasion where people can suddenly recognize themselves in the work of someone "different" from them.

— VIJAY IYER, SOUTH ASIAN MUSICIAN

136 I learned in philosophy that a thing without tension is really not alive, that the essence of life is conflict. Drama is the art form that has the most to do with how to deal with conflict.

— JOHN O'NEAL, BLACK ACTOR

137 Of course, we also want to change the world, or to be the flint by which the sparks of revolutionary thought will be struck.

— RYAN RED CORN, AMERICAN INDIAN GRAPHIC ARTIST

138　But there has to be an appreciation that there are different forms of knowledge—that even the know-nots have a form of knowledge that we, the elite, do not. Call it street knowledge, or some other term for cultural knowledge, but it needs to be respected and brought into the discourse.

　　　　　—Saru Jayaraman, South Asian organizer

139　We cannot minimize culture. We cannot minimize vision. We cannot minimize the internal struggle within all of us to make our mark, to say something that is meaningful, important, and critical. We must be skilled doers in this world, walking and working with a humility that is focused on wellness.

　　　　　—Haki Madhubuti, Black poet

140　I always greet people in my language because I believe that cultural diversity is as beautiful as biodiversity, and that is reflected in language.

　　　　　—Winona LaDuke, American Indian activist

141　Most people who come to the United States will, over some number of generations, assimilate, but the patterns of assimilation will not all be the same; culture persists and, because it persists, determines how people live in new circumstances. Moreover, it determines the circumstances; no culture is immune from loving infection by its neighbors.

　　　　　—Earl Shorris, Latino writer

142　Writers imagine that they cull stories from the world. I'm beginning to believe that vanity makes them think so. That it's actually the other way around. Stories cull writers from the world. Stories reveal themselves to us. The public narrative—the private narrative, they colonize us. They commission us. They insist on being told. Fiction and nonfiction are only different techniques of story telling. For reasons that I don't fully understand, fiction dances out of me, and nonfiction is wrenched out by the aching, broken world I wake up to every morning.

　　　　　—Arundhati Roy, Indian writer

143   When I write, I lay down my weapons and give the book to the reader.

—ARUNDHATI ROY, INDIAN WRITER

144   A clown has always had a function in history. You don't take what he does as seriously because he's a clown, but he might be saying some real truths that hurt. We're clowning, but we're saying something that's very real.

—HERBERT SIGUENZA, LATINO COMEDIAN

145   As long as critics have been around, they have insisted that the artist's life and art are inextricably linked.

—CLAUDIA C. TATE, BLACK WRITER

146   Deliver me from writers who say the way they live doesn't matter. I'm not sure a bad person can write a good book. If art doesn't make us better, then what on earth is it for?

—ALICE WALKER, BLACK WRITER

147   Writing poems is my way of celebrating with the world that I have not committed suicide the evening before.

—ALICE WALKER, BLACK WRITER

148   A writer needs certain conditions in which to work and create art. She needs a piece of time; a peace of mind, a quiet place, and a private life.

—MARGARET WALKER, BLACK EDUCATOR

149   Poetry will always have a life and will always continue to prosper as long as people are being brave and honest and real with their word. There will always be an audience because people are looking for something beyond the materialist, capitalist, superficial world that we live in. They want something that will move their spirits, and as long as the world's like that, we're going to need poetry.

—ISHLE YI PARK, ASIAN AMERICAN POET

150 The playground game is all about improvisation. Within the space of the court, within the very minimal rules of basketball, infinite possibilities exist. Its always the tension between those two, freedom and structure, that improvisation is all about.

—JOHN EDGAR WIDEMAN, BLACK NOVELIST

151 If you sing too often of woe, yours or your sister's, you may be charged with being "too personal," "too autobiographical," too much a woman who cries out, who acknowledges openly, shamelessly, the pain of living and the joy of becoming free.

—NELLIE WONG, ASIAN AMERICAN POET

152 All art is a kind of confession, more or less oblique. All artists, if they are to survive, are forced at least to tell the whole story; to vomit the anguish up.

—JAMES BALDWIN, BLACK WRITER

153 Poetry is music made less abstract.

—AMIRI BARAKA, BLACK POET

154 What is the imagination for if everything requires life experience?

—JULIA ALVAREZ, LATINA WRITER

155   The role of art is to express the triumph of the human spirit over the mundane and material...to express the universal myths and archetypes of the universal family of man.

—JOHN BIGGERS, BLACK ARTIST

156   Art is not simply works of art; it is the spirit that knows Beauty, that has music in its soul and the color of sunsets in its handkerchief, that can dance on a flaming world and make the world dance too.

—W.E.B. DU BOIS, BLACK SCHOLAR AND ACTIVIST

157   I try to catch the character and the mood and feeling of my people. The music of my people is something more than the American idiom. It is the result of our transportation to American soil and was our reaction to plantation days—to the life we lived. What we could not say openly, we expressed in music. The characteristic melancholic music of my race has been forged from the very white heat of our sorrows and from our groping.

—DUKE ELLINGTON, BLACK MUSICIAN

158   The blues is an impulse to keep the painful details and episodes of a brutal experience alive in one's aching consciousness, to finger its jagged grain, and to transcend it, not by the consolation of philosophy but by squeezing from it a near-tragic, near-comic lyricism. As a form, the blues is an autobiographical chronicle of personal catastrophe expressed lyrically.

—RALPH ELLISON, BLACK WRITER

159   I hope all Arabs say it with the dignity of our ancestors: we are human not despite our culture, but because of it, and we refuse to go anywhere.

—STEVEN SALAITA, ARAB AMERICAN SCHOLAR

160   The BEST advice I ever got was also the WORST advice any one ever gave me. In high school I had a very stern English teacher and one gloomy day she summoned me into her gloomy office. She knew I loved English and that I wanted to study literature and perhaps someday become a writer—"Dont study English," she said, "you havent got the talent for it." What a horrible thing to say. What an excellent suggestion. It was an excellent suggestion because it forced me to think for myself.

—SUZAN-LORI PARKS, BLACK PLAYWRIGHT

161   I wanna hear an American poem, an American poem about sharecroppers on the side of the road or families in cardboard boxes, not about kings or majestic lands or how beautiful ugly can be. I wanna hear some American poetry about projects and lead poison, poverty and children in jail...I just want to hear an American poem, something native like the Trail of Tears, Wounded Knee, or small pox in blankets. You know, American, something that represents us: a colorful rainbow, a big black fist, an uncorrected sentence, improper English.

—RAS BARAKA, BLACK POLITICIAN

162   We make art out of our loss.

—LINDA HOGAN, AMERICAN INDIAN WRITER

163   Some people as they write, they might dwell on love, other people on money or the acquisition of great riches, but for some reason I seem to bothered whenever I see acts of injustice and assaults on people's civil liberties. I imagine what I write in the future will follow in that vein.

—IRIS CHANG, ASIAN AMERICAN WRITER

164   Bebop was about change, about evolution. It wasn't about standing still and becoming safe. If anybody wants to keep creating they have to be about change.

—MILES DAVIS, BLACK MUSICIAN

165   I believe every child is born a poet and every poet is born a child.

— PIRI THOMAS, LATINO WRITER

166   I will say, if you're writing to be recognized and to be paid, then you're in it for the wrong reasons. If you write because you're compelled to write, then that becomes the only reward you should look for.

— EDWARD P. JONES, BLACK NOVELIST

167   There is something in language itself that is trying to put a finger or put a hand on something that is ineffable. So when I talk about the slipperiness of language, I think experience itself is difficult to grasp directly . . . For language to be true to experience, it has to have that quality of at once being utterly precise and also a resonating surface.

— LÊ THI DIEM THÚY, ASIAN AMERICAN WRITER

168   A Japanese American writer I know says that those of us who come from marginalized cultures are often bequeathed fragments, brief bits of the past, and nothing more. There are no unbroken threads, no fully developed tales or histories. There are too many secrets and occlusions, there are too many reasons to forget the past. And there are forces which do not want us to remember, do not want us to take those fragments and complete them, to restore them to some fuller life.

— DAVID MURA, ASIAN AMERICAN WRITER

169   Imagination is intervention, an act of defiance. It alters belief.

— DAVID MURA, ASIAN AMERICAN WRITER

CHAPTER 5

Making Change

Organizing and Activism

1   I am here and so are you. And we matter. We can change things.

—ELLA BAKER, BLACK CIVIL RIGHTS ACTIVIST

2   We need to develop our own institutions, strengthen our organizations, and build an infrastructure to support them. We have to write down our own history, our own training manuals, our own models of doing this work.

—JEANNE GAUNA, LATINA ACTIVIST

3   You move into a struggle with certain kinds of visions and ideas and hopes, you transform the situation and then you can no longer go on with the same kinds of visions and hopes and ideas because you have created a new situation for yourself.

—VINCENT HARDING, BLACK SCHOLAR

4   I now believe that activism is like marriage. Commitment to the struggle does not mean being held in a cage. Commitment is the spirit that you hang on to. Hold it like a pigeon in your hand.

—PROSY ABARQUEZ-DELACRUZ, ASIAN AMERICAN ACTIVIST

5   The days were full, the nights too short, and the fellowship was electric with Black love and die-hard commitment.

—Mumia Abu-Jamal, Black journalist

6   You have to tell the truth, even if it's not politically popular or runs against the racist stereotypes people have been taught. When you don't, the consequences are far-reaching... You lay the basis for further attacks against all immigrants and people of color for the sake of tactical considerations which are really illusions.

—Susan Alva, Latina activist

7   The people who dominate the inner cities numerically cannot possibly work out a plan or have any programme by which they can improve their own situation which does not take into consideration the city as a whole. A new situation has arisen for the urban black, for thinking in terms of the whole city means that you are automatically thinking in terms of the state and from the state you find yourself facing the whole nation.

—C.L.R. James, Caribbean scholar

8   Instead of avoiding the state, we need to recognize it as an extremely important site of struggle—one we cannot afford to ignore.

—Robin D. G. Kelley, Black scholar

9   Decent countries are made, not born. While atonement, personal responsibility, and self-transformation are vitally important to our collective spiritual well-being, political struggles do matter. By political struggle, I do not mean simply registering voters and selecting candidates. I am referring to a social movement with a radical democratic vision, a way of imagining and remaking the world in a manner we have never seen.

—Robin D.G. Kelley, Black scholar

10 Things won't ever be the same again—and that's what the American Indian Movement is about. We are the shock troops of Indian sovereignty. We intend to raise questions in the minds of all—questions that have gone to sleep in the minds of Indians and non-Indians alike. AIM is the new warrior class of the century, bound by the bond of the drum, who vote with our bodies instead of our mouths. Our business is hope.

—BIRGIL KILLS STRAIGHT, AMERICAN INDIAN ACTIVIST

11 This is what the Movement does. It tells individuals that they are somebody, that they can make a difference. A movement creates hope, it empowers human beings, advances them to a new plateau of consciousness and self-consciousness, creativity, and social responsibility.

—GRACE LEE BOGGS, ASIAN AMERICAN ACTIVIST

12 It's not for you to go in and solve people's problems for them, but to help people to come together to find a means to bring an end to their own problems.

—STEVE BRADBERRY, BLACK ORGANIZER

13 What I found out when I began to actually do the organizing work is that it wasn't just about turnout numbers, that it wasn't just about the campaigns, but rather the challenges around leadership development and development of political consciousness and crafting it together—what it means to craft an alternative world view.

—VIVIAN CHANG, ASIAN AMERICAN ORGANIZER

14 I think one of the problems on the left is that we tend to get so caught up at times in our own ideology and our own analysis and jargon that we don't actually relate to people as human beings who we know are catching hell but who have a very different language, a very different tradition.

—CORNEL WEST, BLACK SCHOLAR

1 5   When people participate in a political movement, you can't assume their participation means their questions about an issue, its significance, and its meaning in the larger scheme of things are all resolved.

— HARVEY DONG, ASIAN AMERICAN SCHOLAR

1 6   There's a tendency in most strikes, struggles, or movements to confine the battle to their own group. The workers who were the most active and wanted their struggle to win actually saw the need to link right away with other people and other forces.

— HARVEY DONG, ASIAN AMERICAN SCHOLAR

1 7   Activists in any period need to be good listeners, buckle-down, and figure out with the people themselves what the pertinent issues are, and from there, move on to change society.

— HARVEY DONG, ASIAN AMERICAN SCHOLAR

1 8   It is essential that we make an important distinction between issues of politics and problems in psychology. We should see this as a distinction between what we do in order to influence the political and economic relations in the society and what, in a more personal way, we do to achieve self-knowledge and identity. Now I do not think that these are hard and fast categories that totally exclude one another. A just society certainly encourages a healthy psychology, and individuals can find personal fulfillment through political involvement. But I think we must make this distinction, because in periods of great social upheaval—and we are living through such a period—there is a tendency to politicize all things, including scholarship, art, friendship, and love. The most extreme form of this total politicization is totalitarianism, a stage we have not yet reached. But even a moderate form can be dangerous since it can lead to a politics so preoccupied with psychological issues that the goals of political action are obscured and even rendered unobtainable.

— BAYARD RUSTIN, BLACK CIVIL RIGHTS ACTIVIST

19   If we must have justice, we must be strong; if we must be strong, we must come together; if we must come together, we can only do so through the system of organization.

—MARCUS GARVEY, BLACK ACTIVIST

20   I spend a lot of sleepless nights wondering how I'm going to meet the payroll, but I've never spent a sleepless night wondering if I'm doing the right thing.

—ANTONIA HERNANDEZ, LATINA LAWYER

21   And, apart from strategy and tactics, the motivating spirit of our political engagement will determine our success as much as anything.

—JUNE JORDAN, BLACK POET

22   It is an historical fact that privileged groups seldom give up their privileges voluntarily. Individuals may see the moral light and voluntarily give up their unjust posture; but, as Reinhold Niebuhr has reminded us, groups tend to be more immoral than individuals.

—MARTIN LUTHER KING, JR., BLACK CIVIL RIGHTS ACTIVIST

23   Power is the ability to achieve purpose.

—MARTIN LUTHER KING, JR., BLACK CIVIL RIGHTS ACTIVIST

24   One thing that can make a difference is to hear and understand other people's stories. The sharing of stories about each others' lives and families and experiences helps bridge differences of our backgrounds, ethnicities or cultures so that some human understanding really occurs, more understanding of each other as people.

—ALICE ITO, ASIAN AMERICAN ACTIVIST

25   I ain't got time to sit around no more and debate this stuff politically. I want to debate it through education of men and women within our community and fighting for a better society for our children.

—MARIAN KRAMER, BLACK ACTIVIST

26   In order to move a debate, there must be organized forces which help to advance a position and/or facilitate a dialogue. Such dialogues will rarely happen on their own.

—BILL FLETCHER, BLACK ACTIVIST

27   We need to start at the local level and, along with other working class allies (such as worker centers), engage in discussions concerning the nature and shape of a working people's agenda for cities and counties.

—BILL FLETCHER, BLACK ACTIVIST

28   Movements for change, movements to make us well, to create healthy societies—whether tribal or American—are grounded in healing, are grounded in honesty.

—WINONA LaDUKE, AMERICAN INDIAN ACTIVIST

29   Change *will* come. As always, it is just a matter of who determines what that change will be.

—WINONA LaDUKE, AMERICAN INDIAN ACTIVIST

30   I always feel politically optimistic. I believe that there are always people who are struggling for justice and working to eradicate the worst results of inhumanity and exploitation. Think how much stronger our movements could be if more of us who are on the same page could actually sit down with respect and deal with each other. If we worked together, we would be that much closer to freedom.

—BARBARA SMITH, BLACK ACTIVIST

31 You are the movement, they are the movement. I AM THE MOVE-MENT. It lies in our hands and is our responsibility to regain our homes and sacred lands one song and one verse at a time.

— MARCUS FREJO LITTLEEAGLE,
AMERICAN INDIAN HIP-HOP ARTIST

32 The future of the earth may depend upon the ability of all women to identify and develop new definitions of power and new patterns of relating across difference.

— AUDRE LORDE, BLACK WRITER

33 We need to keep in touch with our sisters and bros working both sides of oceans and borders to be better equipped to deal with what's coming around the corner, especially with the ever-quickening pace of globalization.

— MIRIAM CHING LOUIE, ASIAN AMERICAN ACTIVIST

34 My experiences on different sides of the border lead me to believe that war and the rise of a national security state necessitate a new response from movimiento leaders.

— ROBERTO LOVATO, LATINO WRITER

35 Historically, movements against state sanctioned violence—from the anti-lynching movement to the present-day movements against police violence and the prison industrial complex—have been framed within a patriarchal lens.

— KAI LUMUMBA BARROW, BLACK ACTIVIST

36 For its part, the anti-prison movement often acts like only men are in prison. It seems to imagine that the world of crime, policing, and imprisonment are inhabited only by white, uniformed hunters and their black or brown, heterosexual male prey.

— KAI LUMUMBA BARROW, BLACK ACTIVIST

3 7   As long as we agree on objectives, we should never fall out with each other just because we believe in different methods or tactics or strategy.

—MALCOLM X, BLACK ACTIVIST

3 8   In any struggle against those in power, the biggest seduction is to compromise with the status quo, especially in situations where "radicals" depend on institutions like universities or unions for their career advancement.

—WARREN MAR, ASIAN AMERICAN ACTIVIST

3 9   I will march for peace, first, because this war will not bring peace and will only bring more terror. I will march for peace, second, because militarism is wrong. The choice of the bigger bomb; of shooting before thinking, arguing, debating, and talking; of silencing dissent in the name of defense is the most dangerous choice we can make in the nuclear age.

—MARI MATSUDA, ASIAN AMERICAN LAW PROFESSOR

4 0   If design can be used to sell jeans and perfume, then I will use it to fight for democracy and against injustice.

—CHAZ MAVIYANE-DAVIES, BLACK GRAPHIC DESIGNER

4 1   You cannot move this country unless you have consensus. The country's too big, too huge, too diverse, too confused. That's part of what we learned in Mississippi. We learned it on the ground, running.

—TONI MORRISON, BLACK NOVELIST

4 2   Civil society either founders on factions or is founded on coalitions. We all share a stake in the healing of the body politic. We must keep the faith.

—FRANK H. WU, ASIAN AMERICAN SCHOLAR

4 3   What is at stake as each of us decides whether or not to be involved in the struggle is nothing less than what it means to be free.

— PRAMILA JAYAPAL, SOUTH ASIAN ACTIVIST

4 4   We did not wait to be invited to participate. We did not wait to be given power, knowing that marginalized communities rarely are given such power. We took it. Those who believe that these communities can be ignored will have to think again, for these communities have discovered the power of action, of standing together, of creating a new world that does not pit us against them.

— PRAMILA JAYAPAL, SOUTH ASIAN ACTIVIST

4 5   We have the strength and the ability and the intelligence and the wealth to control our own destinies.

— WALTER MOSLEY, BLACK NOVELIST

4 6   A built-in hazard of an aggressive ethnocentric movement which disregards the interests of other disadvantaged groups is that it will become parochial and ultimately self-defeating in the face of hostile reactions, dwindling allies, and mounting frustrations...Only a broad movement for human rights can prevent the Black Revolution from becoming isolated and can insure ultimate success.

— PAULI MURRAY, BLACK LAWYER

4 7   I've pretty much always used my positions as a bully pulpit. What that means is strongly advocating for the things I feel are really important.

— JOYCELYN ELDERS, BLACK SURGEON GENERAL

4 8   Action talks and bullshit walks!

— NICK NAGATANI, ASIAN AMERICAN ACTIVIST

49   We need a language of caring. We need a language that allows caring to be something other than warm and fuzzy. We need a tough vocabulary of caring.

—ANNA DEAVERE SMITH, BLACK PLAYWRIGHT, PERFORMER

50   The power of the people is greater than the man's technology.

—HUEY P. NEWTON, BLACK ACTIVIST

51   There is a strong moralistic strain in the Civil Rights Movement that would remind us that power corrupts, forgetting that the absence of power also corrupts.

—BAYARD RUSTIN, BLACK CIVIL RIGHTS ACTIVIST

52   It was impossible for us not to speak up. We realized that if we speak, the powers will listen. They would have to heed the people's voice. We had a responsibility to contribute, to push for government accountability.

—FATHER THI VIEN NGUYEN, ASIAN AMERICAN PRIEST

53   You throw an anchor into the future you want to build, and you pull yourself along by the chain.

—JOHN O'NEAL, BLACK ACTOR

54   When you interact with an audience, if your interest is to figure out ways to deal with the problems of oppression and exploitation, you can't approach them with canned solutions. You approach them with different ways to look at the problem, with encouragement and celebration about their own history and potential.

—JOHN O'NEAL, BLACK ACTOR

55 Systems of power do not change unless they are forced to. The question for me in organizing has been how do we actually translate a moral assertion of rights into a practical demand on power?

—GIHAN PERERA, SOUTH ASIAN ORGANIZER

56 If we wait around to draft the perfect program for struggle and blueprint for a future society, we will abandon the process of social change and sit on our hands.

—VIJAY PRASHAD, SOUTH ASIAN SCHOLAR

57 American foreign policy issues largely from a domestic mill of competing forces. If the forces are not there competing to cause us to do the right thing, invariably nothing right happens.

—RANDALL ROBINSON, BLACK ACTIVIST

58 When I was a young man, I used to think that good would win out over evil and that good things would happen because good people could not suffer forever and things would change. Now that I am older, I know that one has to chart a course, relentlessly stick to it, and do the job until one has won.

—RANDALL ROBINSON, BLACK ACTIVIST

59 I'm changing the world. I'm making the world a just place. That's what organizing is about. There are many ways of doing that, but in the end that's what it's about. We're helping people change their reality.

—GUILLERMO QUINTEROS, LATINO ORGANIZER

60 The strongest, most effective form of community activism is not complicated. It comes from a sense of family, love and urgency.

—BUSHRA REHMAN, SOUTH ASIAN WRITER

61   I was never working for an organization; I have always tried to work for a cause. And the cause to me is bigger than any organization, bigger than any group of people. It is the cause of humanity . . . The drive of the *human* spirit for freedom.

—Ella Baker, Black civil rights activist

62   When we stop dreaming about what is possible, when we stop imagining a world we all share that is guided by great feelings of love, we become our biggest barrier. We who believe another world is possible have yet to live in it. We have never experienced it. The other world is something we must dream of, it must first be something we feel when we close our eyes and use our imagination.

—Robby Rodriguez, Latino organizer

63   In order for our organizations to become vehicles for change and not obstacles that contribute to the status quo, we need to find new ways of collaboration by sharing vision, learning from each other, planning joint strategies and sharing resources. When we disagree, we need to resolve it and move forward. When we mess up, we need to own it and be forgiving. Our work must be fueled not by scarcity and competition, but by a spirit of abundance and camaraderie!

—Robby Rodriguez, Latino organizer

64   I think it all depends on whether or not you have enough understanding of the movement process that you can take the attitude of the long distance runner instead of a sprinter.

—Jerome Scott, Black activist

65   Organizing allows progressives to get to the ground on which change is being made, to feel the rumble in the earth as the people rise to make a new day.

—Rinku Sen, South Asian organizer

66 When I look back on all the fighting we did against each other in the early seventies during the movement, I realize that we cared about being right more than we cared about each other. We weren't farsighted enough, and we didn't love each other enough to really care, and we didn't love the people enough.

— PAT SUMI, ASIAN AMERICAN ACTIVIST

67 Leadership, I feel, is only incidental to the movement. The movement should be the most important thing. If the leader becomes the most important part of the movement, then you won't have a movement after the leader is gone. The movement must go beyond its leaders. It must be something that is continuous, with goals and ideals that the leadership can build upon.

— PHILIP VERA CRUZ,

ASIAN AMERICAN LABOR ORGANIZER

68 It has become a common feeling, I believe, as we have watched our heroes falling over the years, that our own small stone of activism, which might not seem to measure up to the rugged boulders of heroism we have so admired, is a paltry offering toward the building of an edifice of hope. Many who believe this choose to withhold their offerings out of shame. This is the tragedy of the world. For we can do nothing substantial toward changing our course on the planet, a destructive one, without rousing ourselves, individual by individual, and bringing our small, imperfect stones to the pile.

— ALICE WALKER, BLACK WRITER

69 The task of a good organizer is to understand that when you come to roadblocks, which are set up to keep you from reaching your strategic goal, you need to figure out how to go around it, over it, or ignore it.

— ALFREDO DE AVILA, LATINO ORGANIZER

7 0   We can't play the trade-off game with politicians. Politicians play that game—the game of compromise, the game of choosing the lesser of two evils. But if those of us who are supposedly struggling for collective rights start to play that game, all that we'd be compromising would be our principles. We can't sit there and decide who's going to get in the cattle car first, because the fact is, we'll probably be the next one pushed inside.

—Alfredo De Avila, Latino organizer

7 1   We've only got so much time and so much money—never enough. And so I've come to think that we should be looking for the people who are interested in fighting the big fights, those who want to fight against racism and for justice in society.

—Alfredo DeAvila, Latino organizer

7 2   There has to be an end product. Are hourly wages going up? Is rent coming down? What material change is it going to bring about in people's lives? The only way that's going to happen is if there are organizations to be involved in—something that at the end of the day makes people see that there is power in numbers.

—Boots Riley, Black hip-hop artist

7 3   [It's] part of being involved with life, and not missing things, and being present. And that's the same reason that I have wanted to be part of changing the world. I want to be part of it all. I don't want to just stand by and watch it be however it is.

—Boots Riley, Black hip-hop artist

7 4   Prudent tactical planning for effective social change requires that we keep all options open.

—Jesús Salvador Treviño, Latino filmmaker

75 The society we live in is not cast in stone; it is not immutable. Men and women created the social world we live in, and men and women can also transform and improve that world.

—JESÚS SALVADOR TREVIÑO, LATINO FILMMAKER

76 Will we allow ourselves to become the pliable, exploitable workforce for the burgeoning capitalist expansion known as globalization? Or will we, instead, take a stand to affirm our identity as unique Americans with our own distinct culture and language, who demand respect, equality and justice?

—JESÚS SALVADOR TREVIÑO, LATINO FILMMAKER

77 The struggle for freedom is the next best thing to actually being free.

—ALEJANDRO LEAN, ASIAN AMERICAN ACTIVIST

78 I despair at our failure to wrest power from those who have it and abuse it; our reluctance to reclaim our old powers lying dormant with neglect; our hesitancy to create new power in areas where it never before existed.

—TONI CADE BAMBARA, BLACK WRITER

79 I want to be a part of dismantling the machine of misinformation.

—WAFAA BILAL, ARAB AMERICAN ARTIST

80 We began to boycott buses and form organizations, and go where we weren't wanted, or expected. We began to sit and march. We wanted to live our ideas, involved with various disciplines and religions. We came to understand that frustration was transferable, that energy was itself valuable. That the cool of death, of isolation, and self-imposed alienation was not what it meant.

—AMIRI BARAKA, BLACK POET

81   Now the younger activists are very creative, very alive. They're at the beginning of their lives, so their ability to conceive of new ways of doing things is unlimited. On the other hand, they don't have experience, and they generally don't want to hear about how people did things a long time ago. They tend to be ahistorical and think the world began with them.

—RICHIE PEREZ, LATINO ACTIVIST

82   I'll tell you how I handled white people. There was a shoe store in Raleigh called Heller's. The owner was a Jewish man, very nice. If you were colored, you had to go in the back to try on shoes, and white people sat in front. It wasn't Mr. Heller's fault; this was the Jim Crow law. I would go in there and say, "Good morning, Mr. Heller, I would like to try on those shoes in the window." And I would say, "Where, Mr. Heller?" And he would gesture to the back and say, "Back there." And I would say, "Back where?" Well, I'd just worry that man to death. Finally, he'd say, "Just sit anywhere, Miss Delany!" And so I would sit myself down in the white section, and smile.

—SARAH LOUISE "SADIE" DELANY, BLACK EDUCATOR

83   To speak out against an unjust war was treasonous, to speak against the treatment of Blacks made you a Communist. But if you feel in your heart that you have a responsibility to advance justice and human rights, then do it.

—HARRY BELAFONTE, BLACK ACTOR

84   How different my own activism would be if every time something happened, I asked myself, "What would I do if this was my family?"

—BUSHRA REHMAN, SOUTH ASIAN WRITER

85   The people are generally not yet prepared to understand their own interests in the great work to be done for themselves and their children. We shall be obliged to work sometimes without the popular sympathy we ought to have, but with utterly inadequate resources.

—EDWARD WILMOT BLYDEN, BLACK SCHOLAR

86   If you are open to it, the craft of organizing allows you amazing insight into the human condition.

— FRANCIS CALPOTURA, ASIAN AMERICAN ORGANIZER

87   I am in search of a new organizing paradigm, one where culture is central to the enterprise and which considers the organization as a social space to celebrate and transform cultural norms. And the creation of this space is as important as winning on issues.

— FRANCIS CALPOTURA, ASIAN AMERICAN ORGANIZER

88   We had no more courage than Harriet Tubman or Marcus Garvey had in their times. We just had a more vulnerable enemy.

— STOKELY CARMICHAEL, BLACK ACTIVIST

89   You need some order, but you don't necessarily need Robert's Rules of Order. Who is this Robert guy anyway?

— MEIZHU LUI, ASIAN AMERICAN LABOR ORGANIZER

90   Far too often we become cowards when faced with individuals who have strong leadership abilities, individuals who often do not want social revolution as much as they want personal power. Far too often we follow blindly because what they say they want to do sounds right. We follow because we are afraid that those around us will misunderstand our questions and put us down.

— SHIRLEY CHISHOLM, BLACK POLITICIAN

91   I got involved in protests and I felt very empowered. I learned a new language and for the first time, I was able to identify racism and I learned about pluralism. I felt smart, creative and I thought, "Wow, I'm doing something that makes a difference."

— MEE MOUA, ASIAN AMERICAN POLITICIAN

92   America needs all of our wisdom, strength, attention, and experience to thrive and grow. The lockout of half the population from American politics will not change unless we change it: not just the parties, not just the activists, but ordinary Americans who reach out to their friends, families, and neighbors.

— FARAI CHIDEYA, BLACK JOURNALIST

93   Journalism is not the endgame, it's the beginning. If we have good journalism, what else can we have? We can have good citizenship. We can have the potential for social change.

— FARAI CHIDEYA, BLACK JOURNALIST

94   Believe me, I know there are reasons to be terrified and there are ways that the situation is desperate, but what happens is that only a small percentage of us are motivated by terror and desperation. Terror and desperation are not attractive. Most people just go back into denial and don't want to deal with it. We have to be appealing and we have to create a situation that is desirable, so people want to be a part of it, and where people are welcomed into it.

— AYA DE LEON, LATINA PERFORMER

95   Movements need to move people. It's not just intellectual and it's not just about political organizing. It's not even just about the art—the art begins to scratch the surface of the emotion, but sometimes we've just got to go for the emotion. The emotional transformation.

— AYA DE LEON, LATINA PERFORMER

96   Transformation requires new strategic approaches. I advocate rejecting a politics of seeking incorporation or inclusion, and instead choosing a politics of everyday resistance.

— LAURA HARRIS, BLACK SCHOLAR

97 When some Hispanic millionaires also began to call for brown power, I realized we hadn't thought this out. What we need is a transformation of the whole society.

—RODOLFO ACUÑA, LATINO SCHOLAR

98 If we fail to place fighting electoral racism at the very top of a racial justice agenda, people of color will continue to be effectively disenfranchised, and white people, especially conservative white Republicans, will enjoy electoral privileges that enable them to shape the policies and institutions of this country at our expense.

—BOB WING, ASIAN AMERICAN ACTIVIST

99 What is different from fly-over or drop-in trauma tourism, and inept organizing and political factionalism on the ground (which harbor their own forms of narcissism) is to recognize humanity as we witness suffering (our own and others) and recognize that underneath spectacle is a spark where empathy and compassion—not sympathy or charity—function as precursors for radical activism. Which might explain why deep emotions, so difficult to come by and sustain, have a value that exceeds words, even those of transformative literacy.

—JOY JAMES, BLACK SCHOLAR

100 Coalition work is not easy for anyone. And coalition is not right for everything we do. Perhaps it might help for us to view coalition not as a site of comfort and refuge but as a site of struggle.

—ELAINE KIM, ASIAN AMERICAN SCHOLAR

101 No matter what, in the end there is no real turning away from other people's misery, poverty, or lack of freedom.

—ELAINE KIM, ASIAN AMERICAN SCHOLAR

102   The most successful organizers in this period are those who engage in deep work within specific sectors while simultaneously analyzing conditions and planning for change.

—Kalamu ya Salaam, Black activist

103   We who live below the water line have no choice. Our first priority is to survive. Our second priority is to struggle. Our ultimate responsibility is to win. Survive. Struggle. Win.

—Kalamu ya Salaam, Black activist

104   I've exposed anti-immigrant activists through a lot of different formats —investigative reporting, first-person perspectives—but really the only way to deal with these fools is to make fun of them.

—Gustavo Arellano, Latino writer

105   I don't want to operate in an echo chamber, only working with people who agree with me. I want to jump into the belly of the beast.

—Gustavo Arellano, Latino writer

106   We have an adversarial and entertainment oriented media. You're either engaged in a fight, a game, or some sort of performance. You can't have a conversation in that context.

—Lani Guinier, Black scholar

107   However, I submit that, in point of fact, "we who are dark" have done precious little talking about our pain in this post–civil rights era and probably a bit too much posturing about our plans. If anything, we have a surplus of plans, many of them quite sound and longstanding and unrealized.

—Jared Sexton, Black scholar

108 At one point in my life, I was really against working with the system. I thought, you really can't get anywhere that way. Now I realize, you *really* can't get anywhere that way!

— SARAH JONES, BLACK PLAYWRIGHT, PERFORMER

109 I am struck by how much progressive organizing and creative work is going on. There are struggles around housing, poverty, racism, the war, sexual violence and the list goes on. There are also some amazing spoken-word and visual artists who are inspiring and moving audiences to action. Finally, there are authors and scholars who are researching, analyzing and writing about social movements, about social problems and about history in a way that can help activists crystallize their strategies. It is critical that we link these areas of work. I think we have the ingredients for a powerful social movement, but perhaps we just need a recipe for combining those ingredients.

— BARBARA RANSBY, BLACK SCHOLAR

110 Nonviolence as a method has within it the demand for terrible sacrifice and long suffering, but, as Gandhi has said, "freedom does not drop from the sky." One has to struggle and be willing to die for it.

— BAYARD RUSTIN, BLACK CIVIL RIGHTS ACTIVIST

111 They reject all allies, black and white, within and outside the movement. Racism, they say, is not a negotiable issue; it is absolutely wrong and therefore any compromise, any demand short of total and immediate freedom, is a sellout. Of course racism is absolutely wrong, but the effective implementation of the moral rights of a 10 percent minority requires allies and politics.

— BAYARD RUSTIN, BLACK CIVIL RIGHTS ACTIVIST

112   Our progress is slow; sometimes our allies drag their feet; and sometimes we ourselves fail in leadership and imagination. What is not true is that democracy and nonviolence have irrevocably failed...And the only way to prove that democracy and nonviolence still have meaning is to demonstrate their effectiveness in action by achieving significant change.

—BAYARD RUSTIN, BLACK CIVIL RIGHTS ACTIVIST

113   It will require paying as much attention to the destination as we pay to the journey, but by working one step at a time, one policy at a time, our collective work can build hope and belief in the noblest of our imaginings.

—MAKANI THEMBA-NIXON, BLACK ACTIVIST

114   We cannot limit ourselves to organizing just one group of people, because our vision of society is broader than that. And, if we're trying to organize on a large scale to gain real power, I don't believe there's any one ethnicity that can do it by themselves. Alliances have to be built between different communities and we need to create multicultural organizations and multiracial movements.

—ANTHONY THIGPENN, BLACK ACTIVIST

115   This work is transformational work, and it gives us the opportunity to talk about culture, and not simply the economic system or the political system. We should be creating and practicing what we want to be.

—LEAH WISE, BLACK ACTIVIST

116   The acceptance of our present condition is the only form of extremism which discredits us before our children.

—LORRAINE HANSBERRY, BLACK PLAYWRIGHT

117 I would go to the last house, the last house on the way out...and knock on every door. Twenty houses would turn me down. One would listen. And then I would talk to them about the union and they would look at me, either afraid or disbelieving. And then after I explained, I would get them... I would say why don't you call your friends and let me come back next weekend.

—Cesar Chavez, Latino organizer

118 What if we looked at organizational formations as "political projects" designed to take advantage of concrete historical opportunities for a given period of time? The existence of organizations would be dependent on whether the political opportunities they seek to exploit continue to exist. There would be no permanent organizations with indeterminate shelf lives. This way, people would be loyal and accountable to the politics of the project and not to the vehicle that is used to engage in the fight.

—Francis Calpotura, Asian American organizer

119 Ultimately, we must be accountable not to those in power, but to the powerless.

—Beth Richie, Black activist

120 I've never really had a choice of going out and being some very wealthy corporate lawyer. I knew I was going to be fighting for my land, because that's all we've ever known.

—Gail Small, American Indian activist

121 Finally I realized that activism is not a vocation or a calling. It can be the way we live our lives. It was just how I learned to be in this world, how I learned to live my everyday life. Large numbers of movements in this country have emerged as a result of people's approaching activism in the same way, especially women. It is not a big deal. It is not anything extraordinary.

—Angela Davis, Black scholar

122   Policies are the rules of the world we live in. Changing the world means changing the rules.

—MAKANI THEMBA-NIXON, BLACK ACTIVIST

123   I didn't break the rules, but I challenged the rules.

—ELLA BAKER, BLACK CIVIL RIGHTS LEADER

124   The arc of history is that every generation has to fight the liberation struggle. Every generation. It doesn't matter what the generation before you did or didn't do. You're going to have to deal with it. It helps if there is a connection between the previous generation and the new generation. It helps, it doesn't prevent you from making mistakes. Every generation will make their own mistakes, will create its own organizations, will create its own cultural forms, its own expression, everything. And every generation will have its own rhythm.

—RICHIE PEREZ, LATINO ORGANIZER

125   I don't claim to have any corner on an answer, but I believe the struggle is eternal. Someone else carries on.

—ELLA BAKER, BLACK CIVIL RIGHTS ACTIVIST

Leadership

126   The most difficult task is to turn the relationship between organizer and leader into one between leader and the organization.

—ALFREDO DeAVILA, LATINO ORGANIZER

127 There's a tension between projecting a national leader and creating local leadership...If you're spending all of your energy trying to project the national leader, you have very little energy left over to actually develop a local leadership.

— ROBERT MOSES, BLACK ACTIVIST

128 [The leader] stays behind the flock, letting the most nimble go out ahead, whereupon the others follow, not realizing that all along they are being directed from behind.

— NELSON MANDELA, BLACK PRESIDENT OF SOUTH AFRICA

129 I decided to run when my little 10-year-old niece said, "But Auntie Carol, all the presidents are boys." And I stood there and I said, "Sweetie, girls can be president, too"—knowing I was lying to her. And I just decided I was not going to let that lie stand. That was the reason I got out there to run. And I hope that by doing so it made it a little easier for Barack and for Hillary, and for any nontraditional candidate. We need to open it up so that the American people can tap the best and the brightest in whatever shape they come in.

— CAROL MOSELEY BRAUN, BLACK POLITICIAN

130 Our leadership is just we ourself.

— CLAUDETTE COLVIN, BLACK CIVIL RIGHTS ACTIVIST

131 Turning down the volume of the elites' chatter, we must train our ears to listen harder to hear the vibrant voices and lyrical leadership of grassroots folk on the bottom, the foundation rock of mass movement.

— MIRIAM CHING LOUIE, ASIAN AMERICAN ACTIVIST

132 When leaders have fulfilled their functions, it's time for them to retire.

— NATHAN HARE, BLACK SCHOLAR

133   Fanatics are, for one thing, boring and, for another, unreliable. They tend to burn out just when you need them.

—Nikki Giovanni, Black poet

134   As women, we need to develop our leadership in all senses of the word. In order to become community leaders, first we need to become leaders of our own lives. We need to open our minds, become alert to the problems we face, and help each other realize our potential.

—Claudia Llanos, Latina immigrant activist

135   I think that not only in today's society but in all societies, down through the ages, you have to be somewhat cutting edge or advanced to be in a decision-making position. And there are not many people of color who are involved in the decisions of design and image.

—Delano Greenridge, Black publisher

136   I believe that decision making should not be the exclusive right of the privileged. That those who are affected by policy—not those who by default often stand above it—should be heard in the debate.

—Winona LaDuke, American Indian activist

137   The leadership that can deliver a world from the realm of ignorance toward enlightenment still needs to be demonstrated by someone, somewhere. Will the United States, that place on earth that holds the promise of democracy, peace, and dignity for all—no matter what race, nationality, or religion—be that leader? I, for one, truly hope so.

—Angela Oh, Asian American lawyer

138   Intellectual and political leadership should be neither elitist, nor populist; rather it ought to be democratic, in that each of us stands in public space, without humiliation, to put forward our best visions and views for the sake of the public interest.

—Cornel West, Black scholar

139   Most brothers and sisters born into the confusion of North America who emerge into positions of leadership do so less because we're saints in the purported European sense, and more because we have an intense ability to feel in the African sense. We feel not only for ourselves, but for the entire African family. We feel our people's pain, their torment, their joy, and their happiness. We feel the spirit of our ancestors who challenge us to be more than what white society gives us as standards and limitations.

—Sister Souljah, Black hip-hop artist

140   The children, through their innocence, curiosity, joy, and willingness to take part showed me the power and source of their creative energy. Their participation forced me to figure out a different way of doing things. It was a way that was not taught in my school, not in my family life, nor in the talk of our society. That was when I learned how to be a leader. A real leader understands the art of following. To lead, one must follow the feeling that comes from the heart and the energy that surges forth directly from life itself.

—Lily Yeh, Asian American artist

141   Strong people don't need strong leaders.

—Ella Baker, Black civil rights activist

142   There was an assumption that those who were trained were not trained to be *part* of the community, but to be *leaders* of the community. This carried with it another false assumption—that being a leader meant that you were separate and apart from the masses, and to a large extent, people were to look up to you, and that your responsibility to the people was to *represent* them. This means that the people were never given a sense of their own values.

—ELLA BAKER, BLACK CIVIL RIGHTS ACTIVIST

143   Nobody is going to do for you that which you have the power to do for yourself.

—ELLA BAKER, BLACK CIVIL RIGHTS ACTIVIST

144   In the anatomy of frustration, the long-time leadership is rejected. But heroes must be found somewhere, and so the frustrated adopt heroes of foreign revolutions—not because they believe in their philosophy but because they want to adopt the extreme tactics that they believe have worked for those heroes. Thus Che Guevara, Mao Tse-tung, Castro, and Fanon become heroes. This doesn't make the militants Communists. It means, rather, that they are so desperate for new methods that they reach into completely different kinds of situations, hoping that those tactics can be applied here. Of course, they cannot be, but the frustrated, by the anatomy of frustration, are convinced that the only thing left to do is to give everybody hell, to denounce everybody, and to call for revolt.

—BAYARD RUSTIN, BLACK CIVIL RIGHTS ACTIVIST

145   Chloroform your "Uncle Toms." Unload the leeches and parasitic leaders who are eating the life out of the struggle.

—NANNIE BURROUGHS, BLACK EDUCATOR

146   The tiny minority who act outside the constraints of their times in fact help to define those times.

—THOMAS C. HOLT, BLACK SCHOLAR

147   What is needed is not so much charismatic leaders as ordinary people rising to meet the extraordinary challenges of their time.

—Clarence Lusane, Black scholar

148   What is missing in much of our leadership and community is a moral rebuilding consciousness. We need a home-based regeneration.

—Haki Madhubuti, Black poet

149   The struggle is about the creation of leadership, it is about the generation of a program of social revolution from the bottom up.

—Vijay Prashad, South Asian scholar

150   Contrary to popular belief, we have never been a people who waited for a savior to turn things around.

—Tammy Johnson, Black activist

151   There is an untapped reservoir of leadership and strength in youth seeking a way out of the lives they've been born into or are channeled into through societal norms.

—Magdaleno Rose-Avila, Latino activist

152   We tend to defer too much to the insiders to provide leadership when in fact they are being socialized by their new institutional arrangement to function in traditional ways, not transformative ways.

—Lani Guinier, Black scholar

153   Small-scale responses become necessary in periods of dictatorship and totalitarian rule because large-scale structures and processes are controlled by the dominant power. The small becomes powerful in rebuilding living cultures and living democracies because small victories can be claimed by millions. The large is small in terms of the range of people's alternatives. The small is large where unleashing people's energies are concerned.

— Vandana Shiva, South Asian scientist

154   If we accept these illegal, illegitimate laws, structures, and rules, we will lose our freedom—our living cultures and democracies. As Gandhi taught, freedom can be reclaimed only by refusing to cooperate with unjust, immoral laws. The fight for truth—employing the principles of civil disobediance, nonviolence, and noncooperation—is not just our right as free citizens of free societies. It is our duty as citizens of the earth.

— Vandana Shiva, South Asian scientist

155   If you're going to call yourself a leader, you'd better be building an institution for the community. You'd better have a body of work that is going to change the direction of our situation. You've got to be training young people. Otherwise, you're not really a leader, you're a spokesperson.

— Kevin Powell, Black journalist

156   People are looking for some sort of Grand Poobah, and that's not going to happen.

— Kevin Powell, Black journalist

157   The lack of moral responsibility and leadership in the world is appalling. We know that something's wrong, but why don't we do something to change the way decisions are made?

— Walter Mosley, Black novelist

158   Good leadership listens. And that's why Cesar smart, because he listens. Then there is the tendency that when you become too popular and you think you are somebody, you are still the same shit, you know. But you feel kind of bigger and bigger. That happens to some guys, and then they lose contact of the people. And then they cannot communicate with them anymore.

—Philip Vera Cruz,

Asian American labor organizer

159   True forms of leadership emerge when we take the time and energy to build legitimacy.

—Phoebe Eng, Asian American lecturer

160   I knew that violence was a problem in my life, but I never really saw myself as being a person to do something about it. I would see a story in the news where someone got shot, and I would think to myself, "Man, it's really crazy out here—someone needs to do something about this." But I always overlooked the fact that I was somebody and that maybe the somebody that needs to do something about this was me. When you just stand by and let things happen, you silently condone it.

—Sherman Spears, Black activist

161   Instead of the leader as a person who was supposed to be a magic man, you could develop individuals who were bound together by a concept that benefited the larger number of individuals and provided an opportunity for them to grow into being responsible for carrying out a program.

—Ella Baker, Black civil rights activist

Peace and Justice

162   One of the challenges we have in America is that America is a society based on conquest, not on survival. It is a society, by and large, based on the concept that there is always a West, always a frontier. There will always be someplace to go. We don't necessarily have to give thanks for where we are because we're moving. That's what has happened in this America, is this conceptual framework—there is always going to be someplace we can go or something else we can buy.

—WINONA LaDUKE, AMERICAN INDIAN ACTIVIST

163   The young people of this country haven't experienced a moment in which our government has made a concerted effort to do anything but wage war.

—ANDREA BATISTA SCHLESINGER, LATINA ACTIVIST

164   The time has come, God knows, for us to examine ourselves, but we can only do this if we are willing to free ourselves of the myth of America and try to find out what is really happening here.

—JAMES BALDWIN, BLACK WRITER

165   As long as you keep a person down, some part of you has to be down there to hold him down, so it means you cannot soar as you otherwise might.

—MARIAN ANDERSON, BLACK SINGER

166   The need for change bulldozed a road down the center of my mind.

—MAYA ANGELOU, BLACK POET

167 Can you imagine if this country were not so afflicted with racism? Can you imagine what it would be like if the vitality, humor, and resilience of the black American were infused throughout this country?

— MAYA ANGELOU, BLACK POET

168 Empowerment comes from ideas—our revolution is fought with concepts, not with guns, and it is fueled by vision. By focusing on what we want to happen we change the present. The healing images and narratives we imagine will eventually materialize.

— GLORIA ANZALDÚA, LATINA WRITER

169 It is not enough merely to call for freedom, democracy, and human rights. There has to be a united determination to persevere in the struggle, to make sacrifices in the name of enduring truths, to resist the corrupting influences of desire, ill will, ignorance, and fear. Among the basic freedoms to which men aspire that their lives might be full and uncramped, freedom from fear stands out as both a means and an end.

— AUNG SAN SUU KYI, BURMESE LEADER

170 This is America. Paranoia here is justified.

— NATHAN McCALL, BLACK JOURNALIST

171 Active political participation can only be achieved by the removal of discriminatory election systems.

— JOAQUIN AVILA, LATINO ACTIVIST

172 I know that what I am asking is impossible. But in our time, as in every time, the impossible is the least one can demand—and one is, after all, emboldened by the spectacle of human history in general and American Negro history in particular, for it testified to nothing less than the perpetual achievement of the impossible.

— JAMES BALDWIN, BLACK WRITER

173   The absence of freedom must never make us forsake the path of human love for the path of caged fury.

—DENNIS BANKS, AMERICAN INDIAN ACTIVIST

174   When there are not civil liberties, we cannot make social progress.

—BAYARD RUSTIN, BLACK CIVIL RIGHTS ACTIVIST

175   Let us be enraged about injustice, but let us not be destroyed by it.

—BAYARD RUSTIN, BLACK CIVIL RIGHTS ACTIVIST

176   The triumph of the civil rights movement is a testament to the successful transformation of opinion achieved by millions of individuals who wanted to see an America as good as its promise. Those people understood the essential message and vision of our Declaration of Intent and they gave it life.

—CAROL MOSELEY BRAUN, BLACK POLITICIAN

177   It's too cold to think warmly. Which gives me insight into the European. Where else would colonialism, slavery, capitalism come from except out of the icebox.

—TONI CADE BAMBARA, BLACK WRITER

178   I have no doubt that the forces of justice and peace will prevail over the contemporary incarnation of empire, blood, terror, and greed that is the USA.

—WALDEN BELLO, FILIPINO SCHOLAR

179   They want to bring back in legalized slavery. If you privatize the prisons and you make it extremely hard to get an education, hard to get jobs, the prisons are going to fill up.

—TWILIGHT BEY, BLACK ACTIVIST

180 There will come a time when we need to become more than we are now. When that happens, we will use all of the creativity, physical resources, energy, and history at our disposal to make the changes we want. We need not try to bring that time about; it will choose us when it is ready, and leave us when it is done. The change will create power, which will in turn create change.

— TODD STEVEN BURROUGHS, BLACK SCHOLAR

181 I'm not interested in pursuing a society that uses analysis, research, and experimentation to concretize their vision of cruel destinies for those who are not bastards of the Pilgrims; a society with arrogance rising, moon in oppression, and sun in destruction.

— BARBARA CAMERON, AMERICAN INDIAN WRITER

182 Let us not be narrow. Let us not be small and selfish. Let us aspire to be as great in our communication as were the forefathers of our people, whose struggles made our being here possible.

— ELIZABETH CATLETT, BLACK SCULPTOR

183 Everyone else is represented in Washington by a rich and powerful lobby, it seems. But there is no lobby for the people.

— SHIRLEY CHISHOLM, BLACK POLITICIAN

184 If there's a child on the south side of Chicago who can't read, that matters to me, even if it's not my child. If there's a senior citizen somewhere who can't pay for their prescription and having to choose between medicine and the rent, that makes my life poorer, even if it's not my grandparent. If there's an Arab-American family being rounded up without benefit of an attorney or due process, that threatens my civil liberties. It is that fundamental belief—it is that fundamental belief—I am my brother's keeper, I am my sister's keeper—that makes this country work. It's what allows us to pursue our individual dreams, yet still come together as a single American family: "E pluribus unum," out of many, one.

— BARACK OBAMA, BLACK POLITICIAN

185   Why is it we must change our lives, our way of life, to accommodate the corporations, and they are allowed to continue without changing any of their behavior?

—KATSI COOK, AMERICAN INDIAN MIDWIFE

186   The practice of peace and reconciliation is one of the most vital and artistic of human actions.

—THICH NHAT HANH, VIETNAMESE MONK

187   Jails and prisons are designed to break human beings, to convert the population into specimens in a zoo—obedient to our keepers, but dangerous to each other.

—ANGELA DAVIS, BLACK SCHOLAR

188   We have accumulated a wealth of historical experience which confirms our belief that the scales of American justice are out of balance.

—ANGELA DAVIS, BLACK SCHOLAR

189   The process of empowerment cannot be simplistically defined in accordance with our own particular class interests. We must learn to lift as we climb.

—ANGELA DAVIS, BLACK SCHOLAR

190   Prisons do not disappear problems, they disappear human beings.

—ANGELA DAVIS, BLACK SCHOLAR

191   The practice of disappearing people has become big business.

—ANGELA DAVIS, BLACK SCHOLAR

192 To deliver up bodies destined for profitable punishment, the political economy of prisons relies on racialized assumptions of criminality—such as images of black welfare mothers reproducing criminal children—and on racist practices in arrest, conviction, and sentencing patterns.

— ANGELA DAVIS, BLACK SCHOLAR

193 I know, maybe better than anyone, that there are times when it seems that our nation is too divided ever to heal. There are times when we feel so different from each other that we can hardly believe that we are all part of the same family.

— DONNA BRAZILE, BLACK POLITICAL STRATEGIST

194 At its conception, our nation was dedicated to the proposition of equality. What has given concreteness to this powerful national principle has been our coming together in the creation of a new society.

— RONALD TAKAKI, ASIAN AMERICAN SCHOLAR

195 We are seeing the deepening divide between citizens and non-citizens. Legal, social and economic divides are deepening.

— AARTI SHAHANI, SOUTH ASIAN ORGANIZER

196 We did not ask for a war economy. We did not ask for tax breaks for the rich. We did not ask to have our kids accountable to pass tests that nobody's prepared them for and we sure as hell didn't ask for increased surveillance, racial profiling and incarcerations for young immigrant men. We didn't ask for it—but it is the hand we've been dealt. It is the space and place we live in. We can either accept it—or we can fight it.

— GARY DELGADO, BLACK ORGANIZER

197   Where justice is denied, where poverty is enforced, where ignorance prevails, and where any one class is made to feel that society is in an organized conspiracy to oppress, rob, and degrade them, neither persons nor property will be safe.

—FREDERICK DOUGLASS, BLACK ABOLITIONIST

198   It is clear still today that freedom of speech and of thinking can be attacked in the United States without the intellectual and moral leaders of this land raising a hand or saying a word in protest or defense.

—W.E.B. DU BOIS, BLACK SCHOLAR AND ACTIVIST

199   And when I have my own children, I will teach them to fight, too. Because we are free, but we are not yet finished.

—TANANARIVE DUE, BLACK WRITER

200   It was against the law of America for a black person to be free. So obviously, I don't genuflect before the altar of the law.

—MICHAEL ERIC DYSON, BLACK SCHOLAR

201   Let's only have affirmative action as long as we had slavery. And then we can call it a day.

—MICHAEL ERIC DYSON, BLACK SCHOLAR

202   Everything different is wrong, especially gay people. If you're too tall, you're wrong. If you're too short, you're wrong. The military uses that to dehumanize the enemy. That way, people aren't so averse to killing.

—STEPHEN FUNK, ASIAN AMERICAN CONSCIENTIOUS OBJECTOR

203 When you are a child of wartime, peace is the all consuming fantasy.

— MONIQUE TRUONG, ASIAN AMERICAN NOVELIST

204 So, let it be clear to us now: The desperation of our people, the agonies of our cities, the desolation of our countryside, the pollution of the air and the water—these things will not be significantly affected by the new faces in the old places in Washington D.C. This is the truth we must face...if we are to join our people everywhere in the movement toward liberation.

— GARY DECLARATION, AT THE NATIONAL BLACK POLITICAL
CONVENTION IN GARY, INDIANA 1972

205 Uncover the wrong questions divorced from social reality and raise new questions rooted in it.

— EMMA GEE, ASIAN AMERICAN ACTIVIST

206 Who thinks of justice unless he knows injustice?

— DIANE GLANCY, AMERICAN INDIAN POET

207 We have the power to reinvent ourselves and create institutions that are equitable.

— SHANA GRIFFIN, BLACK SURVIVOR OF HURRICANE KATRINA

208 If it doesn't work for one of us, it doesn't work for any of us. The definition of sovereignty [means that] none of us are free unless all of us are free. We can't, we won't turn anyone away. We've been there. I would hear stories about the Japanese internment camps...and I could relate to it because it happened to us. Or with Africans with the violence and rape, we've been there too. So how could we ever leave anyone behind?

— LAKOTA HARDEN, AMERICAN INDIAN ACTIVIST

209   Whenever the oppressed, for whatever reason, begin to feel too weak to fight their real enemy, the oppressor himself, they turn upon themselves, squabbling over this or that theory while leaving the oppressor free to do anything he chooses.

—NATHAN HARE, BLACK SCHOLAR

210   The life of the land is perpetuated by righteousness.

—HAWAIIAN SAYING

211   Until the killing of black mothers' sons becomes as important to the rest of the country as the killing of white mothers' sons, we who believe in freedom cannot rest.

—ELLA BAKER, BLACK CIVIL RIGHTS ACTIVIST

212   No nation can make itself secure by seeking supremacy over all others. We all share responsibility for each other's security, and only by working to make each other secure can we hope to achieve lasting security for ourselves.

—KOFI ANNAN, BLACK DIPLOMAT

213   In order for us poor and oppressed people to become a part of a society that is meaningful, the system under which we now exist has to be radically changed. This means that we are going to have to learn to think in *radical* terms. I use the term radical in its original meaning, *getting down to and understanding the root causes*. It means facing a system that does not lend itself to your needs and devising means by which you change that system.

—ELLA BAKER, BLACK CIVIL RIGHTS ACTIVIST

214   The one goal is, after all, liberation from physical, psychological and spiritual destruction. Liberation from the decadent values of "the American way of life."

—ELLA BAKER, BLACK CIVIL RIGHTS ACTIVIST

215   The first step is access to power. The second step is how to exercise this power we are getting. The second step is harder—you must think of a larger vision than your own political interest.

—ANDREW HERNANDEZ, LATINO ACTIVIST

216   We must imagine a world without rape. But I cannot imagine a world without rape, without misogyny, without imagining a world without racism, classism, sexism, homophobia, ageism, historical amnesia and other forms and manifestations of violence directed against those communities that are seen as "asking for it." Even the Earth is presumably "asking for it."

—INÉS HERNÁNDEZ-ÁVILA,
NATIVE-CHICANA WRITER AND SCHOLAR

217   I see again the terrifying destructiveness of American life. Everything seems to go—integrity, self-confidence, honor, trust, gratitude, all human values—with awesome swiftness in the struggle for the dollar. And once gone what have you?

—CHESTER HIMES, BLACK NOVELIST

218   Now, in the first decade of the twenty-first century, we have the opportunity to confront twentieth-century racial violence and begin a long-overdue process of truth telling and reconciliation.

—SHERRILYN A. IFILL, BLACK LAW PROFESSOR

2 1 9   Oppressed people resist by identifying themselves as subjects, by defining their reality, shaping their new identity, naming their history, telling their story.

— BELL HOOKS, BLACK SCHOLAR

2 2 0   Societies who do not care for their young people and old people are decadent, decaying societies.

— JOY HARJO, AMERICAN INDIAN POET

2 2 1   When the power of love overcomes the love of power, the world will know peace.

— JIMI HENDRIX, BLACK MUSICIAN

2 2 2   To view the world differently requires a transformative view of liberation. Without this view, we are left with memorable tunes and unfinished business.

— BARBARA HOLMES, BLACK THEOLOGIAN

2 2 3   Today, the limits of rights language have been reached. Rights can't address dysfunction, depression, and low self-esteem. Rights don't have the moxie or the power to uplift whole communities across class lines. Rights are merely recitations of what ought to be in a society of persons who are presumed to be equal.

— BARBARA HOLMES, BLACK THEOLOGIAN

2 2 4   The importance of public discourse about difficult social issues cannot be overemphasized. Public dialogue infuses an issue with energy.

— BARBARA HOLMES, BLACK THEOLOGIAN

225 I'm convinced that we need to get that sense of entitlement back. Call me old-fashioned, but opposing strong government supports in favor of some romantic notion of self-reliance is tantamount to relinquishing our citizenship.

—ROBIN D.G. KELLEY, BLACK SCHOLAR

226 We cannot afford to be embarrassed or afraid to demand massive social investment. After all, it is our money.

—ROBIN D.G. KELLEY, BLACK SCHOLAR

227 Language is also a place of struggle.

—BELL HOOKS, BLACK SCHOLAR

228 To me feminism is not simply a struggle to end male chauvinism or a movement to ensure that women will have equal rights with men; it is a commitment to eradicating the ideology of domination that permeates Western culture on various levels—sex, race, and class, to name a few—and a commitment to reorganizing U.S. society so that the self-development of people can take precedence over imperialism, economic expansion, and material desires.

—BELL HOOKS, BLACK SCHOLAR

229 Given the racist and patriarchal patterns of the state, it is difficult to envision the state as the holder of solutions to the problem of violence against women of color.

—ANGELA DAVIS, BLACK SCHOLAR

230 We must learn how to oppose the racist fixation on people of color as the primary perpetrators of violence yet fiercely challenge the real violence that men of color inflict on women.

—ANGELA DAVIS, BLACK SCHOLAR

231   How can a person tell illegal from legal without first taking away my civil rights?

—DANNY ROMERO, LATINO NOVELIST

232   Perhaps the worst ideological mistake of the mainstream white gay movement is their concept that all we need to fight for is something called "gay rights." And gay rights become narrowly defined as those things that concern wealthy gay white men and those white lesbians with sufficient class privilege and lack of feminist politics to go along with them.

—BARBARA SMITH, BLACK ACTIVIST

233   It has taken a long time to get here. The journey has been hazardous, has been long. But we have come here on our own... Throw open the gates! Tear down the fences! Let all be fair on the grounds!

—LAWSON INADA, ASIAN AMERICAN POET

234   Everybody thought it was a joke for years, thought I was a crackpot. They laughed themselves to death... and when the Japanese got their $20,000 each, then they stopped laughing.

—RAYMOND JENKINS, BLACK REPARATIONS ACTIVIST

235   I want you to initiate correspondence with a person in prison. That act of faith, in and of itself, will be a statement of the responsibility you will have deposited in the heart and soul of a Black man. You will be telling him that you are equipped with the potential to trust, care for, respect and embrace his humanity. And that you, by virtue of your thought and deed, will deserve not one whit less in reciprocation. In most cases, he will learn to value the responsibility, trust and lives you and he will share. It will be a fair exchange, and a mutually rewarding responsibility.

—BRANDON ASTOR JONES, BLACK PRISONER

236 I empathize with everybody who struggles. Unfortunately, that's the whole damn world at this point.

— SARAH JONES, BLACK PLAYWRIGHT, PERFORMER

237 When you go through these prisons, and I've been through prisons, you are forced to come to one of two conclusions: either that young Black men are naturally criminals or that there is something seriously wrong with the system.

— MOHAMEDU JONES, BLACK LAWYER

238 I am a feminist, and what that means to me is much the same as the meaning of the fact that I am Black: it means that I must undertake to love myself and to respect myself as though my very life depends upon self-love and self-respect. It means that I must everlastingly seek to cleanse myself of the hatred and the contempt that surrounds and permeates my identity, as a woman, and as a Black human being, in this particular world of ours. It means that the achievement of self-love and self-respect will require inordinate, hourly vigilance, and that I am entering my soul into a struggle that will most certainly transform the experience of all the peoples of the earth, as no other movement can, in fact, hope to claim: because the movement into self-love, self-respect, and self-determination is the movement now galvanizing the true, unarguable majority of human beings everywhere.

— JUNE JORDAN, BLACK POET

239 In America the most important form of news-lying is simply leaving things out.

— WALTER MOSLEY, BLACK NOVELIST

240 Politics is not separate from lived experience or the imaginary world of what is possible; to the contrary, politics is about these things. Politics comprises the many battles to roll back constraints and exercise some power over, or create some space within, the institutions and social relationships that dominate our lives.

— ROBIN D. G. KELLEY, BLACK SCHOLAR

241   In the current period of demoralization and rollbacks, we have to keep reminding ourselves that politics matters, and that politics without some larger vision of what our society should look like tends to be cynical or reactionary.

—ROBIN D. G. KELLEY, BLACK SCHOLAR

242   I am sure that there are things in our world to which we should never be adjusted. There are some things concerning which we must always be mal-adjusted if we are to be people of good will. We must never adjust ourselves to racial discrimination and racial segregation. We must never adjust ourselves to religious bigotry. We must never adjust ourselves to economic conditions that take necessities from the many to give luxuries to the few. We must never adjust ourselves to the madness of militarism and the self-defeating effects of physical violence.

—MARTIN LUTHER KING, JR., BLACK CIVIL RIGHTS ACTIVIST

243   I am convinced that if we are to get on the right side of the world revolution, we as a nation must undergo a radical revolution of values. We must rapidly begin the shift from a thing-oriented society to a person-oriented society. When machines and computers, profit motives and property rights, are considered more important than people, the giant triplets of racism, extreme materialism, and militarism are incapable of being conquered.

—MARTIN LUTHER KING, JR., BLACK CIVIL RIGHTS ACTIVIST

244   Hunger also changes the world—when eating can't be a habit, then neither can seeing.

—MAXINE HONG KINGSTON, ASIAN AMERICAN NOVELIST

245   We need to read, against the grain, the loose use of words like "freedom" and "justice." Freedom to bomb from on high or freedom to live lives free from attacks? Justice in terms of fierce retribution or justice as the right to live without duress?

—AMITAVA KUMAR, SOUTH ASIAN WRITER

246   Iraq, it seems, is about to trump Vietnam in the American psyche as the reigning metaphor for tragedy.

—ANDREW LAM, ASIAN AMERICAN WRITER

247   As a Vietnamese refugee who became an American writer, I can tell you that you matter, that your sadness matters, the story of how you survived and triumphed matters. For every story that belongs to you, in time, belongs to America.

—ANDREW LAM, ASIAN AMERICAN WRITER

248   Why maintain the status quo if it isn't right? Or, why end up perpetuating a positive stereotype? A stereotype is still a stereotype.

—CORKY LEE, ASIAN AMERICAN PHOTOGRAPHER

249   Liberty protects all citizens' choices from the most direct and egregious abuses of government power, but it does nothing to dismantle social arrangements that make it impossible for some people to make a choice in the first place. Liberty guards against government inclusion; it does not guarantee social justice.

—DOROTHY ROBERTS, BLACK SCHOLAR

250   We're made to believe that one group hinders the other. That's absolutely wrong, and I believe in fighting against it.

—SHELIA JACKSON LEE, BLACK POLITICIAN

251   We need to identify U.S. neoliberal policies as the root cause of our day to day struggles, such as the gutting of welfare, exploitation of immigrants and displacement due to gentrification.

—HYUN LEE, ASIAN AMERICAN ACTIVIST

252   For decades of imperialist wars we have been atomic bombed, we have been napalmed; we have been raped; we have been driven to suicide—and we have built this country from the east to the west. And we have been called the barbarian! . . . Who's the barbarian?

—TANA LOY, ASIAN AMERICAN ACTIVIST

253   The truth as I see it now is that in a war, the bad is often measured against what's even worse, and that, in turn, makes a lot of deplorable things permissible. When that happens, the imaginary line between right and wrong starts to vanish in a heavy fog, until it disappears completely and decisions are weighed on a scale of values that is profoundly corrupt.

—CAMILO MEJÍA, LATINO CONSCIENTIOUS OBJECTOR

254   I'm sorry, wherever there's injustice it's your duty as a human being to speak up and if you don't there's no excuse. You're just a lemming. So if you don't speak out against injustice you're a lemming.

—RUSSELL MEANS, AMERICAN INDIAN ACTIVIST

255   The people who told their stories in spite of tremendous fear, did so not only for themselves and their communities but for all of us. They spoke out because they love America and they believe that public debate is essential for a functioning democracy. They spoke out for freedom for their children and for all of our children. They spoke out because they know that ultimately, the erosion of their rights can summarily be applied to all of us.

—PRAMILA JAYAPAL, SOUTH ASIAN ACTIVIST

256   When you're accused of doing something you didn't do, the first impulse is to feel guilt or unease. Anyone under those circumstances would start behaving badly.

—SUSAN CHOI, ASIAN AMERICAN NOVELIST

257   In our bodies a terrible thunder is building its nest.
—JANICE MIRIKITANI, ASIAN AMERICAN POET

258   The strongest prisons are built / With walls of silence.
—JANICE MIRIKITANI, ASIAN AMERICAN POET

259   It seems to me that one needs an integrated theory or framework to see the world from the point of view of the most disenfranchised. Often times it happens to be women of color, peasant women, tribal women around the world who are the poorest of the poor.
—CHANDRA TALPADE MOHANTY, SOUTH ASIAN SCHOLAR

260   If you are really honest about equity and social justice then you have to start thinking about the transformation of your own framework, of your own ways of thinking in order that people are included, so that people come along with you.
—CHANDRA TALPADE MOHANTY, SOUTH ASIAN SCHOLAR

261   Exclusionary knowledges and ways of seeing and interpreting the world affect the way we understand social and political reality and also how we understand the position of different communities of people in the social pattern. It also clearly affects the way we fight for equity and social justice.
—CHANDRA TALPADE MOHANTY, SOUTH ASIAN SCHOLAR

262   If you're going to hold someone down you're going to have to hold onto the other end of the chain. You are confined by your own system of repression.
—TONI MORRISON, BLACK NOVELIST

263   Short of major wars, mass incarceration has been the most thoroughly implemented government social program of our time.

—ANGELA DAVIS, BLACK SCHOLAR

264   Young people, whether you're in college or in prison, you need to do what you need to do to make the next century belong to the people, because this century has been 100 years more of slavery.

—ASSATA SHAKUR, BLACK ACTIVIST

265   In American society, and British society, in the West and the East, in Islam and Christianity and Judaism and Hinduism, even Buddhism, people are trying to denigrate our earth for power, control and ego, and we can't let it happen.

—ASRA Q. NOMANI, SOUTH ASIAN JOURNALIST

266   It is all about love that knows no boundary of geography or country; it is simply a generation's commitment to what service to humanity is all about.

—CECILE CAGUINGIN OCHOA, ASIAN AMERICAN JOURNALIST

267   If the American people really want to get at an understanding of why violence is such a problem in the inner city these days, they should take a look at the connection between violence in the community and police brutality. A people who are brutalized—economically, spiritually and physically—will start to act that way themselves.

—PARIS, BLACK HIP-HOP ARTIST

268   I just felt so tired of giving in to a system so unjust.

—ROSA PARKS, BLACK CIVIL RIGHTS ACTIVIST

269 If you're considered as "other," you could be subject to being killed, or beaten down, or left on a roof for three to four days, or left to rot in the Superdome. That's not a democracy to me. That's a country that's missing its soul.

—KEVIN POWELL, BLACK JOURNALIST

270 The terror of the frustrated works alongside the terror of the behemoth to undermine the powerful and democratic urges of the people. Both of those terrors must be condemned.

—VIJAY PRASHAD, SOUTH ASIAN SCHOLAR

271 The "realism" that abounds does not empower people; rather, it ensures that they lose sovereignty over their own destinies, and it erodes the basis of fellowship. In struggle, we can re-create our bonds and we can fight, ceaselessly, for what we deem to be our rights and for what we envision, however clumsily, as our freedom, not just for ourselves, but for working people in general.

—VIJAY PRASHAD, SOUTH ASIAN SCHOLAR

272 I'm willing to do whatever is necessary, because I'll be damned if you're gonna walk all over people. I'll be damned if I'll let you.

—JANET ROBIDEAU, AMERICAN INDIAN ACTIVIST

273 We've got a country that never takes any responsibility for anything. It forgets its role and makes everybody else forget what happened, too. And that it is not just dangerous for the victim, but also for the perpetrator.

—ROBBY RODRIGUEZ, LATINO ORGANIZER

274 Resistance is a political act. It is also a nonviolent strategy for changing a status quo that perpetuates race wars and violates civil rights. To resist means that one does not accept the belief system, the data as they are presented, or the rationalizations used to perpetuate the status quo around race relations. Resistance also means refusing to fragment, marginalize, or disconnect ourselves from people and from ourselves.

— MAGDALENO ROSE-AVILA, LATINO ACTIVIST

275   To call someone "anti-American," indeed to be anti-American (or for that matter, anti-Indian or anti-Timbuktuan), is not just racist, it's a failure of the imagination. An inability to see the world in terms other than those the establishment has set out for you. If you're not a Bushie you're a Taliban. If you don't love us, you hate us. If you're not Good, you're Evil. If you're not with us, you're with the terrorists.

— ARUNDHATI ROY, INDIAN WRITER

276   Powerful people—white men and their many-hued and gendered agents —are afraid they may be challenged. Domestic militarization and prison—not education, public health, or good jobs—is their answer.

— RUTH WILSON GILMORE, BLACK SCHOLAR

277   I don't know any other way to say this: it is about time youth were romanticized again. The United States is rightly afraid of the kids it has abandoned, which is to say most of them.

— RUTH WILSON GILMORE, BLACK SCHOLAR

278   In the religious community, we think in generations and that's the way to think because that's how real change happens. Legislation is just the tip of the iceberg—there's deeper things going on under the surface.

— REV. ALEXIA SALVATIERRA, LATINA ACTIVIST

279   We are tired of praying and marching and thinking and learning / Brothers want to start cutting and shooting and stealing and burning.

— GIL SCOTT-HERON, BLACK POET

280   What to do with those whom society cannot accommodate? Criminal-ize them. Outlaw their actions and creations. Declare them the enemy, then wage war. Emphasize the differences—the shade of skin, the accent in the speech or manner of clothes. Like the scapegoat of the Bible, place society's ills on them, then "stone them" in absolution. It's convenient. It's logical. It doesn't work.

—LUIS J. RODRIGUEZ, LATINO WRITER

281   It is necessary to continue to tell white America about us, as white America needs to continue to share and know us. Because this time, we are going to walk down that long road into American history together.

—MONICA SONE, ASIAN AMERICAN ACTIVIST

282   We first fought in the name of religion, then communism, and now in the name of drugs and terrorism. Our excuses for global domination always change.

—SERJ TANKIAN, ARMENIAN AMERICAN MUSICIAN

283   I'm a woman. I'm a black woman. I'm a poor woman. I'm a fat woman. I'm a middle-aged woman. And I'm on welfare. In this country, if you're any one of these things you count less as a human being. If you're all those things, you don't count at all. Except as a statistic. Welfare's like a traffic accident. It can happen to anybody, but especially it happens to women. As far as I'm con-cerned, the ladies of NWRO [National Welfare Rights Organization] are the front-line troops of women's freedom. Both because we have so few illusions and because our issues are so important to all women—the right to a living wage for women's work, the right to life itself.

—JOHNNIE TILLMON, BLACK ACTIVIST

284   I write to fight erasure, to demand a voice, to become visible, to reclaim my history. I write to turn on the light.

—KITTY TSUI, ASIAN AMERICAN WRITER

285   We need to take the discussion to another level. If we talk only about violent offenders—the worst cases—there will never be any forward motion in the direction of prison abolition. Instead, we need to focus on creative dialogue around the possibility of abolishing jails and prisons as the knee-jerk response to every form of crime.

—ANGELA DAVIS, BLACK SCHOLAR

286   Since the arrival of foreigners and their "systems of power," which brought mass death, oppression, and disenfranchisement for Native Hawaiians, we have been degraded to criminal status in our own homeland and become a nation incarcerated.

—HEALANI SONODA, NATIVE HAWAIIAN ACTIVIST

287   I had reasoned this out in my mind; there was one of two things I had a *right* to, liberty or death; if I could not have one, I would have the other; for no man should take me alive.

—HARRIET TUBMAN, BLACK ABOLITIONIST

288   Humiliation is permanent. This isn't to say that once a person is humiliated the humiliation will continue endlessly. Rather, the memory of that humiliation will never dissipate. It will remain with the humiliated person until his or her death. So it is for the Iraqi civilians in Abu Ghraib who were stripped of their dignity by a platoon of soldiers who had the backing of a country whose stock and trade in foreign policy has long been the degradation of Arabs.

—STEVEN SALAITA, ARAB AMERICAN SCHOLAR

289   America is ours as much as it is *theirs*. We have to be clear about that . . . We own this country as much as white people do. In fact, we built this country more than they did. We are not guests at the table called America.

Not when we carved the table, polished it, put the food on it, and did everything else. From that perspective, you know we own this, and in owning it we decide how we press a claim and also how we make our mark.

—JULIANNE MALVEAUX, BLACK ECONOMIST

290 We need political power to protect and defend ourselves as we work to eradicate homophobia. This answer may strike some as paranoid or simplistic; but the necessity of a movement that can defend queer people is urgent.

—URVASHI VAID, SOUTH ASIAN ACTIVIST

291 The situation in Israel and Palestine is often the subject that no one wants to talk about. We have to talk about it and weigh in on it whether we are Black, Latino, Asian or white. In other words, it is not simply a Jewish-Arab question, but a human rights question.

—BARBARA RANSBY, BLACK SCHOLAR

292 "Progress" affects a few. Only revolution can affect many.

—ALICE WALKER, BLACK WRITER

293 You have to read and read and read to really find out the horrors of what people we have entrusted to govern and protect us are doing behind closed doors. I had to decide what I really believed and what I was willing to sacrifice for those beliefs.

—EHREN WATADA, ASIAN AMERICAN CONSCIENTIOUS OBJECTOR

294 There must always be a remedy for wrong and injustice if we only know how to find it.

—IDA B. WELLS, BLACK JOURNALIST

295   One had better die fighting against injustice than to die like a dog or a rat in a trap.

—Ida B. Wells, Black journalist

296   With the vast erosion of civic networks that nurture and care for citizens—such as families, neighborhoods, and schools—and with what might be called the gangsterization of everyday life, characterized by the escalating fear of violent attack, vicious assault or cruel insult, we are witnessing a pervasive cultural decay in American civilization.

—Cornel West, Black scholar

297   The sublime notion that each and every ordinary person has a dignity that warrants his or her voice being heard in shaping the destiny of society remains a revolutionary force in the 21st century—in the face of the power of autocratic empires, plutocratic states, and xenophobic communities.

—Cornel West, Black scholar

298   In every human breast, God has implanted a principle, which we call love of freedom; it is impatient of oppression and pants for deliverance.

—Phillis Wheatley, Black poet

299   I don't want violence to have the last word.

—Cindy Widell, American Indian activist

300   A creole in general means improvisation. It means resistance. Creole creativity can be places for resistance, places where political movements are born, where values are preserved.

—John Edgar Wideman, Black novelist

301 The polemics of right-wing radio are putting nothing less than hate onto the airwaves, into the marketplace, electing it to office, teaching it in schools, and exalting it as freedom.

—PATRICIA WILLIAMS, BLACK LAW PROFESSOR

302 Democracy can never enter a country through a coup or through military tacks. Democracy is a culture that must be created in a society and then progress.

—SHIRIN EBADI, IRANIAN LAWYER AND ACTIVIST

303 History, demographics, and our determination are on our side. What we have learned can't be taken away. We will be full partners in the future of America.

—HELEN ZIA, ASIAN AMERICAN JOURNALIST

304 If we do not now dare everything, the fulfillment of that prophecy, re-created from the Bible in song by a slave, is upon us: *God gave Noah the rainbow sign, No more water, the fire next time!*

—JAMES BALDWIN, BLACK WRITER

305 Nobody can go to war...and win.

—JAMES BALDWIN, BLACK WRITER

306 The world is before you and you need not take it or leave it as it was when you came in.

—JAMES BALDWIN, BLACK WRITER

307   You don't want to stand on a corner and be told to get off it when you got nowhere else to go. And we want somewhere else to go.

—AMA BONTEMPS, BLACK WRITER

308   All Black people are involved in the same struggle. Revolutionaries are not necessarily born poor or in the ghetto. There is a role for every person in the revolution.

—H. RAP BROWN, BLACK ACTIVIST

309   I have done little in this world in which to glory except this one act— and I certainly glory in that. When I ran away from slavery, it was for myself; when I advocated emancipation, it was for my people; but when I stood up for the rights of women, self was out of the question, and I found a little nobility in the act.

—FREDERICK DOUGLASS, BLACK ABOLITIONIST

310   No people that has solely depended on foreign aid or rather upon the efforts of those in any way identified with the oppressor to undo the heavy burdens, ever gained freedom.

—FREDERICK DOUGLASS, BLACK ABOLITIONIST

311   I cannot recall any previous period when the challenges have been so basic, so interconnected, and so demanding, not just to specific groups but to everyone living in this country, regardless of race, ethnicity, class, gender, age, or national origin.

—GRACE LEE BOGGS, ASIAN AMERICAN ACTIVIST

3 1 2   We trace the real cause of this World War to the despising of the darker races by the dominant groups of men, and the consequent fierce rivalry among European nations in their efforts to use darker and backward people for the purposes of selfish gain regardless of the ultimate good of the oppressed. We see permanent peace only in the extension of the principle of government by the consent of the governed, not simply among the smaller nations of Europe, but among the natives of Asia and Africa, the West Indies and the Negroes of the United States.

—W.E.B. Du Bois, Black scholar and activist

3 1 3   Today's real borders are not between nations, but between powerful and powerless, free and fettered, privileged and humiliated. Today, no walls can separate humanitarian or human rights crises in one part of the world from national security crises in another.

—Kofi Annan, Black diplomat

3 1 4   To your tents, Americans! We have gone far enough into the morass of fear, war, hate, lying and crime. We face a crisis and our first duty is here and now. For the time being, never mind the Soviet Union; forget China... Come back home and look at America.

—W.E.B. Du Bois, Black scholar and activist

3 1 5   The cost of liberty is less than the price of repression.

—W.E.B. Du Bois, Black scholar and activist

3 1 6   The bones of injustice have a peculiar way of rising from the tombs to plague and mock the iniquitous.

—Marcus Garvey, Black activist

3 1 7   The national pastime in this country is not sex and it's not baseball. It's lying.

—DICK GREGORY, BLACK COMEDIAN

3 1 8   For above all, in behalf of an ailing world which sorely needs our defiance, may we never accept the notion of "our place."

—LORRAINE HANSBERRY, BLACK PLAYWRIGHT

3 1 9   To resist is the affirmation of our own humanity and the humanity of others. It is a radical political statement in a society that systematically denies the humanity of us on this planet. To open up spaces where people can bring their whole humanity into the room, celebrate it, acknowledge it—that is radical.

—PANCHO ARGUELLES, LATINO ORGANIZER

3 2 0   I dream an America that is a democracy and not a kleptocracy, where we bail out the schools before the airlines.

—FARAI CHIDEYA, BLACK JOURNALIST

3 2 1   We've got to make them know and understand how evil the things are that they did to us over all these years and are still doing to us today. We've just got to let *them* know that we *know what they are doing* and we're not going to lighten up until they stop.

—MILES DAVIS, BLACK MUSICIAN

3 2 2   If the people of the United States had the real story about what their government has done in Iraq, the occupation would already have ended. As a journalist, I continue to hold out hope that if people have knowledge of what is happening, they will act accordingly. If people in my country could hear the stories of life under occupation and put themselves into the Iraqis' stories, they would understand. I hold that hope because the stories of Iraq are our story now.

— DAHR JAMAIL, ARAB AMERICAN JOURNALIST

323 We need to create and support the development of a whole generation of young people who think about war differently, think about the world differently.

— AIMEE ALLISON, BLACK ACTIVIST

324 Caught in a situation where both adversaries in the war on terror claim to be fighting terror with weapons of terror, nothing less than a global movement for peace will save humanity.

— MAHMOOD MAMDANI, SOUTH ASIAN SCHOLAR

325 If we pay attention to and think from the space of some of the most disenfranchised communities of women in the world, we are most likely to envision a just and democratic society capable of treating all its citizens fairly. Conversely, if we begin our analysis from, and limit it to, the space of privileged communities, our visions of justice are more likely to be exclusionary because privilege nurtures blindness to those without the same privileges.

— CHANDRA TALPADE MOHANTY, SOUTH ASIAN SCHOLAR

326 Some of us continue to believe we need a revolution, a complete change in the ruling social order. Progressives across the country have responded to the Katrina disaster not only as volunteers but also in hopes of establishing focal points of organizational development. The truth is, however, that a disaster is not a revolution.

— KALAMU YA SALAAM, BLACK ACTIVIST

3 2 7   I think at this stage the big question is, What is the American society? Is it the kind of society that either black women or black men or anyone who is seeking a dignified existence as a human being, that permits people to grow and develop according to their capacity, that gives them a sense of value, not only for themselves, but a sense of value for other human beings. Is this the kind of society that is going to permit that? I think there is a great question as to whether it can become that kind of society.

—ELLA BAKER, BLACK CIVIL RIGHTS ACTIVIST

Environmental Justice

3 2 8   My vision is for a world in which we have tons of people who can respond to the things that are happening to them in a proactive way, in a sustainable way and in a way that's going to leave a sustainable world.

—ADRIENNE MAREE BROWN, BLACK ACTIVIST

3 2 9   The environmental justice movement has been about people taking control of their own communities. Those most impacted by a problem are also the ones leading the hunt for a solution.

—OMAR FREILLA, LATINO ACTIVIST

3 3 0   We don't have to accept the dictatorship of high-tech. Human beings can make decisions about when and where to use high-tech, low-tech, intermediate-tech, or a mix of these, on the basis of what best develops people and communities and at the same time maintains the health of our ecosystem.

—GRACE LEE BOGGS, ASIAN AMERICAN SCHOLAR

3 3 1   For our own well-being—for the health and safety of our communities, our cities, and our country—we need to accept the awesome responsibility of creating new ways of making a living, new ways of producing for our material needs, and new ways of daily living that reestablish our sacred connection to Mother Earth and to one another.

—GRACE LEE BOGGS, ASIAN AMERICAN SCHOLAR

3 3 2   I have become an environmentalist, because it is over the environment that the last of the Indian Wars will be fought.

—MARY CROW DOG, AMERICAN INDIAN ACTIVIST

3 3 3   The land is our mother, the rivers our blood. Take our land away and we die. That is, the Indian in us dies. We'd become just suntanned white men, the jetsam and flotsam of your great melting pot.

—MARY CROW DOG, AMERICAN INDIAN ACTIVIST

3 3 4   I wasn't born to be rich. I was born to live a good life...I hunt all over. I don't believe the white man has a right to stop us and don't understand what they say and what they do...I just want them to live up to this land, to what they said and to themselves.

—LENNIE BUTCHER,
AMERICAN INDIAN RESIDENT OF
THE WHITE EARTH RESERVATION

3 3 5   You may sit there and ask what we want, but what we want is what you need, too. It's what this society needs, if they want to continue to stay alive on this earth. What we do is for all things, for all people. Because if you don't stop now with the destruction, with the development and the poisoning of the environment, we're all gonna go. So when you ask the question of what we want,

you might as well go ahead and include yourself. Because not only do we want to survive as who we are, I'm pretty sure that you want to survive as who you are, too.

—DANNY BILLIE, AMERICAN INDIAN ACTIVIST

336   The earth is a living thing. Mountains speak, trees sing, lakes can think, pebbles have a soul, rocks have power.

—HENRY CROW DOG, AMERICAN INDIAN ACTIVIST

337   It's incredible, although not surprising, to see the extent to which corporations continue to devise ways to profit from people's increasing concern for their environment and health. I'm sure we'll get a product bottled and sold to us that purports to solve climate change sometime soon.

—ANTONIO DIAZ, LATINO ACTIVIST

338   If you see the world around you as a collection of objects for you to manipulate and exploit, you will inevitably destroy the world while attempting to control it.

—VINE DELORIA, JR., AMERICAN INDIAN WRITER

339   Here's the riddle for Our Age: when the sky's the limit, / how can you tell if you've gone too far?

—RITA DOVE, BLACK POET

340   Mainstream environmentalists would do well to build relationships and alliances with Native groups—but first they must be willing to listen to our point of view.

—WINONA LADUKE, AMERICAN INDIAN ACTIVIST

341   Native communities are not in a position to compromise, because who we are is our land, our trees, and our lakes. This is central to our local and collective work. This is also why the conflicts remain in Native America between corporate interests and our traditional ways, and between segments of our community who embrace the values of industrial society and those who continue to embrace traditional values.

—WINONA LaDUKE, AMERICAN INDIAN ACTIVIST

342   They keep changing what they mean, or changing the terminology. We cannot do that. You can change the terms, you can change the allowable limits, you can do the risk assessment—all these things—but in the end, the fact is that you and I drink that water. You and I breathe that air. You and I live here.

—WINONA LaDUKE, AMERICAN INDIAN ACTIVIST

343   Frankly, these native societies have existed as the only example of sustainable living in North America for more than 300 years.

—WINONA LaDUKE, AMERICAN INDIAN ACTIVIST

344   If we do not get involved, we will end up with eco-apartheid—a society with ecological haves and have-nots. Imagine a world in which wealthy people have clean air, fresh water, healthy food and no-cost energy, thanks to solar panels, organic agriculture and green technology. Meanwhile, poor neighborhoods continue to choke in the fumes of last century's pollution-based industries.

—VAN JONES, BLACK ACTIVIST

345   We're completely surrounded by petro-chemical companies. We're housing the largest pig farm in the county. We're housing one of the largest chicken farms. What I'm saying is that we're completely surrounded, in one form or another, in shit, OK? The opposite side of that coin is that we want to be here. We're very proud of our community. We've raised our families up here. Some would say, "Why don't you pack up your stuff and leave?" Well, it's about standing up for justice.

—RICHARD MOORE, LATINO ACTIVIST

346   It has been proved that the land can exist without the country—and be better for it; it has not been proved that the country can exist without the land.

—ALICE WALKER, BLACK WRITER

347   It must become a right of every person to die of old age. And if we secure this right for ourselves, we can, coincidentally, assure it for the planet.

—ALICE WALKER, BLACK WRITER

348   The animals of the planet are in desperate peril. Without free animal life I believe we will lose the spiritual equivalent of oxygen.

—ALICE WALKER, BLACK WRITER

349   I had assumed that the Earth, the spirit of the Earth, noticed exceptions—those who wantonly damage it and those who do not. But the Earth is wise. It has given itself into the keeping of all, and all are therefore accountable.

—ALICE WALKER, BLACK WRITER

350   I am awed at man's ingenuity and what he can achieve. I recognized what a beautiful and fragile planet we live on. Seeing Earth from 170 miles out in space is not like standing on Earth and looking at the moon.

—GUION BLUFORD, BLACK ASTRONAUT

351 Minorities are the targets of a disproportionate threat from toxins, both in the work place where they are assigned the dirtiest and most hazardous jobs, and in their homes, which tend to be in the most polluted community.

—JOHN CONYERS, BLACK POLITICIAN

352 Sell a country! Why not sell the air, the clouds and the great sea, as well as the earth? Did not the great spirit make them all for the use of his children?

—TECUMSEH, AMERICAN INDIAN CHIEF OF THE SHAWNEES

353 We must pay our debts to the past by putting the future in debt to ourselves.

—ALICE WALKER, BLACK WRITER

354 And the arrogance, saying we're going to save the planet. The planet will take care of herself. It's not about us saving her, it's about us being in syncretism with her. With a sense of interdependence, with respect.

—NILAK BUTLER, AMERICAN INDIAN ACTIVIST

355 We need each other. Each of us is responsible for what happens on this earth. We are each absolutely essential, each totally irreplaceable. Each of us is *the* swing vote in the bitter election battle now being waged between our best and our worst possibilities.

—LEONARD PELTIER, AMERICAN INDIAN ACTIVIST

356 It is absolutely essential that we protect our families, our communities, our environment, our livelihoods. Protection is not protection*ism*, because protection cannot be reduced to a phenomenon of the market place.

—VANDANA SHIVA, SOUTH ASIAN SCIENTIST

357   This we know; the earth does not belong to man; man belongs to the earth. This we know. All things are connected like the blood which unites our family. All things are connected.

—SEATTLE, AMERICAN INDIAN CHIEF OF SQUAMISH TRIBE

358   In contrast to viewing the planet as prviate property, movements are defending, on a local and global level, the planet as a commons. In contrast to experiencing the world as a global supermarket, where goods and serv-ices are produced with high ecological, social, and economic costs and sold for abysmally low prices, cultures and communities everywhere are resisting the destruction of their biological and cultural diversity, their lives, and their livelihoods.

—VANDANA SHIVA, SOUTH ASIAN SCIENTIST

359   It has been my experience that most Americans would rather fight for a rain forest five thousand miles away than join the battle being waged by native peoples right here in their own backyards.

—GAIL SMALL, AMERICAN INDIAN ACTIVIST

360   Someone once said that the first recyclers were poor people.

—ANTONIO DIAZ, LATINO ACTIVIST

361   I've committed myself to feeding people.

—BRYANT TERRY, BLACK ACTIVIST

362   Why should environmentalists care about farmworkers? Well, do you eat? Do you buy plants from a nursery or flowers from a florist? Do you play golf? Or work in a finely landscaped office building? If you do any of these things, chances are that you have been exposed to pesticides. And, the people who made it possible for you to have that food, or those flowers, or who grew the sod on your golf course or the plants in your landscape, were more than likely low-wage farmworkers who, along with their families, were exposed to pesticides in the production processes.

— TIRSO MORENO, LATINO ORGANIZER

3 6 3 I have a stereotype of environmentalists as being rather affluent white people who go around with binoculars to watch birds and don't see the connections between their lifestyles and the poverty in their communities.

— TIRSO MORENO, LATINO ORGANIZER

3 6 4 All places and all beings of the earth are sacred. It is dangerous to designate some places sacred when all are sacred. Such compromises imply that there is a hierarchy of value, with some places and some living beings not as important as others. No part of the earth is expendable; the earth is a whole that cannot be fragmented, as it has been by the destroyers' mentality of the industrial age.

— LESLIE MARMON SILKO, AMERICAN INDIAN WRITER

3 6 5 We need solutions at every level, from people in every sector, if we are to save ourselves from the climate crisis. Indeed, efforts are doomed if they get stuck in elite subcultures instead of including broad, vibrantly diverse coalitions.

— IAN KIM, ASIAN AMERICAN ACTIVIST

3 6 6 Indians believe in the spiritual nature of the environment. The federal agencies charged with helping us protect our physical surroundings cannot do so unless they understand the interdependence of environment, culture, and religion in the tribal way of life.

— GAIL SMALL, AMERICAN INDIAN ACTIVIST

367   Our thinking is that all people throughout the world should re-identify with what our relationship is with this planet that we call Mother Earth. We must re-evaluate our own spiritual relationship. We feel that this world is out of balance. We feel that human beings throughout the world have lost a sustainable ethic to the land. Industrialized man has given up our power as human beings. Industrialized man believes in this false belief that technology is going to save us when it is not.

—Tom Goldtooth, American Indian activist

368   We are really concerned about what we eat. We feel that all humans have a right to know what they are consuming. Our tribal elders tell us the food that is created in laboratories has no spirit. If we keep on eating food with no spirit we are going to lose our spirit. That means that we won't be able to think for ourselves. There's an energy force when we consume that creative principle of our Mother Earth. When civil society can't think for ourselves, then perhaps that is a time when industrialized corporate leaders and technology will take over and be thinking for us.

—Tom Goldtooth, American Indian activist

369   This is what true revolutions are about. They are about redefining our relationships with one another, to the Earth and to the world; about creating a new society in the places and spaces left vacant by the disintegration of the old; about hope, not despair; about saying yes to life and no to war; about finding the courage to love and care for the peoples of the world as we love and care for our own families.

—Grace Lee Boggs, Asian American activist

370   Our fates *are* tied. We have this strange notion on this planet that our fates are *not* tied. If it were not so we would not be here together. It's that simple.

—Luisah Teish, Black performer

CHAPTER 6

Inner Visions

Spirit

1 I don't think a time will ever come when we will dismiss the human spirit.

—Lorraine Hansberry, Black playwright

2 I loved living, physically as well as spiritually.

—W.E.B. Du Bois, Black scholar and activist

3 There is no god but Love and work is his prophet.

—W.E.B. Du Bois, Black scholar and activist

4 The craft of questions, the craft of stories, the craft of the hands—all these are the making of something, and that something is soul. Anytime we feed soul, it guarantees increase.

—Clarissa Pinkola Estés, Latina psychologist

5 For the American Indian, the ability of all creatures to share in the process of ongoing creation makes all things sacred.

—Paula Gunn Allen, American Indian writer

6   The quintessential revolution is that of the spirit, born of an intellectual conviction of the need for change in those mental attitudes and values which shape the course of a nation's development. A revolution which aims merely at changing official policies and institutions with a view to an improvement in material conditions has little chance of genuine success. Without a revolution of the spirit, the forces which produced the iniquities of the old order would continue to be operative, posing a constant threat to the process of reform and regeneration.

—Aung San Suu Kyi, Burmese leader

7   A good spirit is like a muscle. If you do not work and exercise it and massage it in a good and positive way it will eventually wither and die.

—Brandon Astor Jones, Black prisoner

8   We are the peoples who bless being or all of existence, and are blessed by being. Saying we give blessings means that we appreciate, understand and respect the Earth and the universe, both physically and spiritually. We give meaning to being, to the universe, by our self-conscious acts of ceremony, blessings and respect. This worldview differs sharply with some Western philosophical positions, known as materialism or nihilism, where the universe is believed to have no significant meaning or purpose for humans. We can continue on the line of thought by saying we are the peoples who bless becoming. Becoming is the pattern of change and direction of the universe. Becoming is similar to what many indigenous peoples understand as the Great Spirit. We are the peoples who believe there is a plan and purpose to the unfolding of the universe, or becoming. Individuals are part of the overall becoming of the universe, and therefore individuals and nations play a role or purpose in the process of becoming.

—editors of *Indian Country Today*

9   Language is more than just a functional mechanism. It is a spiritual energy that is available to all.

—Simon Ortiz, American Indian poet

10 The word spiritual in English is always connected with religious. For me the spiritual is right there. There is nothing mystical about spirituality. Its everyday life you can see it, you can hear it, you can feel it. That's spirituality.

— BASIL JOHNSTON, AMERICAN INDIAN WRITER

11 There is a psychic wilderness that surrounds each of us, a wilderness of silence and self-evaluation that we spend most of our day avoiding. Only in our sleep do we let go of the packaged spectacles. For most of us, nighttime dreaming brings us closer to our identities and our power than any activity in the waking world.

— WALTER MOSLEY, BLACK NOVELIST

12 Material pursuits and solitary avarice are methodically engendering a great forgetting. We are slowly losing our memories and sections of our souls.

— DAVE STEPHENSON, AMERICAN INDIAN WRITER

13 It can perhaps best be described as a smooth flowing, a continuity of the land and its animals and ourselves, an uninterrupted progression. We are a part of the totality, and we are confident the totality will always remain.

— DAVE STEPHENSON, AMERICAN INDIAN WRITER

14 You can study about organizing, but unless you do it with a full heart and your ceremonies intact and your spiritual people behind you, and your medicine people with you, it won't work. I just believe you have to have spirituality in everything you do.

— PAMELA KINGFISHER, AMERICAN INDIAN ACTIVIST

15 Let your soul do the singin'.

— MA RAINEY, BLACK SINGER

16   No, I wasn't very smart, this I knew, but I was beginning to think that maybe, just maybe, I was some kind of crazy-*loco* genius, *burro* genius. I mean, to have been able to hold on to my Spirit for this long had to mean something.

— VICTOR VILLASEÑOR, LATINO WRITER

17   Is this what enabled me to feel that humming behind my ears? Was this what allowed me to sometimes see the whole world come alive in light and color? Could dyslexia be a gift? Could it be that we were all "dyslexic" back at one time when we all recognized that the Kingdom of God was within and we knew how to bring what was within out into the world?

— VICTOR VILLASEÑOR, LATINO WRITER

18   The main point of any spiritual practice is to step out of the bureaucracy of ego. This means stepping out of ego's constant desire for a higher, more spiritual, more transcendental version of knowledge, religion, virtue, judgment, comfort, or whatever it is that the particular ego is seeking. One must step out of spiritual materialism.

— CHOGYAM TRUNGPA, TIBETAN BUDDHIST TEACHER

19   I believe that if we listen and are open to hear, there are divine voices urging us to action at every moment of our lives…To hear the voices (call it God, a guardian angel, the spirits of those passed on) we must believe that they are real to us, and to listen to them we must have faith in the universe's intentions and in our own ability to know the truth in our bones.

— G. WINSTON JAMES, BLACK WRITER

20   They call me Lady Soul, so let me tell you something about soul. Soul is something creative, something active. Soul is honesty. I sing to people about what matters. I sing to the realists; people who accept it like it is. I express problems, there are tears when it's sad and smiles when it's happy. It seems simple to me, but to some, feelings take courage.

— ARETHA FRANKLIN, BLACK SINGER

21 Fearlessness is the first requisite of spirituality. Cowards can never be moral.

—MOHANDAS GANDHI, INDIAN LEADER

22 *Despair?* Did someone say despair was a question in the world? Well then, listen to the sons of those who have known little else if you wish to know the resiliency of this thing you would so quickly resign to mythhood, this thing called the human spirit.

—LORRAINE HANSBERRY, BLACK PLAYWRIGHT

23 You should know that the movement for Indian rights was first of all a spiritual movement and that our ancient religion was at the heart of it... Christianizing us was one way of making us white, that is, of making us forget that we were Indians. Holding on to our old religion was one way of resisting this kind of slow death. As long as people prayed with the pipe or beat the little water drum, Indians would not vanish, would continue to exist as Indians.

—MARY CROW DOG, AMERICAN INDIAN ACTIVIST

24 All classes of a people under social pressure are permeated with a common experience; they are emotionally welded as others cannot be. With them, even ordinary living has epic depth and lyric intensity, and this... is their spiritual advantage.

—ALAIN LOCKE, BLACK PHILOSOPHER

25 Unlike "New Age" versions of spirituality, which focus almost exclusively on the personal (so that goals become acquiring increased wealth, a "good life," or other solipsistic materialistic items), spiritual activism begins with the personal yet moves outward, acknowledging our radical interconnectedness. This is spirituality for social change, spirituality that recognizes the many differences among us yet insists on our commonalities and uses these commonalities as catalysts for transformation. What a contrast: while identity politics requires holding onto specific categories of identity, spiritual activism demands that we let them go.

—AnaLouise Keating, Latina scholar

26 The spiritual components of life *cannot* be divorced from politics, sexuality, writing, or daily living.

—AnaLouise Keating, Latina scholar

27 Our Earth faces ecological disaster. People continue suffering from social injustices. Alienation from self and communities persists. In this era of capitalist globalization, there is a great necessity for relief from physical, spiritual, and social afflictions. So many of us (re)turn to indigenous and mestiza spiritual knowledges for empowerment—knowledge powerful enough to survive despite patriarchal and colonial efforts at destruction.

—Irene Lara, Latina scholar

28 There is a simple spiritual principle: the meaner you get toward your brother and sister, the meaner it will come back to you.

—Sandra Robertson, Black activist

Faith

29 In this era of increasing multiculturalism, and the social strains this brings into people's lives, our free faith is evidence to the world that pluralism can work. We know it can work because we live it every day. We are living proof that our difference need not divide us.

—Rev. William G. Sinkford, Black minister

3 0   In the native world, major gods come in trios, duos, and groups. It is the habit of non-natives to discover the supreme being, and the one and only head god, a habit lent to them by monotheism.

—PAULA GUNN ALLEN, AMERICAN INDIAN WRITER

3 1   What is religion, you might ask. It's a technology of living.

—TONI CADE BAMBARA, BLACK WRITER

3 2   Our religion and ceremonies have become fads, and a fashionable pastime among many whites seeking for something that they hope will give meaning to their empty lives. . . . after macrobiotics, Zen, and channeling, the "poor Vanishing Indian" is once more the subject of "deep and meaningful conversation" in the high rises.

—MARY CROW DOG, AMERICAN INDIAN ACTIVIST

3 3   Loving God is much like a successful long term relationship. You've got to try a lot of different things, be adventurous in order to keep things interesting.

—MARGARET CHO, ASIAN AMERICAN COMEDIAN

3 4   I have loved a fight and I have realized that Love is God and Work is His prophet; that His ministers are Age and Death.

—W.E.B. DU BOIS, BLACK SCHOLAR AND ACTIVIST

3 5   God's been going deaf. . . . Here God used to raineth bread from clouds, smite the Phillipines, sling fire down on red-light districts where people got stabbed. He even appeared in person every once in a while. God used to pay attention, is what I'm saying.

—LOUISE ERDRICH, AMERICAN INDIAN NOVELIST

36   Ain't no such thing as I can hate anybody and hope to see God's face.

—Fannie Lou Hamer, Black civil rights activist

37   I want to hear prayers that empower people, not prayers that dismiss or degrade people.

—Debbie Almontaser, Arab American educator

38   We talk about it from the pulpit: Being gay and lesbian and still being able to love God and know that God loves us. Our church's motto is "God loves you just as you are."

—Rev. Janyce Jackson, Black minister

39   My faith was always important to me because it's a feeling that there is a higher power that loves me.

—Rev. Janyce Jackson, Black minister

40   If there is a god can she be a committee of women dedicated to wiping out earthly oppression.

—Hattie Gosset, Black writer

41   Faith hasn't got no eyes, but she' long-legged.

—Zora Neale Hurston, Black writer

42   I'll bet when you get down on them rusty knees and get to worrying God, He just goes in His privy-house and slams the door. That's what he thinks about *you* and *your* prayers.

—Zora Neale Hurston, Black writer

43   Nothing that God ever made is the same thing to more than one person.

— Zora Neale Hurston, Black writer

44   Whar did you Christ come from? From God and a woman! Man had nothing to do with him.

— Sojourner Truth, Black abolitionist

45   If there *can* be any thing more diametrically opposed to the religion of Jesus than the working of this soul killing system which is as truly sanctioned by the religion of America as are her ministers and churches we wish to be shown where it can be found.

— Sojourner Truth, Black abolitionist

46   I feel strong because I know that I am not alone. And I know God won't abandon me. And I know that God is not embarrassed when one speaks for truth, for what is just.

— Elvira Arellano,
Latina undocumented immigrant and activist

47   She say, Celie, tell the truth, have you ever found God in church? I never did. I just found a bunch of folks hoping for him to show. Any God I ever felt in church I brought with me. And I think all the other folks did too. They come to church to share God, not find God.

— Alice Walker, Black writer

48   God is inside you and inside everybody else. You come into the world with God. But only them that search for it inside find it. And sometimes it just manifest itself even if you not looking, or don't know what you looking for. Trouble do it for most folks, I think . . . Yeah, It. God ain't a he or a she, but an It.

— Alice Walker, Black writer

49 Despair and hope are inseparable. One can never understand what hope is really about unless one wrestles with despair. The same is true with faith. There has to be some serious doubt, otherwise faith becomes merely a dogmatic formula, an orthodoxy, a way of evading the complexity of life, rather than a way of engaging honestly with life.

—Cornel West, Black scholar

50 Her Episcopalian friends were persuading her to their wishy-washy way of worship. They really believed you could get to heaven without any shouting.

—Dorothy West, Black writer

51 God gave me this physical impairment to remind me that I'm not the greatest, He is.

—Muhammad Ali, Black boxer

52 Blackness is the same as whiteness as far as God and truth is concerned. God has all kinds of colors in his universe and has not condemned any color.

—Clarence L. Franklin, Black minister

53 When you've got so much religion that you can't mingle with people, that you're afraid of certain people, you've got too much religion.

—Clarence L. Franklin, Black minister

54 It's really a wonder that I haven't dropped all my ideals, because they seem so absurd and impossible to carry out. Yet I keep them, because in spite of everything I still believe that people are really good at heart. I simply can't build up my hopes on a foundation consisting of confusion, misery, and death. I see the world gradually being turned into a wilderness, I hear the ever approaching thunder, which will destroy us too, I can feel the sufferings of millions.

—Martin Luther King, Jr., Black civil rights activist

55 Living in a place where we are surrounded by people all the time, but always feel lonely, prisoners are forced to deal with the deprivation of love and freedom. Religion becomes a necessary tool of survival.

—EDDY ZHENG, ASIAN AMERICAN PRISON ACTIVIST

56 I believe that spiritual transformation is a life-long process that requires us to think critically about our relations with each other.

—EDDY ZHENG, ASIAN AMERICAN PRISON ACTIVIST

57 The ability to know what is the right thing to do in a given circumstance is a sheer gift of God.

—HOWARD THURMAN, BLACK THEOLOGIAN

58 One of the most powerful and beautiful aspects of Santeria is that from the moment you enter as an initiate, you are never alone. You have a family of guides and teachers. It is truly a community religion.

—MARTA MORENO VEGA, BLACK PRIESTESS AND SCHOLAR

59 God speaks to us in the Qur'an saying that He will not change our condition until we change what is in our hearts and souls.

—SALEEMAH ABDUL-GHAFUR, BLACK WRITER

60 The Prophet Muhammad taught us that "To know yourself is to know your Lord." And I am closer to my true self than I have ever been.

—SALEEMAH ABDUL-GHAFUR, BLACK WRITER

61 We were ready to strike, and we took a vote and we struck. And we said, "God will provide." That's how it started.

—CESAR CHAVEZ, LATINO ORGANIZER

62   I believe in God. I believe God is spirit and the power of God lives in the soul of every boy and girl, man and woman.

—SISTER SOULJAH, BLACK HIP-HOP ARTIST

Inspirations

63   I wish to live because life has within it that which is good, that which is beautiful, and that which is love. Therefore, since I have known all of these things, I have found them to be reason enough and—I wish to live. Moreover, because this is so, I wish others to live for generations and generations and generations.

—LORRAINE HANSBERRY, BLACK PLAYWRIGHT

64   The world isn't waiting for you to see it; rather, it is waiting to be built by you and others.

—WALTER MOSLEY, BLACK NOVELIST

65   Just don't give up trying to do what you really want to do. Where there's love and inspiration, I don't think you can go wrong.

—ELLA FITZGERALD, BLACK SINGER

66   Talk about it only enough to do it. Dream about it only enough to feel it. Think about it only enough to understand it. Contemplate it only enough to be it.

—JEAN TOOMER, BLACK NOVELIST

67 I am not a special person. I am a regular person who does special things.

—SARAH VAUGHN, BLACK SINGER

68 The ultimate of being successful is the luxury of giving yourself the time to do what you want to do.

—LEONTYNE PRICE, BLACK OPERA SINGER

69 He who is not courageous enough to take risks will accomplish nothing in life.

—MUHAMMAD ALI, BLACK BOXER

70 Hope in the face of difficulty, hope in the face of uncertainty, the audacity of hope: In the end, that is God's greatest gift to us, the bedrock of this nation, a belief in things not seen, a belief that there are better days ahead.

—BARACK OBAMA, BLACK POLITICIAN

71 We may encounter many defeats but we must not be defeated.

—MAYA ANGELOU, BLACK POET

72 You may trod me in the very dirt / But still, like dust, I'll rise.

—MAYA ANGELOU, BLACK POET

73 Self-pity in its early stage is as snug as a feather mattress. Only when it hardens does it become uncomfortable.

—MAYA ANGELOU, BLACK POET

74   Surviving is important, but thriving is *elegant*.

—MAYA ANGELOU, BLACK POET

75   Talent is like electricity. . . . Electricity makes no judgment. You can plug into it and light up a lamp, keep a heart pump going, light a cathedral, or you can electrocute a person with it. Electricity will do all that. It makes no judgment. I think talent is like that. I believe every person is born with talent.

—MAYA ANGELOU, BLACK POET

76   If you have a passion for something take no hesitation to pursue it 110 percent. It's about focus, intensity, perseverance and believing in yourself and what you are capable of.

—ALISSA AUGUSTINE, AMERICAN INDIAN DEEJAY

77   Walls turned sideways are bridges.

—ANGELA DAVIS, BLACK SCHOLAR

78   My future starts when I wake up every morning . . . Every day I find something creative to do with my life.

—MILES DAVIS, BLACK MUSICIAN

79   I think I'm just as good as anyone. That's the way I was brought up. I'll tell you a secret: I think I'm better! Ha! I remember being aware that colored people were supposed to feel inferior. I knew I was a smart little thing, a personality, an individual—a human being! I couldn't understand how people could look at me and not see that, because it was sure obvious to me.

—ANNIE ELIZABETH "BESSIE" DELANY, BLACK DENTIST

80   In seeking to avoid a fight we concede what we're about. We're about justice, fairness, equality—that's our strength. We cannot concede our strength. We must realize, understand and believe that our current conditions do not reflect our ultimate potential. If we limit our choices only to what seems possible or reasonable, we disconnect ourselves from what we truly want. And all that is left is a compromise. In order to move forward we need both the courage of our convictions and the commitment to do the work.

—GARY DELGADO, BLACK ORGANIZER

81   Who can walk into unknown woods and head directly for the other side? Wandering for a spell makes the journey even more exciting.

—VINE DELORIA, JR., AMERICAN INDIAN WRITER

82   Believe that what you have to say, what you have lived and thought and felt, is important and deserves to be told to someone else. That doesn't absolve you from the task of revision. It's not the fact that you've lived it that makes an experience meaningful; that's where you begin.

—RITA DOVE, BLACK POET

83   Beyond the veil lies an undiscovered country, a land of new things, of change, of experiment, of wild hope and somber realization, of superlatives and italics of wondrously blended poetry and prose.

—W.E.B. DU BOIS, BLACK SCHOLAR AND ACTIVIST

84   Create the highest, grandest vision possible for your life because you become what you believe.

—OPRAH WINFREY,
BLACK TALK SHOW HOST AND PHILANTHROPIST

85   Mediocrity is safe.

—NIKKI GIOVANNI, BLACK POET

86   Mistakes are a fact of life / It is the response to error that counts.

—NIKKI GIOVANNI, BLACK POET

87   I try. I am trying. I was trying. I will try. I shall in the meantime try. I sometimes have tried. I shall still by that time be trying.

—DIANE GLANCY, AMERICAN INDIAN POET

88   I am a stranger to half measures. With Life I am on the attack, restlessly ferreting out each pleasure, foraging for answers, wringing from it even the pain. I ransack life, hunt it down. I am the hungry peasants storming the palace gates. I will have my share. No matter how it tastes.

—MARITA GOLDEN, BLACK WRITER

89   Growth is the surviving influence in all our lives. The tree will send up its trunk in thick profusion from land burned black by atom bombs. Children will grow from poverty and filth and oppression and develop honor, develop integrity, contribute to all mankind.

—CHESTER HIMES, BLACK NOVELIST

90   We search for the meaning of life in the realities of our experiences, in the realities of our dreams, our hopes, our memories.

—CHESTER HIMES, BLACK NOVELIST

91   The thing that makes you exceptional, if you are at all, is inevitably that which must also make you lonely.

—LORRAINE HANSBERRY, BLACK PLAYWRIGHT

92 We defeat oppression with liberty. We cure indifference with compassion. We remedy social injustices with justice. And if our journey embodies these lasting principles, we find peace.

—Patricia Roberts Harris,
Black government official

93 The Spirit whispers, the ancestors agree. You are starborn and God loved. The universe awaits your gifts.

—Barbara Holmes, Black theologian

94 When we are fully alert in spirit, mind, and body, we are more than we imagine and can accomplish more than we suppose.

—Barbara Holmes, Black theologian

95 Mama exhorted her children at every opportunity to "jump at de sun." We might not land on the sun, but at least we would get off the ground.

—Zora Neale Hurston, Black writer

96 Grab the broom of anger and drive off the beast of fear.

—Zora Neale Hurston, Black writer

97 The worse it gets, the better you get.

—Sarwat Husain, South Asian publisher

98 I approach the future in a happy and rather adventuresome spirit. It is within my power to make this unknown path a somewhat beaten path.

—Paul Robeson, Black actor

99   Hell, sometimes I can't even finish a book, and now I'm writing one? Oh Lord. I mean, hours and hours of just sitting at the computer, butt cheeks going numb, shoulders getting all cramped up from tension. Then I have to turn the damn thing on...

—WANDA SYKES, BLACK COMEDIAN

100   A difficult birth does not make a baby any less beautiful.

—MILILANI TRASK, NATIVE HAWAIIAN ACTIVIST

101   Life is not intended to be safe. A safe life has too small a name for a creature of eternity. Life at its noblest and highest has a hazard about it; it ponders tomorrow but does not know it; it sounds the depths of the ocean, but knows not the hazards of the bottom. Life at its best takes a chance on righteousness no matter the hazard, no matter the cost. Life, when answering to its true name, lifts on wings, feeling no invisible hands supporting it.

—ETHEL WATERS, BLACK SINGER

102   We need a moral prophetic minority of all colors who muster the courage to question the powers that be, the courage to be impatient with evil and patient with people, and the courage to fight for social justice. In many instances we will be stepping out on nothing, hoping to land on something. That's the history of black folks in the past and present, and of those of us who value history and struggle. Our courage rests on a deep democratic vision of a better world that lures us and a blood-drenched hope that sustains us.

—CORNEL WEST, BLACK SCHOLAR

103   I followed my passion and was guided by the light inside of me. That light does not belong to me alone. It is innate in all of us. Everyone has it. But more often than not, we choose not to see it.

—LILY YEH, ASIAN AMERICAN ARTIST

104   There can be no courage without fear, and fear comes only from the imagination.

— PETER ABRAHAMS, BLACK WRITER

105   I don't let my mouth say nothing my head can't stand.

— LOUIS ARMSTRONG, BLACK MUSICIAN

106   Risk takers often understand that true fearlessness is not the elimination of fear but the transcendence of fear, the movement *through* it and not *against* it.

— PHOEBE ENG, ASIAN AMERICAN LECTURER

107   It's okay to be wrong.

— DAVID HENRY HWANG, ASIAN AMERICAN PLAYWRIGHT

108   Getting information is always key to a risk well taken.

— PHOEBE ENG, ASIAN AMERICAN LECTURER

109   Risk itself is a process of constant unfolding. And taking risks is the process of peeling back the layers of what you are and who you want to be.

— PHOEBE ENG, ASIAN AMERICAN LECTURER

110   The day comes when remaining the same becomes more painful than the risk to grow. And when that happens there are many goodbyes. We leave old patterns, old friends and lovers, old ideas, and some cherished beliefs. Loss and growth are so often one and the same.

— PHOEBE ENG, ASIAN AMERICAN LECTURER

111   I must slide down like a great dipper of stars / and lift men up.

— LUCILLE CLIFTON, BLACK POET

112   Heaven is a place where you get an opportunity to use all the millions of sensitivities you never knew you had before.

— DUKE ELLINGTON, BLACK MUSICIAN

113   Always aim high, never aim low. If you aspire to lofty things, you have accomplished much even though you have not reached the topmost round.

— WILLIAM HASTIE, BLACK FEDERAL JUDGE

114   The willingness to face down passion and fear with reason and courage —and to speak truth to power—is the hallmark of the active citizen.

— DEVAL PATRICK, BLACK POLITICIAN

115   I dare myself to dream of us moving from survival to potential, from merely getting by to a positive getting over.

— JOSEPH BEAM, BLACK WRITER

116   We all need to regain the energy we seem to have lost, drop the pessimism that has filled our souls, and get over the individualism and materialism that has eaten so many of us from within.

— EDUARDO BONILLA-SILVA, LATINO SCHOLAR

117   Our dreams are the North Star by which we navigate. In hard times, they should get bigger rather than smaller. I think of the first enslaved Africans in America standing on auction blocks, someone's dirty thumb checking their teeth as if they were horses. They dreamed of freedom, and passed that dream to children and children's children until some modicum of freedom was achieved. Today we face another freedom struggle. It's time to retake, and remake, American democracy.

—FARAI CHIDEYA, BLACK JOURNALIST

118 Nothing makes me happier than reading or singing or hearing the truth. That's what a movement is about—connecting to something larger than yourself that means hope.

—KIM DIEHL, BLACK ACTIVIST

119 The war will be won when she who is the marginalized comes to speak more in her own language, and people accept her communication as valid and representative. Her need to communicate, formerly unhappy forays into the unfamiliar territory of alternate language discourse, will blossom into flowers that had been dormant in the arid land of the desert of the master discourse. The status quo that assured her that no one would listen, or that they would complain that her enunciation was incomprehensible, will disappear in an ocean of sound.

—JOANNE KILGOUR DOWDY, BLACK EDUCATOR

120 But, here is the miracle. We have been recovering from the moment we began to question, know, and understand. From the instant we began to look for language to *name*.

—INÉS HERNÁNDEZ-ÁVILA,
NATIVE-CHICANA WRITER AND SCHOLAR

121 Ancestors, the good ancestors from the beginning of time to the present, the ones who've gone ahead, the ones who were consumed in violence not of their making, in sickness often passed on through the generations, the children who passed on too early, the ones who had the chance to love and lead full lives, in the Spirit world, they are the light(ness) we need to see and feel. Theirs are the voices we need to hear with the ears of the heart. Theirs are the messages we should welcome with our intuition's blessing, and they are the ones who illuminate our work within and between our respective communities.

—INÉS HERNÁNDEZ-ÁVILA,
NATIVE-CHICANA WRITER AND SCHOLAR

122   Seize the Time.

—GEORGE JACKSON, BLACK PRISONER

123   Grace is the ability to redefine the boundaries of possibility.

—MANNING MARABLE, BLACK SCHOLAR

124   I feel blessed that more than 30 years ago, when I joined the Civil Rights Movement, I enjoined the rest of my life with a commitment to being a fighter for justice and freedom and the right to live celebrating my existence, and the existence of my people—and I come singing!

—BERNICE JOHNSON REAGON, BLACK SINGER

125   Let's start with a fundamental human problem, and I don't mean race or religion or origin. I mean fear. Fright, my young friend, may be the first serious enemy you have to face in our society. It's the most destructive emotional bogeyman there is. Cold feet, panic, depression, and violence are all symptoms of fear—when it's out of control. But this feeling, ironically, can also trigger courage, alertness, objectivity. You must learn not to try to rid yourself of this basic, human emotion but to manipulate it for your own advantage. You cannot surrender to fear, but you *can* use it as a kind of fuel. Once you learn to control fear—to make it work for you—it will become one of your best friends.

—JOSÉ TORRES, LATINO BOXER, WRITER

126 This is a bright *mundo*, my streets, my *barrio de noche*, with its thousands of lights, hundreds of millions of colors mingling with noises, swinging street sounds of cars and curses, sounds of joys and sobs that make music. If anyone listens real close, he can hear its heart beat.

—PIRI THOMAS, LATINO WRITER

127 I had assumed I was more or less free, not realizing that those who are free make and take choices; they do not choose from options proffered by "those out there."

—MITSUYE YAMADA, ASIAN AMERICAN EDUCATOR

128 Let there be everywhere our voices, our eyes, our thoughts, our love, our actions, breathing hope and victory.

—SONIA SANCHEZ, BLACK POET

129 Tomorrow belongs to the people who prepare for it today.

—MALCOLM X, BLACK ACTIVIST

130 We gotta be patient, but we gotta keep moving forward.

—WILL ALLEN, BLACK FARMER

Acknowledgments

I thank my editor at Beacon, Gayatri Patnaik, for presenting me with this opportunity and sticking by me to get it done. The work didn't really get going until assistant editor Tracy Ahlquist and the interns at Beacon (Cristina Rodriguez, Julia Porter, Amanda Pepper, and Joanna Green) set up the database and started the quote collection when I was still buried in other deadlines. Thanks also to assistant editor Allison Trzop; *ColorLines* interns Indigo (Jamee) Eriksen, Aries Hines, and Julianne Ong Hing who contributed research, library trips, their favorite books, entering quotes, labeling and sorting, and many other tasks.

I'm grateful to the Applied Research Center and *ColorLines* magazine, both for housing much of this work while I was on staff and for the many quotes I gleaned from ARC's publications and library.

Also, thanks to Jeff Chang for your sage advice at every turn and constant support. I thank my family—Thinh, Lan, Quynh, Vy and Lynne Nguyen—for seeing me through many evolutions. To Raahi Reddy, Holly Fincke, Andrea Cousins, Monica Hernandez, and Jason Williams, thank you for the laughs and love.

Name Index

Abani, Chris, Black novelist: 4/72

Abarquez-Delacruz, Prosy, Asian American lawyer and activist: 5/4

Abdul-Ghafur, Saleemah, Black writer: 6/59; 6/60

Abrahams, Peter, Black novelist: 1/131; 6/104

Abu-Jaber, Diana, Arab American novelist: 1/166; 1/272; 4/67

Abu-Jamal, Mumia, Black activist, journalist, and prisoner: 5/5

Acosta, Teresa Palomo, Latina poet: 3/47

Acuña, Rodolfo, Latino scholar: 5/97

Adiele, Faith, Black writer: 2/2

Akbar, Na'im, Black psychologist and scholar: 2/93

Al-Amin, Abu Qadir, Black imam: 1/38

Alarcón, Daniel, Latino writer: 4/37

Alejandro, Lean, Filipino activist: 5/77

Alexander, Meena, South Asian writer: 4/73

Alexie, Sherman, American Indian writer: 2/7; 2/8

Ali, Muhammad, Black boxer: 2/77; 2/276; 6/51; 6/69

Ali, Samina, South Asian writer: 2/323

Allen, Paula Gunn, American Indian writer and scholar: 1/1; 1/36; 1/41; 2/277; 3/128; 6/5; 6/30

Allen, Richard, Black abolitionist: 1/19; 1/218

Allen, Will, Black farmer and activist: 6/130

Allen-Taylor, J. Douglas, Black journalist: 1/43

Allison, Aimee, Black activist: 5/323

Almontaser, Debbie, Arab American educator: 6/37

Alva, Susan, Latina activist: 5/6

Alvarez, Julia, Latina writer: 1/258; 2/64; 3/106; 3/138; 3/147; 4/154

Anderson, Ernestine, Black singer: 4/74; 4/75

Anderson, Marian, Black singer: 5/165

Anderson, Mia, Black dramatist: 3/48

Angelou, Maya, Black poet: 1/219; 2/80; 2/193; 2/194; 2/195; 2/253; 3/57; 3/58; 3/59; 3/110; 4/77; 5/166; 5/167; 6/71; 6/72; 6/73; 6/74; 6/75

Annan, Kofi, Black diplomat: 2/290; 5/212; 5/313

Anonymous, migrant: 1/233

Anzaldúa, Gloria, Latina writer: 1/3; 1/45; 2/1; 2/3; 2/5; 2/22; 2/131; 3/60; 5/168

Arellano, Elvira, Latina undocumented immigrant and activist: 1/245; 6/46

Arellano, Gustavo, Latino writer: 2/14; 5/104; 5/105

Argüelles, Pancho, Latino organizer: 4/45; 5/319

Armstrong, Louis, Black musician: 6/105

Augustine, Alissa, American Indian deejay: 6/76

Aung San Suu Kyi, Burmese leader: 5/169; 6/6

Avila, Elena, Latina curandera: 2/211

Avila, Joaquin, Latino lawyer and activist: 5/171

Bailey, Pearl, Black singer and actress: 2/196; 2/269; 2/273; 2/279

Baker, Anita, Black singer: 3/39

Baker, Ella, Black civil rights leader: 2/200; 2/342; 4/1; 5/1; 5/61; 5/123; 5/125; 5/141; 5/142; 5/143; 5/161; 5/211; 5/213; 5/214; 5/327

Baker, Josephine, Black entertainer: 2/171

Baldwin, James, Black writer: 1/220; 2/94; 2/172; 2/197; 2/198; 2/251; 3/5; 4/42; 4/152; 5/164; 5/172; 5/304; 5/305; 5/306

Bambara, Toni Cade, Black writer: 2/203; 2/311; 5/78; 5/177; 6/31

Banks, Dennis, American Indian activist: 5/173

Baraka, Amiri, Black poet and playwright: 1/221; 2/55; 2/91; 2/264; 4/153; 5/80

Baraka, Ras, Black politician and activist: 4/161

Barrow, Kai Lumumba, Black activist: 2/151; 2/152; 5/35; 5/36

Beam, Joseph, Black writer and activist: 6/115

Belafonte, Harry, Black actor, musician and activist: 5/83

Bell, Rosalind, Black playwright: 4/85

Bello, Walden, Filipino activist and scholar: 5/178

ben-Jochannon, Yosef, Black scholar: 1/20

Bennett, Jr., Lerone, Black writer and historian: 1/222; 2/95

Berry, Mary Frances, Black scholar: 1/21

Bethune, Mary Mcleod, Black educator: 3/119

Bey, Twilight, Black activist: 5/179

Bhattacharjee, Anannya, South Asian activist: 2/133

Biggers, John, Black artist: 4/155

Bilal, Wafaa, Arab American artist: 5/79

Billie, Danny, American Indian activist: 5/335

Blige, Mary J., Black singer: 2/267

Bluford, Guion, Black astronaut: 5/350

Blyden, Edward Wilmot, Black educator and diplomat: 5/85

Boggs, Grace Lee, Asian American activist and scholar: 4/46; 5/11; 5/311; 5/330; 5/331; 5/369

Boggs, James, Black activist, and Grace Lee Boggs, Asian American activist and scholar: 1/46

Bond, Julian, Black civil rights leader: 1/133; 4/15

Bonilla-Silva, Eduardo, Latino scholar: 1/146; 6/116

Bontemps, Ama, Black writer: 5/307

Boyd, Herb, Black journalist: 1/223

Boyd, Todd, Black scholar: 1/47

Bradberry, Steve, Black organizer: 5/12

Brant, Beth, American Indian writer: 3/129

Brazile, Donna, Black political strategist: 5/193

Brooks, Gwendolyn, Black poet: 1/49; 1/224

Brown, Adrienne Maree, Black activist: 5/328

Brown, H. Rap, Black activist and prisoner: 1/59; 5/308

Brown, James, Black singer: 1/225

Buckhanon, Kalisha, Black writer: 1/5

Buckley, Gail Lumet, Black writer: 3/49

Bulosan, Carlos, Asian American writer: 1/6; 2/74

Burke, Yvonne Brathwaite, Black politician: 2/312

Burroughs, Nannie, Black educator: 2/313; 5/145

Burroughs, Todd Steven, Black journalist and scholar: 5/180

Bush, Faye, Black community organizer: 3/122

Butcher, Lennie, American Indian resident of the White Earth Reservation: 5/334

Butler, Nilak, American Indian activist: 2/331; 3/126; 5/354

Butler, Octavia, Black writer: 3/61; 4/78

Byron, Don, Black musician: 4/108

Calpotura, Francis, Asian American organizer: 1/263; 1/277; 1/278; 5/86; 5/87; 5/118

Cameron, Barbara, American Indian activist and writer: 1/167; 5/181

Canada, Geoffrey, Black educator and activist: 3/71; 4/60

Carlos, John, Black athlete: 1/32; 1/40

Carmichael, Stokely (Kwame Toure), Black activist: 1/165; 1/226; 5/88

Carson, Benjamin, Black surgeon: 2/314

Carver, George Washington, Black scientist: 2/315

Cary, Lorene, Black writer: 1/168; 3/1

Castaneda, Carlos, Latino writer: 2/204; 2/205

Castillo, Ana, Latina writer: 1/267; 1/284

Catlett, Elizabeth, Black sculptor and printmaker: 4/79; 4/80; 5/182

Cervantes, Lorna Dee, Latina poet: 3/8; 3/9

Chan, Sucheng, Asian American scholar: 2/148; 3/27

Chang, Diana, Asian American novelist and poet: 4/81

Chang, Iris, Asian American writer: 4/163

Chang, Vivian, Asian American organizer: 5/13

Charles, Ray, Black musician: 2/278

Charles, RuPaul, Black entertainer: 2/263

Chavez, Cesar, Latino organizer: 5/117; 6/61

Chideya, Farai, Black journalist: 4/47; 4/48; 5/92; 5/93; 5/320; 6/117

Chin, Marilyn, Asian American poet: 4/84

Chisholm, Shirley, Black politician: 1/53; 1/54; 5/90; 5/183

Cho, Margaret, Asian American comedian: 1/56; 2/199; 3/6; 6/33

Chocano, Carina, Latina writer: 1/241

Choi, Inhe, Asian American activist: 2/150

Choi, Susan, Asian American novelist: 5/256

Chong, Rae Dawn, Black-Asian actress: 1/135

Chrystos, American Indian poet and activist: 1/170

Cisneros, Sandra, Latina writer: 1/172; 3/13; 3/14

Clark, Joe, Black educator: 2/254

Clark, Kenneth B., Black psychologist: 1/57

Clark, Septima, Black civil rights activist: 2/210

Clifton, Lucille, Black poet: 4/89, 4/90; 6/111

Climbing Poetree (Alixa Garcia and Naima Penniman), Black artists: 4/91

Cofer, Judith Ortiz, Latina writer: 1/134

Cole, Johnetta, Black educator: 2/96; 2/97

Coleman, Deborah, Black musician: 4/93

Collier, Eugenia W., Black poet: 2/212

Collins, Marva, Black educator: 2/98

Colvin, Claudette, Black civil rights activist: 5/130

Cone, James H., Black minister: 1/136; 1/137; 1/138

Conyers, John, Black politician: 4/16; 4/17; 5/351

Cook, Katsi, American Indian midwife and activist: 3/104; 5/185

Cook-Lynn, Elizabeth, American Indian writer: 1/58

Corral, Cecilia Betancourt, Latina writer: 3/50

Cosby, Camille, Black philanthropist: 1/140; 2/63; 3/105

Cotera, Martha P., Latina writer: 1/27

Crow Dog, Henry, American Indian activist: 2/213; 5/336

Crow Dog, Mary (Mary Brave Bird), American Indian activist and writer: 1/48; 1/185; 2/190; 3/72; 3/73; 3/132; 4/61; 5/332; 5/333; 6/23; 6/32

Crummell, Alexander, Black abolitionist and minister: 2/317

Cruz, Quique, Latino musician: 4/88

Cruz, Victor Hernández, Latino poet: 1/236

Cuellar, Alberto, Latino music producer: 4/107

Cullen, Countee, Black writer: 1/141

D, Chuck, Black rapper: 3/76

Danticat, Edwidge, Black writer: 1/280; 1/281; 2/134; 4/95

Darraj, Susan Muaddi, Arab American writer: 2/159; 2/160

Davis, Angela, Black scholar and activist: 5/121; 5/187; 5/188; 5/189; 5/190; 5/192; 5/229; 5/230; 5/263; 5/285; 6/77

Davis, Miles, Black musician: 4/164; 5/321; 6/78

Dawes, Kwame, Black poet: 4/96

DeAvila, Alfredo, Latino organizer: 5/69; 5/70; 6/71; 5/126

Dee, Ruby, Black actress: 2/214; 2/215; 3/16; 4/100

Delany, Annie Elizabeth "Bessie," Black dentist: 1/55, 1/59; 2/218; 6/79

Delany, Sarah Louise "Sadie," Black educator: 1/182; 5/82

De León, Aya, Latina performer and writer: 2/135; 3/15; 5/94; 5/95

Delgado, Gary, Black scholar and activist: 1/60; 1/61; 2/300; 5/196; 6/80

Deloria, Jr., Vine, American Indian writer: 1/169; 1/249; 4/28; 5/338; 6/81

Delpit, Lisa, Black scholar: 2/116

Derricotte, Toi, Black poet: 1/173

Desai, Kiran, South Asian novelist: 2/219

Diawara, Manthia, Black scholar: 1/149; 1/243

Díaz, Antonio, Latino activist: 5/337; 5/360

Díaz, Junot, Latino writer: 1/237; 3/17

Díaz, Marcela, Latina organizer: 1/279

Diehl, Kim, Black activist: 6/118

Divakaruni, Chitra Banjeree, South Asian writer: 2/132

Dong, Harvey, Asian American scholar: 5/15; 5/16; 5/17

Douglass, Frederick, Black abolitionist: 2/99; 5/197; 5/309; 5/310

Dove, Rita, Black poet: 1/8; 2/11; 5/339; 6/82

Dowdy, Joanne Kilgour, Black educator and writer: 2/118; 2/125; 6/119

Du Bois, W.E.B., Black scholar and activist: 2/13; 2/318; 4/25; 4/156; 5/198; 5/312; 5/314; 5/315; 6/2; 6/3; 6/34; 6/83

Due, Tananarive, Black writer: 5/199

Dunbar, Paul Lawrence, Black poet: 1/227

Dyson, Michael Eric, Black scholar: 1/62; 1/63; 1/238; 5/200; 5/201

Ebadi, Shirin, Iranian lawyer and activist: 1/288; 2/10; 2/56; 5/302

Edelman, Marian Wright, Black activist: 2/100; 4/43

Edwards, Harry, Black scholar and educator: 1/64; 2/81; 2/101; 3/133

Elders, Joycelyn, former Surgeon General: 1/176; 5/47

Elia, Nadia, Arab American writer: 2/175

Elizondo, Sergio, Latino educator: 1/235

Ellington, Duke, Black musician: 1/23; 2/272; 2/319; 3/40; 4/157; 6/112

Ellison, Ralph, Black writer: 4/158

El Saadawi, Nawal, Arab writer and activist: 2/85; 2/220

Eng, Phoebe, Asian American lecturer: 2/12; 2/30; 2/31; 2/43; 3/33; 3/45; 3/62; 3/63; 3/64; 3/112; 5/159; 6/106; 6/108; 6/109; 6/110

Erdrich, Louise, American Indian novelist: 1/9; 1/174; 1/175; 1/216; 1/217; 2/222; 3/19; 3/20; 3/67; 6/35

Escalante, Alicia, Latina activist: 4/22

Escobedo, Deborah, Latina legal advocate: 3/93

Estés, Clarissa Pinkola, Latina psychologist and poet: 4/76; 4/125; 6/4

Evans, Mari E., Black poet: 3/68

Eyre, Chris, American Indian filmmaker: 4/101

Fanon, Frantz, Black revolutionary: 1/143

Fauset, Jessie Redmon, Black writer: 2/15

Fernandes, Deepa, South Asian journalist: 1/252

Fiol-Matta, Liza, Latina educator: 2/114

Fitzgerald, Ella, Black singer: 6/65

Flack, Roberta, Black singer: 1/178; 4/103; 4/104

Fletcher, Bill, Black activist and writer: 5/26; 5/27

Flores-Ortiz, Yvette Gisele, Latina psychologist: 3/56

Fong-Torres, Ben, Asian American journalist: 3/54; 3/55

Fortune, T. Thomas, Black journalist: 1/144

Franklin, Aretha, Black singer: 3/21; 6/20

Franklin, Clarence L., Black minister: 3/99; 6/52; 6/53

Franklin, John Hope, Black scholar: 2/109

Freeman, Morgan, Black actor: 1/228

Freilla, Omar, Latino activist: 5/329

Fuentes, Carlos, Mexican writer: 1/262

Funk, Stephen, Asian American conscientious objector: 5/202

Gandhi, Mohandas, Indian leader and activist: 2/110; 6/21

Garcia, Antonio, Latino student activist: 2/108

Garcia, Cristina, Latina novelist and journalist: 2/223; 2/224

Garvey, Amy Jacques, Black activist and journalist: 2/321

Garvey, Marcus, Black activist: 2/111; 4/44; 5/19; 5/316

Gary Declaration: 5/204

Gates, Jr., Henry Louis, Black scholar: 1/239; 2/4; 2/61

Gauna, Jeanne, Latina activist: 5/2

Gaye, Marvin, Black singer: 2/274

Gayle, Jr., Addison, Black critic: 2/324

Gee, Emma, Asian American activist: 5/205

Gibson, Althea, Black athlete: 3/125

Gilmore, Ruth Wilson, Black scholar: 5/276; 5/277

Giovanni, Nikki, Black poet: 2/226; 2/227; 2/228; 3/24; 3/25; 3/41; 4/6; 4/109; 4/110; 4/111; 5/133; 6/85; 6/86

Glancy, Diane, American Indian poet: 5/206; 6/87

Glave, Thomas, Black writer: 4/112

Glover, Danny, Black actor: 2/21

Golden, Marita, Black writer: 4/113; 6/88

Goldtooth, Tom, American Indian activist: 2/178; 2/309; 5/367; 5/368

Gomez, Jewelle, Black poet: 2/230

Gómez, Magdalena, Latina poet: 1/180

Gómez-Peña, Guillermo, Latino performance artist: 1/69; 2/25

Gonzales, Patrisia, Latina writer: 3/7

Gonzalez, Gilbert G., Latino scholar: 1/253; 1/254

Gosset, Hattie, Black writer: 6/40

Gossett Jr., Louis, Black actor: 3/101

Grass, Martha, American Indian activist: 1/67

Greenridge, Delano, Black publisher: 5/135

Gregory, Dick, Black comedian: 2/112; 2/113; 2/325; 5/317

Griffin, Shana, Black survivor of Hurricane Katrina: 5/207

Guinier, Lani, Black law professor and scholar: 2/120; 5/106; 5/152

Hagedorn, Jessica, Asian American writer: 4/71

Hajratwata, Minal, South Asian writer: 2/20

Haley, Alex, Black writer: 3/102

Hall, Christine C. Iijima, Black-Asian scholar: 1/77

Hamer, Fannie Lou, Black activist: 4/18; 6/36

Hammad, Suheir, Arab American poet: 2/16; 2/17; 4/114

Handal, Nathalie, Arab American poet: 2/67

Hanh, Thich Nhat, Vietnamese monk: 4/94; 5/186

Hansberry, Lorraine, Black playwright: 2/206; 2/207; 2/326; 2/327; 4/69; 4/70; 5/116; 5/318; 6/1; 6/22; 6/63; 6/91

Harden, Lakota, American Indian activist: 5/208

Harding, Vincent, Black scholar and activist: 1/10; 5/3

Hare, Nathan, Black scholar: 5/132; 5/209

Harjo, Joy, American Indian poet: 4/118; 5/220

Harris, Jessica B., Black cookbook author: 3/109

Harris, Laura, Black scholar: 5/96

Harris, Patricia Roberts, Black government official: 6/92

Hastie, William H., Black federal judge and civil rights activist: 6/113

Hawaiian Saying: 5/210

Hendrix, Jimi, Black musician: 5/221

Hernandez, Andrew, Latino activist: 5/215

Hernández, Antonia, Latina lawyer: 5/20

Hernández, Daisy, Latina writer: 3/88

Hernandez, Yasmin, Latina artist: 4/117

Hernández-Ávila, Inés, Native-Chicana writer and scholar: 1/28; 1/181; 2/333; 3/4; 3/134; 5/216; 6/120; 6/121

Hill, Anita, Black scholar: 2/179

Hill, Barbara Helen, American Indian writer and artist: 3/53

Himes, Chester, Black novelist: 2/18; 5/217; 6/89; 6/90

Hing, Bill Ong, Asian American scholar: 1/244

Hoang, Anh, Asian American fisherman and Hurricane Katrina survivor: 1/285

Hogan, Linda, American Indian writer: 4/162

Holiday, Billie, Black singer: 1/183; 2/328; 2/329; 4/119

Holmes, Barbara, Black theologian: 2/231; 2/232; 2/233; 2/234; 5/222; 5/223; 5/224; 6/93; 6/94

Holt, Thomas C., Black scholar: 1/78; 5/146

Hong, Roy, Asian American organizer: 1/142; 1/148; 4/10

Hong, YK, Asian American activist: 1/184

Hong Kong Fever, Asian American hip-hop artist: 4/120

Hongo, Garrett, Asian American writer: 4/121; 4/122

hooks, bell, Black scholar: 1/68; 1/71; 1/72; 2/19; 2/54; 2/137; 2/139; 2/140; 2/176; 2/177; 2/216; 2/217; 2/229; 3/28; 4/59; 4/123; 5/219; 5/227; 5/228

Hughes, Langston, Black poet: 1/186; 2/262

Hurston, Zora Neale, Black writer: 1/79; 1/80; 1/188; 1/189; 2/26; 2/27; 2/86; 2/235; 2/237; 2/238; 2/240; 2/241; 2/243; 2/244; 2/245; 2/246; 2/248; 2/330; 3/29; 3/30; 3/31; 3/32; 3/42; 3/74; 4/29; 6/41; 6/42; 6/43; 6/95; 6/96

Husain, Sarwat, South Asian publisher: 6/97

Hwang, David Henry, Asian American playwright: 6/107

Ifill, Gwen, Black journalist: 1/42; 4/102

Ifill, Sherrilyn A., Black law professor: 1/30; 5/218

Iijima, Chris, Asian American law professor and singer: 1/11

Iijima, Chris, Asian American law professor and singer, and **Joanne Miyamoto,** Asian American singer: 4/124

Imarisha, Walidah, Black writer: 1/82

Inada, Lawson, Asian American poet: 5/233

Indian Country Today, **Editors of:** 6/8

Ito, Alice, Asian American activist: 5/24

Iyer, Vijay, South Asian musician: 1/14; 1/89; 2/9; 3/22; 4/135

Jackson, George, Black prisoner: 1/230; 6/122

Jackson, Rev. Janyce, Black minister: 6/38; 6/39

Jackson, Jesse, Black politician: 1/83; 4/50

Jackson, John, Black advocate of equitable education: 2/129

Jackson, Mahalia, Black singer: 1/190

Jacques, Geoffrey, Black poet: 2/75

Jamail, Dahr, Arab American journalist: 5/322

James, C.L.R., Caribbean scholar and journalist: 5/7

James, G. Winston, Black writer: 6/19

James, Joy, Black scholar: 5/99

Jayapal, Pramila, South Asian activist: 5/43; 5/44; 5/255

Jayaraman, Saru, South Asian organizer: 4/138

Jen, Gish, Asian American novelist: 1/191

Jenkins, Raymond, Black reparations activist: 5/234

Jiménez, Maria, Latina activist: 1/139, 1/250; 1/271

Johnson, Tammy, Black activist: 5/150

Johnston, Basil H., American Indian writer: 6/10

Jones, Brandon Astor, Black prisoner: 1/192; 5/235; 6/7

Jones, Edward P., Black novelist: 1/88; 4/166

Jones, Mohamedu, Black lawyer: 5/237

Jones, Sarah, Black playwright and performer: 5/108; 5/236

Jones, Van, Black activist: 1/193; 5/344

Jordan, Barbara, Black politician: 1/90

Jordan, June, Black poet: 1/194; 2/6; 2/221; 5/21; 5/238

Ka'ahumanu, Lani, Native Hawaiian poet: 2/28

Kanatakta, Raven, American Indian musician: 4/127; 4/128

Keating, AnaLouise, Latina scholar: 2/68; 2/334; 6/25; 6/26

Keeler, Jacqueline, American Indian writer: 2/123

Kelley, Robin D.G., Black scholar: 1/195; 2/73; 4/7; 4/21; 4/23; 4/24; 4/86; 4/87; 4/126; 4/129; 5/8; 5/9; 5/225; 5/226; 5/240; 5/241

Kennedy, Florynce Rae, Black lawyer and activist: 2/174

Kills Straight, Birgil, American Indian activist: 5/10

Kim, Claire Jean, Asian American scholar: 1/52

Kim, Elaine, Asian American scholar: 1/4; 1/151; 1/152; 5/100; 5/101

Kim, Ian, Asian American activist: 5/365

Kincaid, Jamaica, Black writer: 2/35; 2/36; 2/247

King, Coretta Scott, Black civil rights leader: 4/32; 4/33

King, Jr., Martin Luther, Black civil rights activist: 1/18; 2/255; 3/43; 5/22; 5/23; 5/242; 5/243; 6/54

King, Mel, Black activist: 1/29

Kingfisher, Pamela, American Indian activist: 6/14

Kingston, Maxine Hong, Asian American novelist: 2/88; 3/77; 3/78; 4/8; 5/244

Kong, Grace, Asian American organizer: 3/124

Kono, Stacy, Asian American organizer: 4/4

Kool Herc, DJ, Black hip-hop artist: 1/196

Kramer, Marian, Black activist: 5/25

Kuficha, Dafina, Black healer: 2/242

Kumar, Amitava, South Asian writer and scholar: 5/245

LaDuke, Winona, American Indian activist and writer: 1/24; 1/187; 3/111;

4/140; 5/28; 5/29; 5/136; 5/162; 5/340; 5/341; 5/342; 5/343

Lam, Andrew, Asian American writer: 1/91; 1/197; 1/240; 5/246; 5/247

Lang, Julian, American Indian artist: 1/92

Lara, Irene, Latina scholar: 6/27

Le, Nam, Vietnamese writer: 2/201; 3/85

lê thi diem thúy, Asian American writer: 1/270; 4/167

Lee, Corky, Asian American photographer: 5/248

Lee, Hyun, Asian American activist: 5/251

Lee, Li-Young, Asian American poet: 2/249; 4/130

Lee, Sheila Jackson, Black politician: 5/250

Littleeagle, Marcus Frejo, American Indian hip-hop artist: 5/31

Llanos, Claudia, Latina immigrant activist: 5/134

Locke, Alain, Black philosopher: 6/24

Lok, Rob, Asian American clown: 4/133

Lopez, Adriana, Latina writer: 2/141; 2/142; 2/143; 2/144

Lorde, Audre, Black writer: 1/65; 1/198; 2/37; 2/38; 2/149; 2/250; 2/265; 3/113; 3/114; 3/135; 4/5; 4/134; 5/32

Louie, Miriam Ching, Asian American activist: 5/33; 5/131

Lovato, Roberto, Latino writer: 1/276; 5/34

Loving, Mildred, Black plaintiff: 2/138; 2/169

Loy, Tana, Asian American activist: 5/252

Lozano, Emma, Latina activist: 1/246

Lucci-Cooper, Kathryn, American Indian writer: 1/171

Lui, Meizhu, Asian American labor organizer: 5/89

Lusane, Clarence, Black scholar: 5/147

Madhubuti, Haki, Black poet and scholar: 1/150; 2/119; 3/107; 4/139; 5/148

Malcolm X, Black activist and minister: 3/148; 5/37; 6/129

Malveaux, Julianne, Black economist: 4/57; 4/58; 5/289

Mamdani, Mahmood, South Asian scholar: 1/31; 1/35; 1/153; 1/289; 5/324

Mandela, Nelson, Black president of South Africa: 1/132; 2/92; 5/128

Mar, Warren, Asian American activist: 5/38

Marable, Manning, Black scholar: 1/93; 1/94; 1/154; 1/155; 1/161; 1/199; 2/126; 3/137; 3/141; 4/56; 6/123

Maroon, Bahiyyih, Black writer: 2/40; 2/41; 2/42

Marsalis, Wynton, Black musician: 1/200

Marshall, Jocquelyn, Black survivor of Hurricane Katrina: 1/201

Marshall, Thurgood, Black Supreme Court Justice: 1/96

Martínez, Elizabeth (Betita), Latina activist: 2/153

Martinez, Pam, Latina activist: 2/117

Martínez, Renée M., Latina educator: 2/335; 2/340

Martínez, Rubén, Latino journalist: 1/33; 1/120; 1/255; 1/256; 1/286; 1/287

Matsuda, Mari, Asian American law professor: 5/39

Maviyane-Davies, Chaz, Black graphic designer: 5/40

McCall, Nathan, Black journalist: 1/66; 2/338; 2/339; 4/51; 4/52; 5/170

Means, Russell, American Indian activist: 5/254

Mejia, Camilo, Latino conscientious objector: 5/253

Milczarek-Desai, Shefali, South Asian scholar: 2/69; 2/180

Mirikitani, Janice, Asian American poet: 5/257; 5/258

Mirza, Shazia, South Asian comedian: 1/97

Miyatake, Henry, Asian American redress activist: 1/12

Mohamed, Asha, Black immigrant: 1/98

Mohanty, Chandra Talpade, South Asian scholar: 2/157; 5/259; 5/260; 5/261; 5/325

Momaday, N. Scott, American Indian writer: 2/266

Moody, Anne, Black writer: 1/130

Moore, Richard, Latino activist: 5/345

Moraga, Cherríe, Latina writer: 1/34; 1/251; 3/139; 3/142

Moreno, Tirso, Latino organizer: 4/11; 5/362; 5/363

Morrison, Toni, Black novelist: 1/39; 1/199; 1/100; 1/101; 1/145; 1/202; 1/203; 2/44; 2/65; 2/66; 2/158; 2/189; 2/281; 2/282; 2/284; 2/285; 3/18; 3/79; 3/97; 5/41; 5/262

Moseley Braun, Carol, Black politician: 1/26; 5/129; 5/176

Moses, Omowale, Black educator: 1/103

Moses, Robert, Black activist and educator: 5/127

Mosley, Walter, Black novelist: 1/2; 1/232; 2/191; 2/192; 2/322; 3/3; 3/75; 4/2; 4/9; 4/53; 4/54; 4/55; 4/116; 5/45; 5/157; 5/239; 6/11; 6/64

Moua, Mee, Asian American politician: 2/60; 5/91

Mukherjee, Bharati, South Asian novelist: 1/259; 1/260

Mulligan, Michelle Herrera, Latina writer: 2/58

Mura, David, Asian American writer: 2/70; 4/168; 4/169

Murray, Pauli, Black lawyer, minister, and activist: 5/46

Muwakkil, Salim, Black journalist: 1/104

Nagatani, Nick, Asian American activist: 5/48

Nas, Black hip-hop artist: 1/37

Naylor, Gloria, Black writer: 2/270

Nazario, Sonia, Latina journalist: 1/264; 1/265; 1/266

Newton, Huey P., Black activist: 5/50

Nguyen, Bich Minh, Asian American writer: 4/92

Nguyen, Kien, Asian American dentist: 2/320

Nguyen, Father Thi Vien, Asian American priest: 5/52

Nguyen, Viet Thanh, Asian American scholar: 3/70

Noguera, Pedro, and **Antwi Akom Noguera,** Latino scholars: 2/89

Nomani, Asra Q., South Asian journalist: 1/105; 2/39; 2/162; 5/265

Obama, Barack, Black politician: 5/184; 6/70

Ochoa, Cecile Caguingin, Asian American journalist and activist: 5/266

Oh, Angela, Asian American lawyer: 5/137

Omatsu, Glenn, Asian American educator and scholar: 2/130

Omi, Michael, Asian American scholar: 1/81

O'Neal, John, Black actor and director: 4/136; 5/53; 5/54

Ortiz, Simon J., American Indian poet: 4/68; 6/9

Paris, Black hip-hop artist: 5/267

Park, Ishle Yi, Asian American poet: 1/283; 2/49; 2/136; 3/140; 4/149

Parks, Rosa, Black civil rights activist: 5/268

Parks, Suzan-Lori, Black playwright: 4/160

Patel, Eboo, South Asian activist: 2/76

Patrick, Deval, Black politician: 6/114

Payes, Mayron, Latino organizer: 3/123

Peltier, Leonard, American Indian activist and prisoner: 5/355

Perdomo, Willie, Latino poet: 2/286

Perera, Gihan, South Asian organizer: 5/55

Perez, Joe, Latino writer: 2/235

Perez, Richie, Latino activist: 4/27; 5/81; 5/124

Pham, Andrew X., Asian American writer: 2/53

Piepzna-Samarasinha, Leah Lakshmi, South Asian writer: 2/45

Pitts, Stephen, Black economist: 4/12

Poitier, Sidney, Black actor and director: 3/127

Portales, Marco, Latino scholar: 2/258; 2/259; 2/260

Powell, Kevin, Black journalist: 5/155; 5/156; 5/269

Prashad, Vijay, South Asian scholar: 1/106; 1/124; 2/127; 4/19; 4/62; 5/56; 5/149; 5/270; 5/271

Price, Rev. Frederick K.C., Black minister: 1/17

Price, Leontyne, Black opera singer: 1/107; 1/108; 6/68

Queypo, Kalani, Native Hawaiian actor: 4/34

Quintanales, Mirtha, Latina writer: 1/109

Quinteros, Guillermo, Latino organizer: 5/59

Rainey, Ma, Black singer: 6/15

Ransby, Barbara, Black scholar: 5/109; 5/291

Reagon, Bernice Johnson, Black singer and scholar: 2/280; 3/143; 6/124

Red Corn, Ryan, American Indian graphic artist: 4/137

Rehman, Bushra, South Asian writer: 3/144; 3/145; 5/60; 5/84

Richie, Beth, Black activist and scholar: 2/155; 5/119

Riley, Boots, Black hip-hop artist: 4/35; 4/131; 4/132; 5/72; 5/73

Roberts, Dorothy, Black scholar: 2/161; 3/83; 5/249

Robertson, Sandra, Black activist: 6/28

Robeson, Paul, Black performer, writer, and activist: 1/25; 6/98

Robideau, Janet, American Indian activist: 1/162; 3/98; 5/272

Robinson, Eugene, Black journalist: 1/110

Robinson, Jackie, Black athlete: 1/147; 2/283; 3/103

Robinson, Randall, Black activist and writer: 1/7; 1/111; 5/57; 5/58

Rodriguez, Arturo, Latino labor activist: 2/128

Rodriguez, Luis J., Latino writer: 1/282; 3/100; 3/136; 5/280

Rodriguez, Robby, Latino organizer: 5/62; 5/63; 5/273

Rollins, Brent, Black-Asian graphic designer: 1/112

Romero, Danny, Latino novelist: 5/231

Root, Maria P., Asian American psychologist and scholar: 1/113

Roppolo, Kimberly, American Indian scholar: 1/85; 1/86

Rose, Tricia, Black scholar: 2/156; 2/187; 2/302; 3/46; 3/65; 3/66

Rose-Avila, Magdaleno, Latino activist: 1/157; 5/151; 5/274

Ross, Diana, Black singer: 2/288

Roy, Arundhati, Indian novelist and activist: 2/289; 4/142; 4/143; 5/275

Russell, Bill, Black athlete and coach: 3/44

Rustin, Bayard, Black civil rights activist: 1/50; 1/51; 2/84; 2/225; 2/256; 4/3; 4/30; 4/31; 5/18; 5/51; 5/110; 5/111; 5/112; 5/144; 5/174; 5/175

Saed, Khalida, Iranian American activist: 2/46; 2/185

Salaam, Kalamu ya, Black activist and writer: 5/102; 5/326

Salaita, Steven, Arab American scholar: 1/95; 1/102; 3/94; 4/159; 5/288

Salaman, Wanda, Black organizer: 2/90

Saliba, Therese, Arab American scholar: 1/122

Salvatierra, Rev. Alexia, Latina activist: 5/278

Sanchez, Sonia, Black poet: 6/128

San Miguel, Celia, Latina writer: 2/47

Santiago, Roberto, Latino writer: 2/32

Saunders, Charles R., Black writer: 1/204

Schlesinger, Andrea Batista, Latina activist: 5/163

Scott, Jerome, Black activist: 1/163; 5/64

Scott-Heron, Gil, Black poet and musician: 5/279

Seattle, American Indian chief of Squamish tribe: 5/357

Sen, Rinku, South Asian organizer and writer: 5/65

Sexton, Jared, Black scholar: 5/107

Shabazz, Betty, Black educator: 2/271

Shah, Sonia, South Asian writer: 1/22

Shahani, Aarti, South Asian organizer and writer: 5/195

Shakur, Assata, Black activist: 5/264

Shange, Ntozake, Black playwright and performance artist: 1/205; 2/51; 2/163; 2/291; 2/292

Sharpley-Whiting, T. Denean, Black scholar: 2/181; 2/182

Sharpton, Rev. Al, Black minister: 1/70

Shimura, Tom (aka Lyrics Born), Asian American hip-hop artist: 2/52

Shiva, Vandana, Indian scientist, activist, and writer: 4/49; 4/64; 5/153; 5/154; 5/356; 5/358

Shorris, Earl, Latino writer: 1/234; 1/268; 1/269; 2/87; 2/102; 2/103; 2/104; 2/105; 2/106; 4/141

Siguenza, Herbert, Latino comedian: 4/144

Silko, Leslie Marmon, American Indian writer: 1/247; 1/248; 2/145; 2/316; 3/120; 3/121; 5/364

Simmons, Aishah Shahidah, Black activist filmmaker: 2/165; 2/183

Simone, Nina, Black singer-songwriter: 1/114

Sinkford, Rev. William G., Black minister: 1/159; 6/29

Small, Gail, American Indian activist: 1/231; 3/115; 5/120; 5/359; 5/366

Smiley, Tavis, Black talk show host: 3/26

Smith, Andrea, American Indian activist and scholar: 1/229

Smith, Anna Deavere, Black playwright, performer: 1/121; 5/49

Smith, Barbara, Black activist and scholar: 2/146; 2/147; 2/154; 2/184; 5/30; 5/232

Smith, Bessie, Black singer: 2/293

Smith, Tommie: 1/44

Smith, Zadie, Black novelist: 1/116

Solomon, Akiba, Black journalist: 3/82

Sone, Monica, Asian American novelist and activist: 5/281

Sonoda, Healani, Native Hawaiian activist: 5/286

Soto, Gary, Latino poet: 3/69

Souljah, Sister, Black hip-hop artist: 2/29; 2/62; 2/164; 2/341; 3/10; 3/11; 3/12; 3/95; 5/139; 6/62

Souza, Caridad, Latina scholar: 2/173

Spears, Sherman, Black activist: 2/107; 5/160

Star, Kinnie, American Indian musician: 2/294

Stephenson, Dave, American Indian writer: 6/12; 6/13

Stringer, C. Vivian, Black coach: 1/84

Strong, Ted, American Indian activist: 1/215

Sudler, Monnette, Black musician: 2/166

Sumi, Pat, Asian American activist: 1/115; 5/66

Supremes, The, Black singers: 1/206

Suzuki, Shunryu, Roshi, Japanese Buddhist teacher: 2/287

Sykes, Wanda, Black comedian: 6/99

Tajima-Peña, Renee, Asian American filmmaker: 4/105

Takagi, Dana, Asian American scholar: 1/158; 2/115

Takahashi, June Oyama, Asian American activist: 3/80

Takaki, Ronald, Asian American scholar: 2/23; 2/24; 3/130; 5/194

Tan, Amy, Asian American novelist: 2/296; 2/336; 2/337; 4/97; 4/98; 4/99

Tankian, Serj, Armenian American musician: 5/282

Tate, Claudia C., Black scholar: 4/145

Tate, Greg, Black journalist: 4/106

Tatum, Beverly Daniel, Black educator and scholar: 1/73; 1/74; 1/75; 1/76; 3/116; 3/117

Taylor, Mildred, Black writer: 1/13

Taylor, Susan L., Black writer: 1/207

Tecumseh, American Indian chief of the Shawnees: 5/352

Teish, Luisah, Black writer, priestess, and performer: 4/20; 5/370

Terry, Bryant, Black activist and writer: 5/361

Themba-Nixon, Makani, Black activist: 3/92; 3/146; 4/38; 4/39; 5/113; 5/122

Thigpenn, Anthony, Black activist: 5/114

Thomas, Hank Willis, Black artist: 4/36

Thomas, Piri, Latino writer: 1/164; 2/78; 2/79; 2/261; 4/26; 4/165; 6/126

Thomas, Sheree Reneé, Black writer, editor, and publisher: 1/117; 2/167

Thornton, Wiley Steve, American Indian writer: 3/131

Thurman, Howard, Black theologian: 2/297; 2/298; 2/332; 3/34; 3/51; 3/52; 6/57

Tillmon, Johnnie, Black activist: 5/283

Toomer, Jean, Black writer: 2/202; 2/299; 3/2; 6/66

Torres, Gerald, Latino scholar: 1/177; 2/239

Torres, José, Latino boxer and writer: 6/125

Trambley, Estela Portillo, Latina writer: 3/35

Trask, Mililani, Native Hawaiian activist and lawyer: 6/100

Treviño, Jesús Salvador, Latino director: 2/33; 2/34; 5/74; 5/75; 5/76

Trungpa, Chögyam, Tibetan Buddhist teacher: 2/301; 6/18

Truong, Monique, Asian American novelist: 4/115; 5/203

Truth, Sojourner, Black abolitionist: 4/40; 6/44; 6/45

Tsui, Kitty, Asian American writer: 5/284

Tubman, Harriet, Black abolitionist: 5/287

Turner, Tina, Black singer-songwriter: 2/257

Tutu, Desmond, Black archbishop: 2/295

Uchida, Yoshiko, Asian American writer: 3/84

Ulen, Eisa Nefertari, Black writer: 3/81

Underbaggage, William, American Indian activist: 1/179

Vaid, Urvashi, South Asian activist and writer: 5/290

Van Peebles, Melvin, Black filmmaker: 4/65; 4/66

Vaughn, Sarah, Black singer: 6/67

Vega, Marta Moreno, Black priestess and scholar: 6/58

Velasquez, Baldemar, Latino organizer: 1/273; 1/274; 1/275

Vera Cruz, Philip, Asian American organizer: 4/13; 4/14; 5/67; 5/158

Villaseñor, Victor, Latino writer: 2/82; 2/83; 2/121; 2/122; 3/23; 6/16; 6/17

Walker, Alice, Black writer: 1/16; 1/208; 2/168; 2/170; 2/303; 2/304; 2/305; 2/306; 2/307; 2/308; 3/36; 3/86; 3/87; 4/146; 4/147; 5/68; 5/292; 5/346; 5/347; 5/348; 5/349; 5/353; 6/47; 6/48

Walker, David, Black abolitionist: 1/87

Walker, Margaret, Black educator and writer: 1/118; 1/119; 3/89; 4/41; 4/148

Walker, Rebecca, Black activist and writer: 3/108

Walters, Anna Lee, American Indian writer: 3/118

Washington, Harold, Black politician: 1/123

Watada, Ehren, Asian American conscientious objector: 5/293

Waters, Ethel, Black singer: 2/310; 6/101

Weahkee, Laurie, American Indian activist: 3/90

Weems, Renita, Black minister and writer: 3/91

Wells, Ida B., Black journalist and activist: 1/242; 5/294; 5/295

West, Cornel, Black scholar: 1/125; 1/209; 2/268; 5/14; 5/138; 5/297; 5/298; 6/49; 6/102

West, Dorothy, Black writer: 1/15; 6/50

Wheatley, Phillis, Black poet: 5/298

White Hawk, Sandra, American Indian activist: 3/96

Widell, Cindy, American Indian activist: 5/299

Wideman, John Edgar, Black novelist: 4/150; 5/300

Wiley, Kehinde, Black painter: 2/48

Williams, Patricia, Black legal scholar: 2/50; 2/71; 2/72; 5/301

Williams, Saul, Black poet and musician: 4/82; 4/83

Williams, Sherley Anne, Black writer: 1/210; 1/211

Willis, Jan, Black writer and scholar: 1/212; 1/213

Wilson, August, Black playwright: 2/252

Wilson, Harriet E., Black novelist: 3/37; 3/38

Wilson, Phill, Black activist: 1/214

Winfrey, Oprah, Black talk show host and philanthropist: 2/208; 2/209; 6/84

Wing, Bob, Asian American activist and writer: 5/98

Wise, Leah, Black activist: 5/115

Wong, Nellie, Asian American poet and activist: 4/151

Woo, Merle, Asian American writer and activist: 1/126

Wright, Kai, Black journalist: 2/186

Wright, Richard, Black writer: 2/275

Wu, Frank H., Asian American scholar: 1/129; 1/156; 1/160; 1/257; 2/57; 2/124; 5/42

Yamada, Mitsuye, Asian American writer and activist: 1/127; 6/127

Yeh, Lily, Asian American artist: 5/140; 6/103

Young, Phyllis, American Indian activist: 2/188

Yu, Henry, Asian American legal scholar: 1/261

Zheng, Eddy, Asian American prisoner and activist: 6/55; 6/56

Zia, Helen, Asian American journalist: 1/128; 5/303